M000113792

THE VIEW
from the
UPPER DECK

SportsPickle Presents
the Funniest Collection
of Sports Satire
Ever

DJ GALLO

THOMAS DUNNE BOOKS
ST. MARTIN'S GRIFFIN
NEW YORK

This is a work of sports humor and satire. It is intended to entertain, not to portray the actual conduct of any of the public sports figures mentioned in the book.

All quotes are genuine fakes unless otherwise noted. The use of any names of real people who are not public figures is purely coincidental.

The reader therefore shouldn't take anything in this book seriously.

THOMAS DUNNE BOOKS.
An imprint of St. Martin's Press.

THE VIEW FROM THE UPPER DECK. Copyright © 2007 by DJ Gallo. All rights reserved. Printed in the United States of America. No part of this book may be used or reproduced in any manner whatsoever without written permission except in the case of brief quotations embodied in critical articles or reviews. For information, address St. Martin's Press, 175 Fifth Avenue, New York, N.Y. 10010.

www.thomasdunnebooks.com
www.stmartins.com

Design by Level C

LIBRARY OF CONGRESS CATALOGING-IN-PUBLICATION DATA

Gallo, DJ.
 The view from the upper deck : SportsPickle presents the funniest collection of sports satire ever / DJ Gallo.
      p. cm.
  ISBN-13: 978-0-312-36363-5
  ISBN-10: 0-312-36363-X
1. Sports—Humor. I. Title.
  PN6231.S65G35 2007
  818'.602—dc22

                                                                                2006037825

First Edition: May 2007

10 9 8 7 6 5 4 3 2 1

For everyone along the way

CONTENTS

CONTENTS

ACKNOWLEDGMENTS

First off, a huge thank you to Adam Reisinger,
SportsPickle.com's longtime webmaster. There would be no
SportsPickle without his willingness to help out—and continued
willingness to help out for cents an hour.

Another thank you to Thaddeus Pasierb
for doing great work on the illustrations.
(Check him out at www.thaddeusexmachina.com.)
And also to Gina Fanelli for helping me
with the SportsPickle logo.

Thanks to Pete Wolverton and Katie Gilligan at
St. Martin's/Thomas Dunne for taking a shot on the book
and their support and patience along the way.
And the same goes for Jim Ornstein and Lisa Grubka at
William Morris: thanks for all you've done.

To my family: as always, thank you for your love and support.

To Ray-Ray, Peyton, Eli, Phil, and all the rest: thank you for all
your inspiration along the way. I never could have
accomplished this without you. You guys are the best.

And, finally, to Emily: I can never thank you enough for
being cool with me taking a shot at this highly
lucrative career called writing. Love you, girl.

(Noah, I'd thank you, too, but you can't read.)

INTRODUCTION

What a year it was in sports. One unlike any other we've seen before.

Baseball, cycling, and track and field were all rocked by performance-enhancing drug scandals. The college football season was tainted by controversy surrounding the BCS system. College basketball saw Bob Knight gain headlines for boorish behavior, while the NCAA Tournament featured a slew of upsets, including a heavily favored Duke team falling short of the title. In horse racing we fell tantalizingly short of seeing a Triple Crown winner, just as NFL quarterback Peyton Manning played poorly in the playoffs again. The New York Yankees threw financial responsibility aside and went on an out-of-control off-season spending spree in a desperate attempt to win a championship. And the sport of boxing lost some of its luster thanks to mismanagement at its highest levels. Several members of the Baltimore Ravens, Portland Trailblazers, and Florida State and Miami football teams got into legal trouble, and men's tennis struggled to uncover a marketable star. The New York Knicks spiraled into oblivion, and superstar receiver Terrell Owens turned fans against him with his outrageous behavior.

Yes, it was a crazy year. A unique year. A year that definitely could not be confused with any other year from, say, 2000 to 2010 or so.

So let's take a look back at all the news and newsmakers that made it such a memorable year with SportsPickle.com's first-ever book.

SportsPickle has long had an established web presence, but times are changing and the Internet is out and a new technology called "books" is in. So SportsPickle.com is jumping on the bandwagon before it's too late.

So what you hold in your hands is the result of SportsPickle .com's bold step into book writing. (Unless you're reading this while on the toilet, and then you hold in your hands both the result of SportsPickle.com's bold step into book writing *and* your junk.)

I am confident you will enjoy what is in the pages that follow. But don't take my word for it. Listen to the recommendations from some of my friends in the sports world.

"Pookie, Ray-Ray, Moesha, my baby's daddy . . . they all reading this, ya heard? Oh, and I would kick myself later if I didn't add this: Boo-yah!" —Stuart Scott, sportscaster

"This is a great book to kick back with after a long day of murdering. Uh, ball carriers. Murdering opposing ball carriers." —Ray Lewis, linebacker

"If this book doesn't sell a million copies, not only will it be disrespectful to the author, but also to the New England Patriots." —Tom Brady, quarterback

"It's no Kenny Chesney album, but it's still good." —Peyton Manning, quarterback

"Whoop! Whoop! Whoop! I love Sports 'Dill' Pickle! Whoop! Back, back, back. Whoop! Rumbling, stumbling. I find the book to be very humorous . . . bone. It could . . . go . . . all . . . the . . . way . . . to the top of the bestseller list." —Chris Berman, broadcaster

"In all honesty, I didn't read the book but I wanted to provide a quote since it's another way to get my name in print." —Terrell Owens, wide receiver

"I love this book. It's a lot like the books I put out, only in my books the sugar content is enough to kill a diabetic." —Mitch Albom, sportswriter and author of Tuesdays with Morrie *and other sappy, unreadable tripe*

"This book is horrible. An absolute disgrace."
—Bill Walton, sportscaster and former basketball player

(Author's note: If you ever write a book, don't ask Bill Walton for a recommendation. He's a bit of a dick.)

THE VIEW
from the
UPPER DECK

SPORTS THROUGH HISTORY

It may seem that sports have never been a bigger part of society. But they've always played a role in major world events.

Take a look.

20 MILLION B.C. Apelike creatures evolve to the point of living out of the trees and walking upright. At the same time, these creatures cast off elementary sports—like soccer, which only requires use of the feet—for those which require full-body dexterity, like baseball, basketball, and football.

40,000 B.C. The first cave paintings are made.

4000 B.C.   Cain kills Abel in the first-ever boxing match.

2000 B.C.   The world's first metallic money appears and, with it, the world's first sports agents.

508 B.C.   Democracy is developed in Athens, putting the selection of the All-Star teams in the hands of the fans for the first time.

387 B.C.   Plato and Aristotle gain recognition through their debates on *SportsCenter*'s Fact or Fiction segment.

7 B.C.   Jesus Christ comes to earth so he can help his favorite athletes and teams win games.

1250   Armor is developed, including metal caps for the elbows and knees, conical helmets, the jockstrap, and the single-bar face mask.

1445   Johannes Gutenberg invents the printing press, allowing mass production of NCAA Tournament brackets.

1492   Spain sends Christopher Columbus in search of the New World in hopes of finding untapped soccer talent for its national team.

1533   John Calvin spreads the idea of predestination, claiming that all blacks are destined to be basketball players, Hispanics baseball players and boxers, and Caucasians golfers and lacrosse players.

1621   The first Thanksgiving is held, but tensions quickly mount between the Pilgrims and Indians when all there is to watch on television is the Detroit Lions.

1665   Sir Isaac Newton "discovers" gravity after being struck in the head by a foul ball at a baseball game. He then sues the league for pain and suffering, wins, and uses the money to further his gravity research.

1692 The town of Salem, Massachusetts, is torn apart in a witch hunt that accuses more than one hundred different people of being Yankees fans.

1776 Adam Smith pens *The Wealth of Nations*, which espouses the benefits of free trade, free enterprise, and no salary caps.

1776 American colonists file for free agency.

1803 U.S. President Thomas Jefferson agrees to the Louisiana Purchase with an eye toward establishing the Big 12 conference.

1804 Lewis and Clark set out on a scouting trip for the Big East conference.

1819 Factory work is outlawed for children under nine in England, forcing Nike to close its British operations.

1830 Abolitionists establish the Underground Railroad as means of smuggling black slaves from the South to play for bigger contracts for northern NBA teams.

1844 Samuel F. B. Morse transmits the first message across a telegraph line. Sent to his bookie, the message read: "Jets +6. Stop. And the over on the Patriots-Chargers. Stop."

1859 In his book *The Origin of Species*, Charles Darwin points to the three-month NBA play-offs to advance his theory of natural selection.

1860 The Pony Express opens for service, delivering the first *Sports Illustrated* swimsuit editions to the American West.

1867 Concrete is invented, leading to the construction of Philadelphia's Veterans Stadium.

1876 Searching for a way to make it easier for baseball managers to communicate with their bullpens, Alexander Graham Bell invents the telephone.

1901   The first Nobel Prizes are awarded in an attempt to compete with the prestigious ESPYs.

1917   Leon Trotsky leads the October Revolution in Russia, gaining the nickname "Mr. October."

1924   While in prison, Adolf Hitler writes *Mein Kampf*, espousing his political ideology, as well as a second book, *Mein Training Kampf*, a collection of drills and tips on how to run a successful football training camp.

1949   The Council of Europe, a forerunner of the European Union, is organized so European countries can combine forces in hopes of beating the United States at the Ryder Cup.

1950   Former FDR advisor Alger Hiss is convicted of stealing signs.

1963   U.S. President John F. Kennedy is assassinated in Dallas in what is the first in a long line of criminal acts committed by Cowboys players.

1964   The Golf of Tonkin Incident pushes the U.S. to the brink of war in Vietnam, as North Vietnamese leader Ho Chi Minh steps in the line of U.S. President Lyndon Johnson's putt on the eighteenth green during a round of golf between the two dignitaries.

1969   The United States puts a man on the moon, eight years after President Kennedy promised that the United States would beat the Soviet Union in the race to hit the longest drive in golf history.

1973   The U.S. Supreme Court rules that abortion is legal in hopes of cutting down on the number of illegitimate children fathered by NBA players.

1989   The Berlin Wall comes down after an eight-foot-four, 723-pound East German female Olympian knocks it over with a shot put.

1990   The Americans with Disabilities Act becomes law, opening the door for many future sports broadcasters.

1992   Rioting erupts in South-Central Los Angeles after Rodney King fails to properly execute a hit-and-run.

BASEBALL

THINKING OF BASEBALL DOESN'T LESSEN
SEXUAL AROUSAL OF SPORT'S NUMBER-ONE FAN

Jason Tyson, baseball's self-appointed number-one fan does not become less sexually aroused when he thinks of baseball, he announced today.

Married for seven years, Tyson, thirty-four, said he actually performs worse in bed when he thinks of baseball during heightened sexual excitement. "I've always heard that you should think about baseball or your mother-in-law in order to last longer in bed," Tyson said. "Thinking about my mother-in-law is downright disgusting, and having baseball pass through my mind makes me finish even quicker."

Tyson said he does not have sex with his wife if there is a baseball game on television or if *Baseball Tonight* is being aired. "That's a strict policy I have," he said. "I love the game and will allow nothing to come between it and me."

And if Tyson feels he needs to slow down in the marriage bed, he does his best to separate his love of baseball from his thought patterns. Thinking of a perfectly executed double play, hit-and-run, or squeeze play only puts him over the edge quicker.

Tyson said he is not bisexual and primarily thinks of specific baseball plays, not certain players. "Sure, Mickey Mantle, Barry Bonds, Nolan Ryan—those guys have entered my mind at orgasm, but it's purely because of my appreciation of their skills, not a sexual attraction to them."

Margie Tyson said she has been able to able to make her husband last longer in bed by whispering things in his ear about steroids or a labor dispute. "I say things like 'BALCO' or 'Don Fehr' sporadically while we're making love," she said. "He could go forever when I do that."

U.S. INTELLIGENCE OFFICIALS DETECT INCREASED INFIELD CHATTER

U.S. intelligence officials reported this morning that they have detected increased chatter, much of it coming from our nation's infields, that may cause the terrorist alert to be increased again to Code Orange.

"We have uncovered a very high amount of infield chatter, especially as the Little League season has progressed," said a senior Homeland Security Department source. "The increased chatter has caused us to worry that al-Qaeda may be targeting our youth athletes for its next attack."

Intelligence officials are especially worried about a phrase repeatedly picked up in its monitoring: "Hey, Batta Batta, Sa-wing Batta, HeCan'tHitHeCan'tHit, Sa-wing Batta."

"So far we have been completely unable to determine what that phrase means," the source said. "We're not even sure what language it is."

CUBS HUNDRED-YEAR REBUILDING PLAN RIGHT ON TRACK

The Chicago Cubs—in the final years of the hundred-year rebuilding plan the franchise set in action after losing the 1910 World Series—are starting to reap the benefits of their patience.

With winning records in three of the last four seasons—including advancing to the verge of the World Series in 2003—the Cubs are nearing the position to make a run at their first World Series championship since 1908, a title that team management didn't target until 2010 after dismantling the Series-losing squad of 1910 in favor of a ten-decade rebuilding plan.

"Honestly, any success we have in the postseason prior to 2010 is a bonus," said Cubs general manager Jim Hendry. "At this point in our rebuilding plan we just want to show improvement from year to year. We really don't want to get ahead of the program."

The organization is on track for achieving its goal of seriously contending for a World Series title in 2010, based on the rebuilding plan that has been kept under lock and key in Cubs offices since it was drawn up in 1910.

"By this time in the process we wanted to be a competitive team, an above .500 team, with designs on putting it all together for Year 100," said Hendry. "A trip to the play-offs before then would actually mean we are a bit ahead of schedule."

Hendry said he expects no more than five or six members of the Cubs' current twenty-four-man roster to be part of the 2010 World Series challenger. "We can't have a team that's too old if we plan to challenge for a title in 2010 and a few years beyond," he said. "I expect maybe Kerry Wood or Mark Prior will still be around, but Derrek Lee might be too old by that time, of course. It's really unfortunate for him, but Ernie Banks and Ryne Sandberg dealt with the same thing. Heck, Ernie was about fifty years short of our target year for building a title contender."

During the Cubs rebuilding, the Yankees have won twenty-six World Series titles, the Athletics and Cardinals nine each, and the Dodgers six. "Those teams have never had the need to start from square one as we did in 1910," said Hendry. "That's the difference between us and them. Sure, it would have been nice to go for broke and try to buy a championship here or there, but we wanted to do this the right way."

If the hundred-year plan pans out, the Cubs expect it to be a model for all future rebuilding plans by struggling baseball franchises.

"You can't just hope to fix things like your minor league system or your starting rotation overnight," said Hendry. "Stuff like that takes time. We just hope this plan pans out for 2010. If not, we'll go back to the drawing board and look at winning another Series early in the twenty-second century."

YANKEES NOT EVEN SURE WHO THEY'RE IN
A BIDDING WAR FOR

With the Red Sox firing the first shot of the off-season by signing several high-profile free agents, the Yankees are hurrying to counter with some moves of their own, going as far as to engage in bidding wars for numerous free agents they have no interest in or can't even identify by name.

"This is standard operating procedure for us," said general manager Brian Cashman. "Mr. Steinbrenner has always made it clear, if a free agent is being offered a contract by a competitor, we submit a much more lucrative counteroffer. Doesn't matter who it is."

Cashman says that specific scenario is currently being played out with nearly a hundred different free agents.

"We just offered some guy—I think he's a shortstop or maybe a reliever on the Padres, or is it the Mariners?—anyway, we offered him six years, $90 million because we heard rumors that the Mets and Red Sox were interested in possibly signing him to a minor-league contract," said Cashman. "We're committed to not letting him slip away to our rivals, whoever he is."

The architect of the Yankees' big-spending philosophy, team owner George Steinbrenner, has mandated a standard response if the team is contacted by an available player's agent.

"I've told Brian and all the guys this," said Steinbrenner. "If some agent tells us he has an offer on the table from another team, just say: 'We'll triple the dollar amount and double the years. Think it over and get back to us.' That approach usually lets us get our man in the end."

Such an aggressive style has enabled the Yankees to land some of the biggest free agents over the years, from Gary Sheffield to Hideki Matsui, but has also stuck the franchise with some stinkers.

"Granted, it backfires on us from time to time," said Cashman. "That's what happened with Tony Womack. We gave him two years, $4 million after I got an anonymous call that Boston was about to sign him. Turned out it was just a prank call from Theo Epstein."

In addition to the bidding war over the shortstop or possibly reliever from the Padres or Mariners, the Yankees have multiyear, ten-figure offers on the table to—according to Cashman—"this one starter who used to pitch for the Devil Rays," "a Dominican out-fielder from an NL West club, or at least I hope he's Dominican," "a few Royals players," "and an infielder named Jack or Jim or something like that with a J," among others.

Cashman said the Yankees are specifically focused on the Jack or Jim guy.

"I don't want us to be kicking ourselves come next September because what's-his-name with the J name is starring for the Red Sox," he said.

PLAYER TO BE NAMED LATER ACQUIRED FOR PLAYER TO BE NAMED LATER

The St. Louis Cardinals and Seattle Mariners pulled off a major trade, or perhaps a minor one, minutes before last Thursday's trade deadline when St. Louis dealt a player to be named later to Seattle for a player to be named later.

"We needed to get pitching for the play-off chase and this trade may or may not have gotten it for us," said Walt Jocketty, St. Louis general manager. "We're potentially very excited."

"People have given us flack over the years for not acquiring players that we need before the trade deadline," said Bill Bavasi, Seattle general manager. "This year that can't be said. If and when we get this player, he could make a very big impact for us. Or not, I suppose."

Both Jocketty and Bavasi said the players to be named later have not been agreed on, and neither knows if the deal will be consummated before the end of the season.

"It would be great if we got someone really good, though," said Jocketty.

ALBERT PUJOLS'S THIRTY-FIFTH BIRTHDAY PARTY A LOW-KEY AFFAIR

St. Louis Cardinals slugger Albert Pujols celebrated his thirty-fifth birthday last night with a select group of close friends and family at a St. Louis restaurant, with those in attendance told not to speak of the purpose of the gathering or, at the very least, not to say Pujols's actual age aloud.

"This is just typical Albert," said a friend, Martin Guerrero. "He doesn't like a lot of attention drawn to himself. He's very humble. Although in this case, in regard to his age, I think there might be some other factors involved—if you know what I'm saying. You didn't hear that from me, though."

Pujols—listed as born January 16, 1980, in the Dominican Republic—exploded onto the scene in 2001 as a "twenty-one-year-old" rookie, exhibiting the poise and production rarely seen in a player so young. He has continued playing well straight through to this season, and is on the verge of eclipsing numerous records for a player "under the age of thirty."

Cardinals manager Tony LaRussa said he still is amazed by what Pujols does on the field day after day.

"People forget that Albert is still only twenty-six years old," said LaRussa, adding "bullsh-t", and then breaking into a coughing fit. "When he first came up, I remember saying to one of my coaches that his size, maturity, and baldness made him seem much older, but I was quickly reminded that what I was saying was crazy talk because no Latino players have ever lied about their age. So even though Albert looks like he's in his thirties and the birth certificate of his that we have on file is a piece of tablet paper that says in pen: 'Albert Pujols is not in his thirties. No, really, he was born in 1980,' I'm going to take him at his word."

Pujols's longtime friend, Hector Ortiz, claims the rumors that Pujols is older than his reported age are absurd.

"I've known Albert my whole life," said Ortiz, thirty-five. "And I know he's not a liar. I remember he was on my Little League team back in Santo Domingo in 1978 and I knew right away that he was a stand-up guy. And when we moved up to a twelve-to-fifteen-year-old league in 1983, he had my back then, too. Oh, no. Oh, crap—wait. I meant 1988, not '78. And he was in that twelve-to-fifteen-year-old league in the early '90s—yeah, that's how it was. The '90s. I was his babysitter. Yep, his babysitter because he's so young. Yep. Okay, I have to go now."

Even though he is only twenty-six, Pujols claims he may s⁺ away from baseball before he is thirty.

"I'm very active in charities and I'd like to give mor⸱ he said. "Plus, for reasons I'm not willing to get in to, I ⸱

I have many more good seasons left in me. Sometimes my body just doesn't feel like it's twenty-six anymore. Or even thirty-four."

"I take offense when people say that I'm injury prone and brittle . . . Aw, crap, my jaw just broke as I was saying that."
                                                            —Ken Griffey Jr.

"Phuck oph!"
            —the Phillie Phanatic, to a fan who threw beer on him

SportsPickleNation Poll

What is the most memorable moment in MLB All-Star history?

6%   1944: With rosters depleted due to World War II enlistments, the name of the contest is briefly changed to the All-Coward Game

12% 1949: Black players finally get good enough to make an All-Star team

4%   1954: Senator Joseph McCarthy accuses anyone who voted for Reds of being Communist

37% 1966: Tim McCarver appears in the All-Star game, marking the first time a mentally disabled person has played in the midsummer classic

12% 1970: Pete Rose bowls over Ray Fosse at home plate because Fosse had given him a bad tip on a horse race

9%   1993: The American League wins its sixth straight All-Star Game, proving once again how great America is at baseball

20% 2002: With the public faced with not knowing which league is superior due to the game ending in a tie, the country erupts into civil war

BASEBALL FUN FACT

"Gaylord Perry" is a sexual term used in the homosexual community to refer to putting a foreign substance on another man's testicles, as in: "I got out the cocoa butter and Gaylord Perryed my partner's balls."

BASEBALL FUN FACT

The busts of Gary Carter and Don Sutton are the only two in the Hall of Fame's prestigious Perm Wing.

BASEBALL FUN FACT

Former A's and Cardinals slugger Mark McGwire was born Andrew Stein-Dionne in 1963 to French and Jewish parents.

GREAT MOMENTS IN BASEBALL HISTORY

JUNE 19, 1889 Washington outfielder Dummy Hoy, who was deaf, throws out three base runners in one inning. Hoy's feat is less impressive considering he threw out Gimpy McNolegs, Fats Slowstein, and Peg-Leg Pete Van Retard.

MARCH 2, 1904 The *Official Playing Rules of Professional Base Ball Clubs* are adopted. The first section of the rule book laid out "gentlemanly ways in which players can repeatedly adjust their manhood with nary a spectator taking note."

OCTOBER 30, 1919 The Professional Baseball Association rules that spitballs and shineballs are illegal. The Association did not ban snotballs, however, leading to a period of dominance by pitchers with hay fever.

APRIL 17, 1953 Mickey Mantle of the Yankees hits a 565-foot home run against Washington, with the ball coming to rest in a backyard one block from the stadium. Unfortunately, the mean old man whose lawn the ball landed in refused to return it and the game had to be called off.

APRIL 19, 1960 Baseball jerseys began displaying players' last names on the back. The change came after longtime Boston Red Sox pitcher Gary Vaginalicker finally retired.

MARCH 5, 1973 New York Yankees pitchers Mike Kekich and Fritz Peterson tell reporters that they traded wives during the off-season. Peterson also picked up a daughter to be named later in the deal.

OCTOBER 15, 1980 George Brett of the Kansas City Royals misses a World Series game due to hemorrhoids. Brett is able to return for the next game after treating his hemorrhoids by smearing pine tar all over his anus.

MARCH 30, 1993 *Peanuts* character Charlie Brown hits a game-winning home run, his first in forty-three years of the comic strip. In a series of comics released by *Peanuts* creator Charles Schulz in 2005, it is revealed that Brown was on steroids when he hit his blast.

SEPTEMBER 28, 1996 Roberto Alomar of the Orioles is suspended five games for spitting on umpire John Hirschbeck. Alomar got the last laugh, however, when Hirschbeck tested positive for herpes.

NOVEMBER 13, 2003 Major League Baseball announces that only 5 to 7 percent of its players tested positive for steroids. The league was later forced to admit that 93 to 95 percent of its players were never tested.

JANUARY 13, 2005 Major League Baseball announces plans for a steroids testing program. The league also announced that it would stop recording 'Roid Rages (RR) as an official major-league statistic.

FEBRUARY 21, 2005 Retired slugger Jose Canseco releases his book: *Juiced: Wild Times, Rampant 'Roids, Smash Hits, and How Baseball Got Big,* shocking the baseball world that he is literate.

PEOPLE TO KNOW

HANK AARON Race played a major role in the career of Hank Aaron. In 1952 he became the last player to make the jump from the Negro League—a league that was racist to its core and did not allow any white players—to major-league baseball, which welcomed players of all races and creeds with open arms. He is best known for breaking Babe Ruth's career home run mark, a feat he accomplished despite receiving thousands of pieces of racist hate mail. His historic, record-breaking 715th came on the night of April 8, 1974, a blast that knocked in three runs—Aaron himself and two hippies who were near the second base bag. In recent years, Aaron has become one of baseball's greatest ambassadors. In his spare time he has taken to sending racist hate mail to Barry Bonds.

YOGI BERRA One of the greatest catchers of all time, the Yankees legend is perhaps better known for his many malaprops—or Yogiisms—including: "It ain't over 'til it's over"; "When you get to a fork in the road, take it"; "I didn't really say everything I said"; and "Please, for the love of God! Why does everyone laugh when I talk? Can't you see I have Alzheimer's? Please get me some help!" *Fun Fact*: In 2005 Berra filed a lawsuit against TBS for using the word "Yogasm" in billboards advertising the show *Sex and the City*, but the case was thrown out after the judge vomited while thinking of Yogi Berra having an orgasm.

BARRY BONDS Perhaps the greatest player ever, Bonds's career has unfortunately been tainted by a cloud of steroids allegations, causing many to hope the slugger would speak candidly about his past; or, at the very least, tear the cloud of allegations apart in a steroids-induced rage. What's worse, the skepticism surrounding him has attached a black mark to one of the sport's premier records: the single-season record for intentional walks, which Bonds set in 2002 with 120. (Interestingly enough, he also holds the single-season home run record.) Even before the steroid allegations Bonds was not a fan favorite and has stated for years that the media is out to get him—which is proved by the fact that the media has only awarded him seven MVP awards during his career and that ESPN gave him his own reality\propaganda show. Despite all the

All photos of Barry Bonds are slightly blurry because the gravitational pull of his head affects camera lenses.

doubters, Bonds has never tested positive for steroids, although his first league-required urine test revealed he has a rare, skull-enlarging disease.

ROGER CLEMENS The Rocket's career will be remembered as one of greatness and longevity. The Boston Red Sox infamously gave up on Clemens after the 1996 season, thinking he was past his prime, a surprisingly bad management decision for a franchise that has so frequently won championships. The hard-throwing righty went on to dominate for another decade as a Blue Jay, Yankee, and Astro, signing with Houston in 2004 after a lengthy three-month retirement. Clemens says he will return again next season if he is allowed to pitch from home.

TY COBB A true legend of America's pastime, Cobb was born in 1886 in Georgia. He immediately developed a reputation for being surly by cussing out his mother for not pushing hard enough to free him from her womb. The deadball-era star was nicknamed the Georgia Peach, though most of Cobb's contemporaries referred to the outfielder as the Georgia Pi-atch. Upon his retirement in 1928, Cobb was the holder of ninety major-league records, the most famous being the mark for career hits, which Pete Rose broke in 1986. But the record Cobb was most proud of was for most infielders spiked in the crotch, with 638—a mark many think will never be broken. *Fun Fact*: Before a game in 1925 against St. Louis, Cobb announced that he would swing for the fences to prove that he could be a home run hitter like Babe Ruth if he put his mind to it, and proceeded to hit three home runs. The next day Ruth countered by announcing he could be a big pussy like Cobb if he wanted, and then hit three singles.

JOE DiMAGGIO Owner of the greatest feat in baseball history, a 56-game hitting streak in 1941, the Yankees outfielder is also admired for the 56-day sex streak he went on after marrying Marilyn Monroe in 1954. Their marriage ended after just 274 days, however, driven apart by DiMaggio's rage over Monroe's refusal to stop walking over subway grates when wearing skirts so passersby could leer at her cootch. DiMaggio remained in the public eye long after his playing career ended, and as most people know, the famous lyric "Where have you gone, Joe DiMaggio?" was written after the Hall of Famer left the legendary folk trio Simon, Garfunkel & DiMaggio in 1968.

LOU GEHRIG A Yankees legend whose career bridged the gap between Babe Ruth and Joe DiMaggio, Gehrig is remembered for playing in 2,130 consecutive games, as well as for suffering from

Lou Gehrig's disease under a microscope.

ALS, a disease that is now commonly known as Lou Gehrig's disease. The Hall of Famer's streak ended in 1939 and, to this day, many medical researches believe consecutive games streaks are an early symptom of ALS. In 1941, at the age of thirty-seven, Gehrig finally succumbed to the disease, his final words being: "Today I consider myself the unluckiest man on the face of the earth. Seriously, this blows."

VLADIMIR GUERRERO Although he is one of the top talents in baseball, Guerrero is thought to be highly underexposed to the average fan. In fact, the national media writes or airs more than 6,000 stories each year about how underexposed the Angels outfielder truly is. Guerrero is the game's premier five-tool player—excelling in average, power, speed, defense, and being Dominican. A very free swinger, he has been known to lace pitches down the line while still waiting in the on-deck circle for his turn at the plate or to strike out on three straight intentional-walk pitches.

TONY GWYNN As pure a hitter as there has been in the game, Gwynn excelled for twenty years in the majors thanks to his strict off-season regimen of not doing sit-ups and eating until he vomited. The Gold Glove outfielder was one of the first players to spend hours analyzing his swing via videotape, but many former teammates say he spent most of his time in the video room masturbating to the Food Network. Gwynn is also one of the rare modern players to spend his entire career in the same uniform, that of the San Diego Padres, although the waist of the pants had to be let out routinely. Fun Fact: Tony Gwynn is a big fatty.

RICKEY HENDERSON Henderson is baseball's career leader in stolen bases, walks, runs, and third-person references. He last played in the majors in 2003 at age forty-four, but he has knocked around various independent leagues since then, and is considering trying out for your son's T-ball team next season in hopes of opening some eyes.

ICHIRO A Japanese superstar, Ichiro came to the U.S. major leagues in 2001 and instantly established himself as one of the best players in the league. He is perhaps the most photographed athlete in the world, but that probably has more due to do with the Japanese people's love of photographing everything than it does with his abilities on the diamond. In 2004 Ichiro broke George Sisler's eighty-four-year old single-season hits record, a feat that, while impressive, failed to capture the nation's consciousness; not a single person took the time to send Ichiro even one piece of racist hate mail as he neared the mark. In 2006 Ichiro led Team Japan to the championship in the inaugural World Baseball Classic, a victory that spawned joyous bukkakeing throughout Japan.

DEREK JETER A very solid player during the regular season, Jeter has a reputation for turning his play up a notch in the postseason and single-handedly willing his team to championships through his un-matched leadership qualities. So solid is this reputation that it has withstood more than a half decade of that not happening, even though Jeter is routinely "leading" a team with a payroll well over $200 million. While Jeter's detractors might say he would not be thought of as a superstar if he played in a smaller market, by no fault of his own he has been able to capitalize on the opportunities New York offers, so much so that each morning there's a line of media members outside his door, all waiting to polish his balls. *Fun Fact*: Derek Jeter is dreamy.

RANDY JOHNSON Nicknamed "Big Eunuch" due to his lack of testi-cles, his reduced package is all the more noticeable in its smallness when contrasted to his six-foot-ten frame. Johnson uses his height to his advantage on the mound to intimidate batters, but not nearly as much as he uses his face, which forces most batters to avert their eyes from the mound in disgust as a 90-plus fastball or slider hurtles toward them. A sure first-ballot Hall of Famer when his career is over, Johnson's will be the first mulleted plaque in Cooperstown.

GREG MADDUX While he may look like an accountant, Maddux throws like a . . . well, he also throws like an accountant. But de-spite not having eye-popping stuff, the right-hander has forged a Hall of Fame career for himself by relying on location, location, loca . . . zzzzzz . . . "Oh, jeez—three strikes on me already? I must have nodded off there." A career National Leaguer, Maddux prefers the title "baseball player" to "pitcher" and takes great pride in his ability at the plate despite a career average well below .200—making perhaps the best argument yet for the existence of the designated hitter. Maddux enjoyed his best success with the Atlanta Braves, but signed with the Chicago Cubs before the 2004 season, proving he was content with being on just one World Series champion in his career.

MICKEY MANTLE Taught as a young boy to be a switch-hitter (not the bisexual kind) by his father, Mantle became the greatest-ever over an eighteen-year career with the Yankees. In addition to hitting 536 home runs and winning the 1956 Triple Crown, Mantle is responsible for the longest home run in history—a 643-foot blast in 1960 over Tiger Stadium's right-field roof, which he hit after his teammates bet him a case of whiskey that he couldn't hit it out of the stadium. Damaged by years of alcoholism, Mantle received a liver transplant in 1994 and succumbed to cancer one year later. But before he passed away he did a lot of good, campaigning for organ donation, urging children to live a clean life, and leading the Betty Ford Clinic slow-pitch softball team to back-to-back league titles.

PEDRO MARTÍNEZ Martínez burst onto the scene in 1997 when he posted a 17–8 record with a 1.90 ERA and 305 strikeouts for the Montreal Expos. The following year he was called up to the majors by the Boston Red Sox and continued his dominance there. One of the most intimidating pitchers in baseball, Martínez has no problem pitching inside or even beating up the elderly, as he proved in the 2003 ALCS when confronted by Yankees coach Don Zimmer. *Fun Fact*: Pedro's daddy is Paolino Jaime Martínez.

WILLIE MAYS Every aspect of the game seemed to come easily for Mays. Except perhaps for fielding, in which he often found himself out of position and forced to make a basket catch. Most credit Mays's long career to his healthy lifestyle, while others surmise he must have known someone at BALCO long before his godson, Barry Bonds, became involved with the company. Mays may be best remembered for a play known as "the Catch" in the 1954 World Series when Cleveland's Vic Wertz smashed a ball to center field. Frightened at how hard the ball was hit and that it seemed to be coming directly at him, Mays immediately turned his back and fled in fear as fast as he could, only to have the ball miraculously land in his glove when he was just feet away from dropping into a fetal position at the base of the outfield wall. The Giants legend sadly ended his career in 1973 with the New York Mets—"sadly" not so much because his skills were depleted by then, but because no has ever dreamed of ending his career with the Mets.

DAVID ORTIZ The Red Sox signed Ortiz from the Twins before the 2003 season and he immediately filled the vacancy left by Mo Vaughn as the fat guy who is too immobile to play in the field. Ortiz's best season came in 2005 when he hit 47 home runs and drove in a remarkable 148 runs but lost out on American League MVP voting to Alex Rodríguez of the Yankees. This "snub" enraged Boston fans, at least it did those who somehow forgot about that whole wearing-a-glove-and-fielding part of baseball. Ortiz has become a cult hero in his brief time in New England due his affable demeanor and propensity for delivering clutch hits. In fact, he holds the all-time Red Sox record for clutch hits with 114, 114 more than the next closest player.

ALBERT PUJOLS One of the rare Dominican players who has panned out as a major leaguer, the Cardinals' first baseman came out of nowhere to win the 2001 National League Rookie of the Year at age twenty-one. Many predicted Pujols would be struck by a sophomore slump, but that didn't pan out. Then it was thought he'd have a junior slump, then a senior slump, and now the conventional wisdom is that there's an outside chance for a third-year post-doctorate slump. Other skeptics have questioned the veracity of Pujols's age—pointing to his many accomplishments and maturity at such a young age, as well as his premature balding—but since no Latin player has ever been untruthful about his age in the past, this charge holds very little water. *Fun Fact:* In Spanish, "Pujols" means "one with multiple anal openings."

MANNY RAMÍREZ No other player proves the truth of Yogi Berra's famous quote that one "can't think and hit at the same time" more than Manny Ramírez. The Red Sox slugger relies on his instincts on the field; if he relied on his intelligence he would likely be a career .000 hitter. Despite being one of the best right-handed bats in the game, Ramírez was offered up to any team in the league for free on waivers by Boston GM Theo Epstein before the 2004 season, sparking concern that Ramírez was afflicted with a rare communicable form of moron-ness that had been contracted by Epstein. Ramírez returned to the Red Sox in 2004, however, and hit .308, with 48 home runs and 130 RBIs, on the way to a World Series trophy— something he was especially excited to win because, like many mentally challenged people, he is transfixed by shiny things. *Fun Fact:* Ramírez's attorneys have beaten dozens of murder charges for their client using the "That's just Manny being Manny" defense.

CAL RIPKEN JR. Remembered most for breaking Lou Gehrig's consecutive-games streak, Ripken was more than just durable—he was one of the best all-around shortstops to ever play. He became the prototype for shortstops that followed after him, such as Derek Jeter and Alex Rodríguez—tall, athletic, powerful, and extremely egotistical. But Ripken was also a force off the field as one of the sport's most marketable stars. In fact, long before the likes of Rafael Palmeiro or Mike Ditka endorsed erectile dysfunction products, Ripken Jr. made millions on his "Iron Man Erection Pills," which guarantee that users will consistently achieve a rock-hard penis: "From Night 1 to 2,131." Ripken retired from baseball after the 2001 season but he has stayed active and has even set more longevity streaks, including most consecutive days not watching a Kevin Costner movie with his wife. *Fun Fact:* Bill Ripken : Cal Ripken :: barnacle : whale.

JACKIE ROBINSON Not only a great player but a great American, Robinson broke baseball's color barrier in 1947. (Black players were finally allowed to play in the majors after World War II, because the powers-that-be felt that, when you looked at the big picture, at least they weren't Nips or Krauts.) Robinson was a surprise choice as the first black major leaguer, partly because—at age twenty-eight—he was relatively old for a rookie, and partly because he had a temper and many in baseball thought a more even-tempered player like Roy Campanella would deal better with the racial abuse sure to come. But performance was also important, and the Dodgers didn't feel the wheelchair-bound Campanella would play very well, so Robinson it was. And he did not disappoint, handling himself with dignity and grace in the face of racism while at the same time becoming an All-Star on the field. In 1997, fifty years after his debut, major-league baseball honored Robinson by retiring all black players from every team. *Fun Fact:* Most fans who heckled Robinson during his career did it not because of the color of his skin, but because Jackie is kind of a girl's name.

ALEX RODRÍGUEZ Despite his undeniable talent, A-Rod does not get due respect from his baseball peers. In fact, he routinely is forced to stamp out flaming poo bags that are left in front of his locker. But while Rodríguez has detractors, he is establishing himself as an all-time great—a player many think will one day hold the career home run mark. (By the age of thirty he already held the career marks for nonclutch hits and home runs.) The slugging Yankees third baseman is also well known for the record ten-year, $252 million contract he signed with the Texas Rangers before the 2001 season. A-Rod is said to be saving most of this money in hopes of one day buying himself a personality, something he was tragically born without. *Fun Fact:* Rodríguez is the world slap fighting champ.

PETE ROSE Born Charles Hustle in 1941, baseball's career hit king changed his name in his teens as a way to avoid being found by bookies he was in debt to. Rose is banned for life from baseball because of how horrifically ugly a Hall of Fame plaque with his face on it would be. His reputation was forever tarnished when it was revealed in 1989 that he had bet on baseball while a player and manager. Perhaps more damaging to his reputation, however, was the disgusting disclosure that he engaged in a regular game of strip poker with Reds owner Marge Schott. In 2004, in an attempt to come clean and pave the way for his reinstatement, Rose released his autobiography, *My Prison Without Barbers*. *Fun Fact:* Rose dove headfirst out of his mother's vagina at birth.

BABE RUTH Born George Herman Ruth but better known as "Babe" or the widely used nicknames "the Bambino," "the Sultan of Swat," and "Babe: Pig-Faced Man in the City," Ruth was an unparalleled player and an American icon. The greatest power hitter the game has ever seen, Ruth actually began his major-league career as a starting pitcher with the Boston Red Sox, using his days off between starts to keep his competitive fires burning by entering eating contests. After the 1919 season Ruth was sold to the New York Yankees, setting off the "Curse of the Bambino," which peculiarly cursed the Red Sox organization to terrible management decisions and whiny fans for eighty-six years. It was with the Yankees that Ruth became a legend, piling up home run records and leading the team to four World Series titles. The Bambino's career came to a close after the 1935 season when he decided he had grown tired of keeping himself in the kind of shape required to be an elite athlete. *Fun Fact:* Upon Ruth's birth in Baltimore in 1895, doctors were amazed to see his umbilical cord was link sausage.

CURT SCHILLING The smartest person ever about everything, Schilling has been one of baseball's most consistent starting pitchers since the early 1990s. He didn't burst onto the national scene, however, until he won the 2004 World Series as a member of the Boston Red Sox, courageously winning Game 6 of the ALCS while pitching with hemorrhoids so severe the blood ran down his right leg and saturated his sock. Schilling thankfully blesses humanity with his unmatched talent and intellect off the field, as well, working with ALS sufferers for more than a decade—although it's widely believed he likes spending time with ALS victims because they are unable to leave the room when he starts talking, as most people do. *Fun Fact:* Curt Schilling thinks spiked hair has never gone out of style and never will.

SAMMY SOSA Despite suffering from a rare disease that causes him to randomly forget how to speak English, the Dominican outfielder has secured his place as one of baseball's greatest power hitters. Signed at sixteen in 1985 by the Texas Rangers, Sosa was traded to the White Sox in 1989 along with Wilson Alvarez for Harold Baines—a deal that George W. Bush, the Rangers owner at the time, signed off on and has called his "biggest mistake." While some might say that Bush has made bigger mistakes with Iraq, the economy, the environment, health care and social security reform, public speaking, bike riding, and eating pretzels, such people have no idea what a horrendous trade that really was. Three years later Sosa was traded to the Cubs, a deal White Sox owner Jerry Reinsdorf has called "Just another enormous mistake among the thousands I've made." It was with the Cubs that Sosa had his best years, climaxing in 1998 when he and Cardinals slugger Mark McGwire captivated the nation in a race to see what mixture of illegal performance-enhancing drugs was most effective. *Fun Fact:* In 2001, Sosa costarred with *Saturday Night Live* alum Chris Kattan in the comedy flop *Corky Dominicano.*

TED WILLIAMS Without a doubt one of the greatest hitters in history, Williams was also a world-class pilot, fisherman, and a-hole. In 1941 he hit .406, the last time anyone has hit over .400 for an entire season, and in 1958 became the highest paid player in baseball with a $135,000 annual salary, most of which he invested in a cryonics company in Arizona. His career totals would have been even more impressive had he not served in the Marine Air Corps in both World War II and the Korean War, and in the latter suffered being shot down by friendly fire coming from a planeload of Yankees fans. Truly a legend, Williams is remembered to this day and he is honored every time someone eats ice cream out of a mini helmet at a baseball game. *Fun Fact:* The label on the freezer in which Williams's body is stored reads "There froze the greatest hitter who ever lived."

CY YOUNG Raised from birth to be a pitcher, as evidenced by his parents naming him after the award given each year to the best major-league pitchers in each league, the Ohio native did not disappoint—although, sadly and somewhat ironically, he never did win the Cy Young Award during his career. Young holds the career mark for wins (511), innings pitched (7,356), games started (815), and complete games (749), all records which are sure to go unbroken since modern pitchers are giant pussies who have to come out of the game and ice their arms if their pitch counts get above eighty.

EIGHT-YEAR-OLD AMBIDEXTROUS PITCHING PHENOM ABLE TO BOTH PITCH AND BELLY-ITCH

Dustin Winters, an eight-year-old ambidextrous Little League pitching phenom, is baffling fans and fellow players with his ability to both pitch and belly-itch at the same time.

"His uncanny ability has left him essentially immune to one of the greatest weapons in youth baseball, the cry of 'We need a pitcher, not a belly-itcher.' I can't tell you what an enormous advantage that is," said Jim Strong, Dustin's coach. "He has speed and accuracy, and can strike out batters and field his position all while itching his belly. It's quite amazing."

For an eight-year-old, Dustin is very aware of the trailblazing status his performance has earned: "I pitch to prove that pitching and belly itching is not an either-or proposition. Someone suffering from belly itch can also be a great pitcher."

Dustin's mom, Karen, said she has an appointment set with a dermatologist for May 18 to get her son's chronic eczema checked.

GMS' TRADE CONVERSATION
SOMEHOW DEVOLVES INTO PHONE SEX

Talks over the phone between Pirates general manager Dave Littlefield and Phillies GM Pat Gillick about acquiring Pittsburgh pitcher Zach Duke took a dramatic turn late last night when the pair found themselves engaged in phone sex.

"I'm not sure exactly how it happened, but it happened," said Littlefield. "We've been spending a lot of time on the phone together recently and I guess it's one of those things like in any workplace where sparks can fly and two people can end up building an intense sexual tension between one another simply because of all the hours spent together working toward a common goal. It was late, we were on the phone, and one thing just led to another."

"I was getting tired and told him I wanted to get out of my work clothes and put on something more comfortable," said Gillick. "He asked me what I was wearing. I told him Dockers and a polo shirt and it turned out he was wearing the same thing. And before I knew it, my pants were down around my ankles and I was muttering: 'Oh, yeah. You want me to pick up 100 percent of Duke's contract, don't you? Come on, you know you want it. Tell me you need another prospect to make this deal happen. That's right, make me work for it.' "

Gillick said he doesn't think the incident says anything about the sexual preference of either executive.

"It was simply a voice on the other end of the line," he said. "A welcoming voice that I had become accustomed to talking to. It was nothing more than a means to relieve stress and hopefully break down barriers between us and finally get a deal worked out that will get Duke here to Philadelphia. And to be honest, I enjoyed it. I hope to deal with Dave again in the future."

But Littlefield isn't so sure.

"For me at least it was extremely awkward when it was over. I felt used," he said. "Doing something like that is totally unlike me. Especially to engage in that kind of behavior with another man. And a fellow GM, no less. I honestly don't know if I'm going to be able to get myself to speak to him again, so I really doubt if this trade with Philadelphia is ever going to come off. I'm going to have to look more closely at offers from other teams and promise myself it won't go beyond a business relationship with their general managers."

MIDDLE SCHOOL BOYS DECLARE: "POO-HOLES OUR FAVORITE MLB STAR"

A study released today by Major League Baseball to gauge middle school boys' interest in baseball has found that St. Louis Cardinals first baseman Albert Pujols is the most favorite player among the age group.

"Poo-holes! Poo-holes! Poo-holes!" yelled Billy Thomas, age twelve, when asked who his favorite player was. His pronouncement received a chorus of agreeing giggles at his lunch table.

"Some people like Bonds, others say A-Rod is the best," said Johnny Oldham, age eleven, "but I've got two words for you: Poo and Holes." Oldham went on to say that he has suffered for his devotion to his favorite player. His social studies teacher, Mrs. Mandlebrew, has sent him to the office several times after he has declared his love for Pujols.

The study found that many of the boys were unclear as to the correct spelling of Pujols name. When told that the Cardinals star spelled his name "P-u-j-o-l-s" and not "P-o-o H-o-l-e-s" as all the boys had written on their surveys, Garret Wilson, age twelve, looked distraught before loudly declaring: "I don't care. He'll always be a big, stinky poo hole to me!" He then turned and skipped off down the hall.

Former Baltimore Orioles star Boog Powell was voted the most fa-

vorite retired player among the age group. Dick Trickle won for favorite non–team sports athlete.

SHOELESS JOE'S BROTHER, PANTS-LESS TED, WAS BETTER, SAY BASEBALL HISTORIANS

Shoeless Joe Jackson, the former Chicago White Sox star, apparently had a stepbrother named Pants-less Ted Thomas, who many
baseball historians feel was a better player than his older brother.

"Pants-less Ted had it all," said Eli Mender, librarian for the Base-
ball Writers' Club. "Size, speed, power, strength—everything. Joe
Jackson was a heck of a player, but he was nothing compared to
Pants-less Ted."

But while Joe Jackson made a name for himself by playing baseball without wearing shoes, his stepbrother Ted insisted on playing
without pants, including no underwear, and was blackballed from
most every professional league in the country.

"Pants-less Ted would have been known as one of the greatest
ever," said Mender. "Ruth, Cobb, Mays, Pants-less Ted—he was in that
same league. It's just that nobody could get him to wear pants when
he played. He insisted on not wearing pants. He was weird like that."

Joe Jackson, banned from the majors after being involved in the
Black Sox scandal of 1919, was two years older than Ted. They had
the same mother, Martha Jackson, who married Jake Thomas, Ted's
father, after Joe's father died in 1890. But due to unclear record
keeping, it only recently became clear that Shoeless Joe and Pants-
less Ted were related.

"I can't even imagine the games those two must have played as
kids," said Mender. "Joe shagging flies without any shoes on. Ted
roping line drives naked from the waist down. It was probably quite
a sight."

When Joe left their boyhood home in South Carolina in 1906 to
pursue a baseball career, Ted soon went after him. But due to his insistence on playing without pants, he couldn't stick with many
teams in the conservative early 1900s.

"People just weren't ready in those days for a player with his penis hanging out," said Mender. "The strange thing was, Ted always
wore shoes."

While Joe toiled in semiprofessional leagues after being banned from the game, Pants-less Ted spent his entire career playing in nudist leagues, where the competition was well below his level.

"It's a sad story, those two," said Mender. "It makes you wonder what kind of upbringing they had. One boy doesn't wear shoes and the other goes pants-less. They must have had some issues at home."

TOMMY JOHN FORCED TO ENDURE HIS 386th SURGERY

Former major-league baseball player Tommy John was forced into his 386th surgery last week in order to remove a malfunctioning gall bladder.

John's string of surgeries began in 1974 when he went under the knife to fix a shoulder ligament in a replacement procedure that extended his pitching career. Since then, various ailments have required Tommy John surgery nearly four hundred times.

"Tommy is a very ill man," said Dr. Frank Marcallow, John's general practitioner. "Tommy John surgery is so common because his body has always been very frail and sickly. He is still healthy enough to conduct daily activities, but he is essentially no more than a walking pile of scar tissue."

RIES TOP STORIES   TOP STORIES TOP STORIES **IN OTHER NEWS . . .**

Devil Rays off to disappointing 38–117 start . . . Sick boy dies after hero fails to homer for him . . . Tom Emansky wins back-to-back-to-back AAU national championships . . . 81 percent of baseball players test positive for being Latino . . . Nostalgic cheapo returns from concession stand with nothing but peanuts and Cracker Jacks . . . Bullpen not sure if it's worth running all the way in for bench-clearing brawl . . . God relents to Ronan Tynan's repeated demands that he bless America . . . "Turn Back the Clock" games to ban "Negroes" . . . Great American Ballpark a little cocky . . . Carl Everett suddenly retires after discovering baseball isn't in the Bible . . . Jason Giambi has horrific nightmare in which everyone remembered he used steroids . . . Coors Field blamed for 475-foot home run . . .

NFL

PEYTON MANNING READY TO PROVE ALL HIS DOUBTERS WRONG AT THE PRO BOWL

Still haunted by critics who say he isn't a clutch performer in the playoffs, Peyton Manning is ready to step up and show he is a dominant, big-game quarterback with a masterful performance in this Sunday's Pro Bowl.

"I hear the whispers. I hear people saying I can't win the big game," said Manning. "But what game is bigger than the Pro Bowl? All of the best players are there, and I light it up against them every year."

Manning has lost only one Pro Bowl start in his National Football League career, a fact he says his detractors have conveniently ignored.

"Sure, I don't have much in the way of championships in high school, college, or the NFL, but people who truly know football know the Pro Bowl is what really counts," said Manning. "That's what my dad has always told me, at least."

Other players may disagree, however.

"I see Peyton's performances in the Pro Bowl as further proof of what a total dork he is," said Patriots quarterback Tom Brady. "He actually takes the game seriously. The rest of us are just there 'cause we get to go to Hawaii for free and get drunk, while that loser is squirreled away watching game film of past Pro Bowls."

RAY LEWIS EXCITED TO UNVEIL HIS GAYEST
PREGAME DANCE ROUTINE YET

Baltimore Ravens linebacker Ray Lewis is ecstatic to be just days away from the first game of the NFL regular season, a game in which he plans to debut the most homoerotic pregame dance routine yet of his illustrious career.

"I've been working all off-season on my new dance, and it's absolutely fabulous," said Lewis. "I just can't wait any longer to unveil it to the world. I feel I have so much to express about myself through my movements, and anyone who doesn't like it is just a hater."

Lewis has been working with a top Broadway choreographer since February in preparation for the season.

"Ray is dedicated to executing the gayest dance ever outside of what's seen at certain leather bars in Greenwich Village and San Francisco," said Blaine DuBose, Lewis's choreographer, whose résumé includes work on *Cabaret*, *Cats*, and *West Side Story*. "Ray has made me swear to secrecy, but I can tell you this—expect lots of pelvic thrusting and even more jazz hands. There will be tons of jazz hands in this year's routine. Even more so than in the past."

Sources close to Lewis have disclosed additional details of what to expect in the opener and throughout the season.

"Ray told me he is going to use a lot of glitter this year on his face and forearms. He said it makes him feel pretty and sparkly," said a Ravens player who wished to remain anonymous.

"All I know is that I saw Ray doing some moves where he seductively ate a banana and two cherries," said a member of the Ravens front office. "I'm not sure if it made the final cut and will be in his dance, but it was probably the most homoerotic thing I've ever seen, and that's including everything from Ray's dances throughout the years, if you can believe that."

Dayn Reveran, a rookie linebacker who was cut last week by the Ravens, says he saw Lewis practicing a routine that ended with him simulating a sex act on former Baltimore defensive back Deion Sanders, another lover of modern, sensual dance. "Let's just say it was extremely gay," said Reveran.

Other details pulled from those close to the Ravens about Lewis's new routine hint that the linebacker pulled inspiration from a rhythmic gymnastics competition he saw on television.

"Ray was watching rhythmic gymnastics one night at camp and he couldn't stop raving about how fantastic the ribbons and hoops were that the girls used in their routines," said a fellow Ravens linebacker. "He was totally psyched about using some of those elements in his dance."

In addition to the jazz hands, glitter, simulated homosexual sex acts, and use of ribbons and hoops, Lewis reportedly will skip in a circle at one point of the routine, tossing rose petals into the air as he does homage to his favorite childhood game of ring-around-the-rosy; each skip is to be accentuated by a dramatic, midair scissor kick.

"As always, my fans know that I've worked hard in the off-season to get ready for this year," said Lewis. "This is most evident in my pregame dance routine. I promised myself after last season that I'd get this team back to the Super Bowl and do it while executing the most homoerotic dancing ever seen on a football field before each game. I plan to deliver on both promises. Terrell Owens's womanly dances won't even be close to mine this year."

MEMBERS OF PACKERS OWNERSHIP GROUP
REPORTEDLY DRUNK IN PUBLIC

Mired in one of the worst stretches in franchise history, the Green Bay Packers season hit a new low this week when it was reported that several part owners of the team were visibly intoxicated and acting loud and belligerent outside Lambeau Field before Sunday's game.

"I couldn't believe what I was seeing. They were pounding beer after beer in the parking lot and were clearly very drunk. I even saw one of the owners throw up on himself. Another passed out in the bed of his pickup truck and never even made it inside the stadium to see the game," said Claire Holt, who recently moved to Green Bay. "Then I saw another owner hang a bratwurst out of his fly as though it was a giant penis. I felt it was extremely inappropriate behavior for the ownership group of an NFL team. Quite unprofessional."

Sunday was just the latest of many reported incidents of public drunkenness by Packers owners, an increasing trend that troubles the league office.

"The NFL expects all of its owners to act at all times with the utmost dignity and professionalism and with respect for the sport and the league," said a statement from the commissioner's office. "What I've been hearing out of Green Bay is unacceptable. I realize they are the only team owned entirely by public stockholders, stockholders who are just average fans, but with that unique arrangement comes responsibility. I no more expect them to be wandering around, half-loaded outside the stadium than I would Dan Rooney or Robert Kraft."

Former commissioner Paul Tagliabue says he has experienced the loutish behavior of Packers owners firsthand.

"I was up there for a game three years ago and as I was walking from my car to the stadium entrance and one of them yelled out: 'Hey! Taglia-POO!' and then threw a chunk of cheese that hit me right in the back of the head," said Tagliabue. "Needless to say, I gave the guy the total cold shoulder at that spring's owners meetings."

But while Tagliabue and many others may find the behavior of Green Bay's ownership group to be inappropriate, the owners themselves believe they are doing nothing wrong.

"I'm as old school an owner as there is in the NFL," said Daniel Schonfeld. "My grandfather was in on the first team stock issue in 1923, and it's been passed down over the years from him to my father to me. We're like the Rooneys or the Maras. Only we get completely hammered before each home game and I'm guessing they probably don't."

Another Packers part owner, Daryl Samuelsson, purchased his first share of Packers stock at age sixteen in 1974 from money he saved up mowing lawns around town.

"I'd be happy to wear a suit and not get drunk just like all the other owners in the NFL," said Samuelsson. "After they give me the same amount of control over player signings and drafts. Until then, I'm going to get bombed in the parking lot before games and then drink out of my flask once I'm inside. And let's not kid ourselves— it's not as though the likes of Al Davis and Georgia Frontiere aren't just as drunk as we are at games, if not more so."

NFL FACING ANOTHER JERSEY DILEMMA IF ED DICKFACE IS SELECTED IN THE DRAFT

Forced to deal with various controversies in regard to jerseys personalized with inflammatory words and sold on its NFLShop.com in recent months, league officials are crossing their fingers that Ed Dickface, a linebacker for Texas State, will not be selected in this weekend's NFL draft.

Dickface—projected as a mid- to late-round pick—could force the league to add yet another entry to the list of words and names banned from NFL-licensed jerseys, an increasingly common practice and something that has brought unwanted attention and embarrassment to the league over the past year. In February 2005, a controversy erupted when it was reported that the league did not allow the word "GAY" on its jerseys, even though an actual NFL player—Randall Gay of the Patriots—has the name. Then came removal of MEXICO in April when customers tried to order number 7 Falcons jerseys personalized with the name Vick reportedly used as a pseudonym to get treated for genital herpes.

DICKFACE could be next.

"That Dickface could really muck things up for us again," said NFL spokesman Brian McCarthy. "As of now, Dickface isn't one of our banned words, but it very well might be if he gets drafted. We can't have thousands of people across the country walking around in NFL apparel with Dickface across the back. I don't care if that's his real name or not—it's not a positive image for us to be projecting."

Most scouts think it's almost a certainty that Dickface will be drafted and that the NFL will be forced to deal with the jersey implications.

"Hey, nobody wants a dickface on their team," said Kevin Colbert, the Steelers director of football operations. "But most everyone would want this Dickface on their team. He can really play. If he's still available in the later rounds, we'll gladly call his name and slap DICKFACE across the back of a Steelers jersey."

Dickface has dealt with jersey issues throughout his football career.

"Our team had player names on the back of jerseys for years," said Tom McGee, Dickface's high school coach at Plains Park High in Omaha, Nebraska. "But when Ed made varsity his sophomore year, we ended the practice until he graduated. We're in a pretty conservative area and a lot of people were offended by the thought of having Dickface on a jersey, even though that is his name. I think it might be Welsh."

Dickface said he just wants to play in the NFL, and won't let his unusual surname cause a distraction. He even hopes to see his name and number retired by an NFL team some day.

"People have razzed me since I was a little kid because of my name," said Dickface. "It was always 'Dickface this' and 'Dickface that.' Although, now that I think about it, maybe they weren't making fun of me at all and were just calling me by my name. It's hard to tell."

Dickface says he once considered changing his last name to his mother's maiden name, but then decided against it.

"My mom's name was Fartsmith, and that's probably no better than Dickface," said Dickface.

"For the record, if we ever win the Super Bowl, I'd like to be doused with gravy instead of Gatorade."
—Andy Reid, Philadelphia Eagles head coach

SportsPickleNation Poll

Where do you normally watch the Super Bowl?

13%   At a Super Bowl party

6%   40° latitude, 73° longitude or thereabouts

17%   With Peyton Manning at his house, same as every year

52%   As far away from Ray Lewis and his friends as possible

12%   Wouldn't you like to know, pervert!

SportsPickleNation Poll

What is the most memorable incident in Terrell Owens's career?

6%　September 24, 2000: After scoring against the Cowboys, Owens sprints to midfield to get as far away as possible from Jerry Jones's horrific, oozing, pus-covered face on the sidelines

20%　October 24, 2002: Following a touchdown on *Monday Night Football,* Owens pulls a Sharpie out of Jeff Garcia's butt and signs the ball

41%　October 31, 2004: After scoring against the Ravens, Owens mocks Ray Lewis by fleeing the scene in a blood-spattered limousine

11%　November 15, 2004: Owens hurts his relationship with Donovan McNabb by having a naked Mrs. McNabb leap into his arms during a *Monday Night Football* intro. He also hurts his back.

12%　December 19, 2004: Owens breaks his leg due to a stress fracture caused by repeated beanings from McNabb's many underthrown ducks

10%　November 3, 2005: Owens states the Eagles would be better with Brett Favre. He also says he believes it's 1995.

20%　September 26, 2006: Owens overdoses on painkillers after seeing Cowboys coach Bill Parcells walk out of the shower naked.

GREAT MOMENTS IN NFL HISTORY

JANUARY 9, 1977 Super Bowl XI sets a Super Bowl attendance record. CMMMCDXXXVIII people purchased tickets.

NFL FUN FACT

Despite his background and appearance, Byron Leftwich is not considered to be a black quarterback due to his lack of mobility.

JULY 11, 1987 Bo Jackson signs a five-year contract to play football for the Los Angeles Raiders. Jackson would go on to become the all-time leading rusher in Tecmo Bowl history.

FEBRUARY 25, 2004 A federal grand jury indicts Ravens running back Jamal Lewis on drug conspiracy charges, prompting Lewis to ask the Ravens to pay him in cigarettes during the 2004 season.

FEBRUARY 5, 2006 The Pittsburgh Steelers defeat the Seattle Seahawks, 21–10, to win Super Bowl XL, but many in the Seahawks organization blame the loss on the officials. The officials, in turn, blame the Seahawks' loss on the Seahawks.

PEOPLE TO KNOW

BILL BELICHICK Belichick is regarded as one of the greatest NFL coaches of all time—especially by those who choose to completely disregard his five years with the Cleveland Browns from 1991 to 1995 that accounts for more than 40 percent of his head coaching career. Upon becoming head coach of the New England Patriots in 2000, he led the team to three Super Bowl titles in his first five years, nearly cracking a smile after each of the championship victories. But Belichick is not all Xs and Os. He also likes to have fun. For instance, he derives great pleasure from cutting loyal, longtime veterans and then re-signing them at a much lower salary. *Fun Fact:* Belichick's turn-ons are hooded sweatshirts, the color gray, obese coordinators, and MILFs.

TERRY BRADSHAW Bradshaw won the most Super Bowls by a quarterback in NFL history with four, as he almost single-handedly piloted a Steelers team in the 1970s that was woefully short on talent. Since his career ended, he has worked as an in-studio football analyst, cementing his celebrity status as well as his reputation as an unabashed moron. In recent years Bradshaw disclosed that he has suffered from depression—depression brought on by watching his spot as Steelers quarterback be filled in the years since he vacated it by the likes of Cliff Stoudt, Mark Malone, Bubby Brister, Neil O'Donnell, Mike Tomczak, Kordell Stewart, and Tommy Maddox.

TOM BRADY Despite being called "slow, clumsy, stupid, too fat, too short, excessively skinny, too hairy, smelly, candy-armed, cleft-lipped, impotent, blind, and a paraplegic" in scouting reports before entering the NFL draft in 2000 out of Michigan, Brady has somehow managed to forge a fairly decent career for himself, winning multiple Super Bowls as the quarterback of the New England Patriots. In fact, Brady has been so successful and proved his many doubters wrong to such a great degree that it is widely rumored that his solid waste does not even smell. In fact, it is said to smell of roses. (But not on a football Sunday, of course. Then it smells of a manly musk.) Brady has been endlessly compared to Colts quarterback Peyton Manning during his career, but there are many differences between the two. For instance, the Patriots star has the clear edge in titles while Manning puts up better stats, and while Manning likes to spend hours analyzing game film, Brady likes to analyze hot Asian sluts during his many online porn sessions.

JIM BROWN The former Cleveland Browns running back is arguably the greatest football player of all time. However, he stepped away from the game in 1965 after just nine years in the NFL, mainly because he's a huge pussy. And yeah, I'd say that to his face. (Because he's in his seventies now and has bad knees so he wouldn't be able to catch me.) But Brown was not only a football star—he also excelled in lacrosse at Syracuse and is thought to be the sole reason the sport is so wildly popular today among urban blacks. *Fun Fact:* Brown claims the proudest moment of his life was appearing in the 1996 film *Mars Attacks!*

DICK BUTKUS The Hall of Fame linebacker developed his legendary toughness as a child, as he withstood countless taunts about his name, like: "Ha-ha, Dick Butkus—you kiss butts with your dick." (Clever, I know.) Fueled by rage from those schoolyard jabs and the anger over why his parents hated him, Butkus channeled his fury onto the football field, where he went on to be a two-time All-American at Illinois and an eight-time Pro Bowl selection with the Chicago Bears. Many Bears fans compare Butkus to current Chicago defense star Brian Urlacher, one of the only differences being that Butkus was often able to play more than three consecutive plays without getting hurt.

BILL COWHER The longtime Steelers head coach had many detractors who said he was unable to win the big game before he broke through and guided Pittsburgh to victory in Super Bowl XL. But, to be fair, his critics were on point, as it was Cowher who told Neil O'Donnell to hit Larry Brown in the chest with two passes in Super Bowl XXX, and it was also Cowher who told both Kordell Stewart and Ben Roethlisberger to throw three interceptions in the 2001 and 2004 AFC Championship games, respectively. So, bad coaching decisions there on his part. Cowher is known for his intensity on the sidelines, but is very popular around the league and has therefore never been fined or suspended for spitting on a referee, a despicable act he has done countless times. Despite all his on-field success, Cowher also makes time for family life. He is the husband of a former college basketball star, and the father of two daughters who also play college basketball, meaning he has suffered through more women's basketball than any man should be forced to see.

JOHN ELWAY A standout prep athlete in baseball and football, Elway was drafted by both the NFL and major-league baseball. He was the number-one overall pick by the Baltimore Colts in 1983, but he and his daddy forced a trade to the Broncos—charting a path for all future spoiled, crybaby, douche-bag, daddy's-boy quarterbacks to follow. Once in Denver, he would go on to stake his place among the quarterback greats. The Broncos legend holds the NFL record for most come-from-behind victories, thanks to his unique ability to fall behind so often, and won* two Super Bowl titles at the end of his career. But things were not always as easy for Elway as they appeared. In 2004, he disclosed his courageous fight against

*Elway didn't so much win two Super Bowls as not blow them by staying out of Terrell Davis's way.

acid reflux disease in a series of commercials for Prevacid. His brave battle inspired millions around the world. *Fun Fact:* Elway's favorite foods are sugar cubes, carrots, oats, and hay.

BRETT FAVRE The quarterbacking legend of the Green Bay Packers ranks near the top in numerous career passing categories, and holds the record for most consecutive starts by a quarterback, with more than 200. His durability is even more impressive considering he seems to be surrounded by near-constant disaster—deaths of loved ones, destructive hurricanes, the proclivity to chuck interceptions in play-off games, having to live in Green Bay, Wisconsin, during the coldest months of the year, etc. Favre has a Super Bowl to his credit and won three straight league MVP awards from 1995 to 1997. Sadly, in a freak accident in 2002, the MVP trophies fell off of his mantel and killed his dog. Through it all, Favre has been adamant that he be thought of as a "gunslinger," feeling that term makes it all right for him to throw tons of interceptions at the most inopportune times.

CHAD JOHNSON The attention-grabbing Bengals receiver is the highest-profile Bengals player since . . . uh, since . . . well . . . he's the first-ever high-profile Bengals player . . . unless that month that Ickey Woods was famous back in the eighties counts. While very productive, Johnson has gained fame almost solely for his antics off the field and after the whistle sounds. Some fear he worries too

You may see a receiver in quadruple coverage and an almost sure interception, but a great quarterback like Brett Favre sees opportunity.

much about his image—and that may be true, as he now only agrees to run routes that send him in the direction of TV cameras. And as much as Johnson likes to dance after scoring a touchdown, he may enjoy making predictions even more. His latest is that you will soon be very sick of seeing and hearing about Chad Johnson. *Fun Fact:* Johnson's agent is Drew Rosenhaus, the same man who represents Terrell Owens. So that should be good.

RAY LEWIS Known for his killer instinct, Lewis was trained from childhood in classical dance. Forced to help support his struggling family as a teenager, he worked after school in the knife store at the mall. But for all of his abilities in dance and with cutlery, it was in football that he would make a name for himself. A standout linebacker at the University of Miami, Lewis was drafted by the Baltimore Ravens in 1996. He quickly made their defense one of the most dominant in the league and even saw the team win the Super Bowl in 2001. Along the way he was inconvenienced by a double murder charge that he plea-bargained out of. But luckily, the NFL has been able to capitalize on the brutal deaths of two people by marketing Lewis as a scary individual who is not to be messed with. There is more to Lewis than many think, however. In 2006 he launched a stock car racing team, hoping to learn how to flee murder scenes more quickly. And he even oversees the Ray Lewis Foundation, which provides assistance to at-risk children. (These children are put at-risk, of course, by being in proximity to Ray Lewis.) *Fun Fact:* Lewis can gut and fillet a fish in less than eight seconds.

VINCE LOMBARDI The two-time Super Bowl–winning Green Bay Packers coach is said to have once said: "Winning isn't everything, it's the only thing." Obviously, it goes without saying that he was a very laid-back coach who kept sports in their proper perspective. Lombardi's name is so closely associated with winning that the NFL awards to its Super Bowl champion the Lombardi Trophy. The Super Bowl runner-up receives the Vince Lombardi-Thinks-You're-a-Complete-Failure Trophy. *Fun Fact:* Lombardi often free-balled it under his trench coat during games.

PEYTON MANNING Without a doubt, Peyton Manning is the greatest dork quarterback of all time. His best season came in 2004 when he set a single-season NFL record by throwing for 49 touchdowns and became the first quarterback in league history to audible out of every play called in the huddle. That historic campaign was preceded by Manning's signing the richest contract in NFL history— seven years and $98 million with a $34.5 million signing bonus. Luckily for the Colts star, his agent demanded that none of the money be tied to play-off-related performance bonuses. *Fun Fact*: In his spare time, Manning likes to write fictional stories with his father, Archie, and younger brother, Eli, about a family of ultra-cool quarterbacks who are loved and admired by everyone and who always come through in the clutch on the way to championship after championship.

DAN MARINO The most prolific passer in NFL history, Marino holds the career records for most completions, most yards, and most passing touchdowns. Unfortunately, he was never able to win a Super Bowl despite being paired with such great running backs as Andra Franklin, Tony Nathan, Sammie Smith, Bernie Parmalee, and Karim Abdul-Jabbar. The Dolphins legend is responsible for revolutionizing the quarterback position, using his legs to scramble and make plays just as much as his arm. In fact, Marino rushed for nearly 9 yards over his career. Today he works as an NFL analyst for CBS and HBO. Marino is so talented on-screen he almost never uses the teleprompter, mainly because he is well prepared and quick on his feet, but also because he can't read.

DONOVAN McNABB Since being drafted out of Syracuse University in 1999, McNabb has quarterbacked the Philadelphia Eagles to the most successful stretch in the franchise's history, just narrowly beating out the stretches that came before it that also were highlighted by not winning a Super Bowl. McNabb is given partial credit for changing the quarterback position in the NFL, as he can lose a big game with his arm or his legs. Despite that, McNabb is without a doubt one of the toughest quarterbacks in the NFL. Although, admittedly, I'm only saying that because as a quasi media member, I want to see a black quarterback succeed. The affable star is one of the few athletes in sports whom people of all backgrounds can get behind. And behind him is a smart place to be because then he can't throw up on you.

JOE MONTANA The only successful quarterback to ever come out of western Pennsylvania, Montana is thought of as one of the greatest quarterbacks ever. Over his fifteen-year career, he threw for 40,551 yards and 273 touchdowns and had a remarkable 63 percent completion rate—remarkable because something the West Coast offense does *not* allow for is short, easily completed passes. The most memorable moment of his career may be "the Drive," when he led the 49ers on a 92-yard, game-winning drive against the Bengals in Super Bowl XXIII (younger readers, the mention of the Bengals is not a joke; they actually were a real NFL team before 2005 and even once made it to a Super Bowl), or "the Catch" in the 1982 NFC title game, when Dwight Clark saved Montana's reputation by reeling in a pass he badly overthrew.

RANDY MOSS As talented and temperamental a wide receiver the game has seen, Moss has been a star since his rookie year, after the Vikings selected him with the twenty-first pick in the 1998 draft. Moss immediately set about making the twenty teams who passed over him regret it by acting like a complete ass. During his time in Minnesota, the Vikings tried to assuage him by implementing the "Randy ratio," which was a plan to throw Moss 40 percent of the team's passes. This "ratio" also applied to other areas, as Moss was also allowed to smoke 40 percent of the teammates' weed, leave 40 percent of their games early, and short-arm 40 percent of the passes thrown to him over the middle. The receiver eventually wore out his welcome in Minnesota and after the 2004 season was traded to the Oakland Raiders. Within forty-eight hours of the trade going down, every rapper in America owned his new Raiders jersey.

TERRELL OWENS Owens is among the greatest receivers and self-promoters in NFL history. He is also rather injury-prone, including numerous muscle pulls, a broken ankle, and an infamous incident in which he severely sprained his neck while trying to dislodge it from his hindquarters. An NFL star during his eight years in San Francisco, Owens became a household name across America during his first season with the Philadelphia Eagles in 2004. Unfortunately for Owens, that breakout season was marred when he suffered a broken leg late in the regular season. Remarkably, though, he returned for the Super Bowl and credited his remarkable recovery to personal intervention by God. (Of note, God immediately held a press conference to deny any involvement in Owens's recovery.) With his hero status secured among Eagles fans, he quickly went about trying to destroy it by threatening to hold out before the 2005 season and eventually getting suspended by the team midway through the season. Thankfully, it was easy to ignore all of this because the media gave the story zero play. Owens eventually signed a three-year, $25 million contract with the Cowboys prior to the 2006 season. But that figure can grow to $50 million if Owens manages to not completely destroy the franchise before the second year of the deal.

BILL PARCELLS One of the most respected coaches in the modern game, Parcells demands discipline from his players—the same level of discipline he shows with his daily eating habits. Throughout his career, Parcells has had a knack for rebuilding poor teams into play-off contenders. He won two championships with the New York Giants, the second coming in 1990 when the Giants became the only team to ever knock off the mighty Buffalo Bills in the Super Bowl. After stints with the New England Patriots and New York Jets sandwiched (mmm . . . sandwich) by semiretirements, Parcells was hired by the Dallas in 2003. *Fun Fact*: In his spare time, Parcells talks to Japanese people to see if they have any ideas for trick plays.

WALTER PAYTON Payton may be the greatest running back in NFL history, totaling 16,726 yards and 110 touchdowns during his thirteen-year career with the Chicago Bears. His power and quickness made him difficult to bring down, especially in the latter portion of his career, when his body was greased by the runoff from his Jheri curl. His legacy is responsible for launching the running-back factory the Bears organization has become, featuring such legends as Neal Anderson, Rashaan Salaam, Raymont Harris, Curtis Enis, and Anthony Thomas since Payton retired in 1987. Sadly, Payton passed away in 1999 at age forty-five after a long battle with cancer. His death greatly grieved Bears fans, especially those who had hoped that one day the Chicago Bears Shufflin' Crew would have a reunion concert.

JERRY RICE Arguably the best wide receiver to ever come out of Mississippi Valley State University, Rice holds almost every NFL receiving record. He also scored the most touchdowns in NFL history and has a league and Super Bowl MVP to his credit. His best days came as a member of the San Francisco 49ers, but after being released by the team in 2001 for salary cap reasons, he extended his career another four years by playing with the Oakland Raiders and then the Seattle Seahawks. Many in the media claimed that Rice was destroying his legacy by continuing to play past his prime—this from a bunch of toads who never had a prime and will still be recycling the same crappy columns when they're seventy-five. Rice's career finally came to an end before the 2005 season when he failed to latch on as a third receiver with the Denver Broncos. He then decided he would show everyone how to really taint a legacy and signed up to compete on *Dancing with the Stars.*

BEN ROETHLISBERGER Drafted by the Steelers in 2004 to be their quarterback of the future, Roethlisberger struggled mightily out of the gate, losing four games in his first two seasons. He also put up a less-than-stellar performance in leading Pittsburgh to a win in Super Bowl XL and becoming the youngest quarterback in NFL history to win a championship, causing many in the Steelers organization to worry that they may have made a poor choice in drafting him and should have traded up for Eli Manning. The Steelers almost got a break when Roethlisberger was hit by a car while riding his motorcycle without a helmet before the 2006 season, but he recovered quickly and it appears the team is stuck with him for a while.

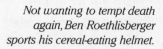
Not wanting to tempt death again, Ben Roethlisberger sports his cereal-eating helmet.

Fun Fact: Roethlisberger dated LPGA golfer Natalie Gulbis for a time, but broke up with her after misinterpreting her request for a foursome with John Daly and Laura Davies.

BARRY SANDERS The most exciting running back ever to play the game, Sanders was so elusive that many opponents went as far as stapling their jocks to their taints so as not to be faked out of them. Third on the career rushing list with 15,269 yards, Sanders also scored 99 touchdowns. He shocked Lions fans by retiring after the 1998 season, although it was no surprise to the rest of the league, as it's almost inconceivable to imagine how emotionally and physically draining it must be to play for the Lions for ten years. Sanders's best season came in 1997, when he rushed for 2,053 yards, becoming just the third back to rush for over 2,000 yards in a season, and just the second back to have done it without then going on to murder anyone.

DEION SANDERS Successful in two sports, Sanders is one of the greatest athletes of all time. He played nine seasons of major-league baseball as an outfielder and fourteen seasons in the NFL as a Hall of Fame–caliber defensive back. He would have been considered a three-sport star as well, but being a cocky a-hole is not considered an athletic endeavor. Sanders stepped away from the NFL in 2000 but returned four years later with the Baltimore Ravens. Upon his return, he showed no signs of rust, tying his career high in tackles in his first game back with zero. *Fun Fact*: His 1994 hip-hop album, *Prime Time,* is so bad that even Shaquille O'Neal makes fun of it.

LAWRENCE TAYLOR Taylor was as dominant a defensive player as football as ever seen. But for all he did on the field, the Giants linebacker was often even more destructive off, as he had a serious drug problem and got into several scrapes with the law. Thankfully, though, his coach, Bill Parcells, suspended Taylor numerous times, proving he was a man of his word and would not give any individual players special treatment. (Actually, hmm . . . no, it turns out Parcells didn't do that and is actually a huge fraud. What a surprise.) But for all of the negative things Taylor did during his career, the worst is without a doubt breaking Joe Theismann's leg in a 1985 game, an injury which sent the tool into the broadcast booth, where he has tortured the nation with his idiocy ever since. *Fun Fact*: Lawrence Taylor thinks that dangly earrings on men are totally rad.

JOHNNY UNITAS The premier quarterback of the 1960s, Unitas was a man defined by his era, as he was an enormous hippie with long hair and a beard, a general disregard for authority, and an unyielding thirst for casual sex and recreational drugs. Despite all that, Unitas was still able to find time to forge a Hall of Fame career on the field, winning three league MVP awards and a Super Bowl for the Baltimore Colts. Despite his successes in Baltimore, his career has been all but forgotten there in recent years, as the city has been treated to quarterback play far superior to anything Unitas ever did behind a seemingly endless parade of Canton-worthy Ravens quarterbacks.

MICHAEL VICK The Atlanta Falcons star is the most exciting player in the NFL today. He can bring fans to their feet when he runs with the ball, and fans of his opponent to their feet when he passes it. (In all fairness, however, it should be noted that Vick holds the all-time record for most touchdown passes thrown by a running back.) In 2006 Vick ran for 1,039 yards, the most in league history by a quarterback, ahead of Randall Cunningham's 942 and Ron Mexico's 968. Vick has almost single-handedly revived pro football in Atlanta, although many fans still keep their distance from him so as not to get herpes. In fact, the Falcons equipment manager labels Vick's water bottle with a Mr. Yuck sticker so other players don't carelessly use it. *Fun Fact*: If you think Michael Vick is overrated, you are a racist.

REGGIE WHITE Nicknamed "the Minister of Defense," White was a sack machine during his career with the Philadelphia Eagles and then later with the Green Bay Packers. He tragically passed away in 2004 at age forty-three and was immediately sent to heaven, where God placed him in a tiny house with twenty Mexicans for his first few days just to teach him a lesson. White's passing was especially mourned in Green Bay, where he is remembered as a great contributor to Green Bay's black community by Green Bay's other black guy.

CONGRESS TO INVESTIGATE RULING ON THE FIELD THAT IT WAS A FUMBLE

Having held investigations into steroids and college football's BCS system in recent years, it was announced today that the U.S. Congress will again be intervening in the sports world to investigate the ruling on the field that it was a fumble.

Cliff Stearns (R.-Fla.), the chairman of the House Subcommittee on Commerce, Trade, and Consumer Protections, told the press this morning that the investigation will focus on Sunday's Dolphins-Chargers game, in which a fumble by Miami running back Ronnie Brown at the goal line was challenged by the Dolphins and upheld upon review.

Representative Stearns, a lifelong Dolphins fan, said he was watching Sunday's game on television and became incensed when Brown coughed the ball up.

"We were about to put the game away and take a thirteen-point lead and then Brown goes and fumbles. It really pissed me off," said Representative Stearns. "And then they show the replay and it looks, to me at least, that he didn't even fumble. So why would the officials say it was a fumble? It was right then that I thought: 'Hey, I'm a powerful congressman. Since I don't have much else better to do, I can pull these refs before Congress and make them answer for their decision.' And that's exactly what I plan to do."

Referee Tony Corrente, replay official Bob Mantooth, and the rest of the nine-man crew that worked Sunday's game will be forced to testify this Friday before Stearns's subcommittee—the same subcommittee that looked into steroids and the BCS.

"The American people need to know that we are here in Washington looking out for them and being ever vigilant about the issues that truly matter to them," said Representative Stearns. "We will not rest until that call is overturned and the Dolphins receive an official apology."

Corrente, who made the fumble ruling on the field, said he is willing to cooperate with the investigation, but doesn't see its importance.

"Congress continues to overstep its bounds," he said. "And regardless of that, it was clearly a fumble. And the replay showed it, too. This is such a waste of our time and a waste of taxpayers' money."

But Representative Stearns disagrees.

"The NFL is a multibillion-dollar industry that plays in taxpayer-funded stadiums," he said. "It is most definitely the business of Congress to make sure that they get their fumble rulings correct. Plus, we really enjoy doing these investigations into sports. It's not nearly as boring as all that war-and-taxes junk, but even better is that a lot of the times we get to meet and talk to famous athletes. I had Mark McGwire sign a bunch of stuff for my kids when he was here. It was totally awesome."

CRAPPY THIRD-STRINGER WISHING HE HAD AN OUTLET FOR HIS AWESOME TOUCHDOWN DANCE

LeShawn Lewis, the sixth wide receiver on the Tennessee Titans, is hoping somehow, some way he can get into the end zone this year so he can unveil a touchdown dance he has developed and claims would be the talk of the league for weeks.

"I'm not going to go into any details of what the dance would be, but—trust me—the creativity and choreography would be unlike anything anyone has ever seen," said Lewis. "I'd immediately become a legend. Unfortunately, I kind of suck at football and I probably have a better chance of being cut before the season is over than I do of scoring a touchdown."

Lewis claims he is just one of many like him around the league who could dance circles around the likes of Terrell Owens, Chad Johnson, and Ray Lewis, if given the opportunity, but don't have the game to get on the field, grab the spotlight, and become famous.

"My role model is Freddie Mitchell, that receiver on the Eagles a few years ago," said Lewis. "I mean, that guy sucked about as much as you can in this league and still have a roster spot. But since the Eagles were so short at wide receiver, he was able to get on the field and when he got the ball in his hands he made the most of it, dancing and gyrating after every catch, never mind waiting for touchdowns. Doing that made him a household name, even though he blew at football. That's what it's all about, really. Screw winning the Super Bowl or whatever. The NFL is about getting on TV."

So, desperate for his moment in the sun, Lewis said he has stooped to working on his game and studying his playbook more than practicing his dance moves.

"If the only way for me to become known around the league is by first becoming a better player so I can get in the game and then score, I guess I'm going to have to do that—even though I'm worried it will leave my touchdown dance a bit rusty when and if I'm ever able to debut it," said Lewis. "In all honesty, I almost feel like a sellout working so hard on my game, but if I don't share this dance with the public before my career is over I'll regret it the rest of my life."

KURT WARNER CREDITS GOD FOR HIS DRAMATIC DECLINE

Arizona Cardinals quarterback Kurt Warner, once one of the NFL's greatest rags-to-riches stories as a member of the Rams, has struggled mightily since leading St. Louis to Super Bowl appearances in 2000 and 2002, piling up losses and turnovers at a startling rate.

And Warner credits all of it to God.

"I wouldn't be able to play this way without God's strength," said Warner, whose dramatic decline has in part been due to a chronically injured thumb on his throwing hand. "I'm only able to compete every week because of my faith."

Warner said his willingness to pin his horrendous play on God is due to a desire to be consistent in his spiritual walk.

"If I'm going to give God all the credit when I'm throwing for five touchdowns and winning Super Bowls, then he's going to get an equal share when I suck," he said. "I've prayed about this and am going to keep pinning my play on God until I turn it around. After that, I might just be more private in my faith from then on. We'll see."

Warner also said he plans to make it a habit to point to the heavens after each turnover he commits, just as he does when he throws a touchdown.

OSAMA BIN LADEN'S DORMANT FANTASY FOOTBALL TEAM BROKEN UP

Osama bin Laden's inactive fantasy football team is being broken up.

Bin Laden's team, which competed in the Philly All-Starz league on CNNSI.com, has been inactive for five weeks. League rules state that any team which is not accessed for more than four weeks will be declared dead and its players dispersed among the league in a special draft.

Though in fifth place in the ten-team league, bin Laden's team—Allah Way to the Super Bowl—has not been updated since Week 8. Bin Laden was in third place at that time. Fellow league members assume bin Laden has been on the run from forces seeking his capture since then, and unable to gain Internet access.

Jimmy Steever, age fourteen and owner of the second-place PA Terminators, said it was obvious bin Laden was inactive. "He's had Fred Taylor at starting running back the whole season even though Taylor has been hurt for weeks. That's just not like Osama to keep a hurt player in the lineup."

Steever said that bin Laden's inactivity gave him a much needed win last week. "I only beat Allah Way by two points last week, 87–85. If he had someone else in place of Taylor I probably would have lost."

Other league members say bin Laden was a master at picking up steals off the waiver wire.

"He got Frank Gore and Drew Brees off the free agent list," said Garry Inruit, owner of the sixth-place East Side Ballerz. "If he hadn't been forced to leave his cave I bet he would have won the whole league."

Inruit said bin Laden's only flaw was coveting certain players too much.

"Osama offered me Peyton Manning and Terrell Owens for Muhsin Muhammad," Inruit said. "I accepted, of course, but the trade didn't pass league approval."

TEAM SUCCUMBS TO LOCKER-ROOM CANCER

The Dallas Cowboys died of locker-room cancer on Sunday following a battle with the disease that rapidly spread among the team after wide receiver Terrell Owens was first diagnosed last year. The entire team succumbed at approximately 5:05 P.M. EST, less than an hour after the Cowboys lost 21–10 to the Redskins.

"I was as distraught as anyone to learn that the team had contracted locker-room cancer," said coach Bill Parcells. "But I was proud of the way they held their heads high and fought it. I can only trust now that they are in a better place."

The NFL announced it will help the Cowboys rebuild their team by granting the team two extra draft picks in each round of next April's draft. Dallas will play the remainder of this season's schedule with a roster of free agents; 50 percent of gate revenues will go to support locker-room and clubhouse cancer research.

STORIES TOP STORIES   TOP STORIES TOP STORIES **IN OTHER NEWS . . .**

Brave man records game without the express written consent of the NFL . . . Undefeated '72 Dolphins squad gathers to go to a strip club . . . Jon Bon Jovi's Arena Football team sets attendance record on "Kick Bon Jovi in the Nuts Night" . . . Report: NFL teams interviewing the same black guy to skirt minority hiring requirements . . . Archeological dig turns up world's first-known Bengals joke . . .

COLLEGE FOOTBALL

CHARLIE WEIS'S ENTIRE CONTRACT TO BE PAID IN ICE CREAM

According to sources with inside knowledge of the negotiations between Notre Dame and Charlie Weis, the Irish's head coach only agreed to a ten-year contract extension after the university promised to pay him the entire worth of his deal in ice cream and other delicious dessert treats.

Now signed through 2015, Weis's deal is worth between $30 million and $40 million—enough to allow him to ingest some 15 million desserts and more than 10 billion calories over the life of the deal.

"Let's just say I haven't stopped smiling since the deal was finalized," said Weis. "I have an intense hunger to bring Notre Dame a national championship—a hunger that's matched only by my love for ice cream sundaes, ice cream cones, fried ice cream, ice cream cakes, donuts, pie, Tasty Kakes, Mallomars, cookies, fudge, brownies, fudge brownies, cupcakes, Snickers, icing, whipped cream, chocolate, heavy whipping cream, Cadbury crème eggs—shall I continue?—deep-fried Twinkies, bear claws, sticky buns, pastries, Smores, Kit Kats, marshmallows, and chocolate-covered lard balls. And I also can put away a few dozen donut holes if need be, although they're not my favorite. Too small."

Faced with speculation in recent weeks that NFL teams would try to lure the former Patriots assistant away after the season, Notre Dame moved to lock up their first-year coach for the long term and quickly hammered out a deal. But it was only after the school acceded to Weis's unorthodox demand of dessert payment that the extension was finalized.

"Charlie told them it was dessert money or he was walking—or shuffling in his case," said a source close to Notre Dame athletic director Kevin White. "He claimed the Raiders were interested in him, and that the job intrigued him because Oakland is only a few hours away from Nestlé's U.S. headquarters in Glendale. That showed them he was serious, and they immediately contacted several large food-service companies to determine the logistics of keeping Weis sated. Aramark won the bidding, and within hours the deal was done."

Weis is reportedly overjoyed with the deal.

"His lifelong dreams were to coach Notre Dame and gorge himself on delicious dessert foods to his heart's content," said a friend of the coach. "He never dreamed them both to be possible, but when Notre Dame offered him an extension, he decided he'd go for it."

Notre Dame's White is simply hopeful Weis can continue producing results on the field.

"To be honest, we don't expect him to live the full length of the deal," he said. "I mean, jeez—look at the friggin' guy, he's enormous. We just hope he wins a few more games for us while he's still alive."

GEORGIA'S UGA DELIGHTS CROWD BY MAULING INFANT IN LSU PAJAMAS

Georgia's 34–14 upset victory over LSU on Saturday in the SEC Championship game may have sent their fans away happy from the Georgia Dome, but it was the actions of the school's famed mascot—Uga—before kickoff that truly riled up the Bulldog faithful.

As the two teams went through pregame warm-ups, Uga trotted on to the sidelines with his official handler, seemingly calm and collected. But suddenly, spotting a toddler dressed in an LSU outfit near the Tigers cheerleaders, the famed bulldog sprang into action, ripping and tearing into the child's face and midsection.

After five to ten seconds of the unchecked carnage, the little boy's screams finally ceased when the enraged Uga tore out his voice box, after which shocked witnesses managed to pull the dog away.

But it was too late.

The child's LSU purple-and-yellow pj's saturated deep red with his own blood, his face—where a Tigers logo was stenciled just seconds before—mangled beyond recognition, his left arm almost completely torn away. He was dead.

And the Georgia partisans immediately rose to their feet in joyous applause.

"That was the most awesome thing I've ever seen," exclaimed Paul Ruth, a Georgia alum. "What a way to get up for a game! Nothing has ever gotten me more pumped to watch the Bulldogs."

"We all thought Uga couldn't be loved any more than he already was by the Georgia faithful, but then he goes and does something like this. Just outstanding," said Mary Robinson, president of the school's alumni association. "I guess this should serve as a warning to everyone out there. Look at Uga wrong and he'll rip you apart, even if you're a little kid."

Those fans who weren't lucky enough to see the attack with their own eyes were able to watch more than a dozen replays of the bloody mauling on the arena Jumbotron. Each replay was met with a chorus of boos from LSU fans, while Georgia backers continued to applaud and high-five.

"Sure, some might say showing the attack over and over and over was in bad taste, but my job here is to give fans what they want and keep them entertained," said Michael Rivera, the Georgia Dome's facilities media director. "And that's all I was trying to do. Plus, that was just the coolest attack ever. I immediately downloaded a copy to my computer and put it up on my blog."

Atlanta police are currently trying to find Uga and his handler to euthanize the animal and possibly make an arrest, but the dog has been difficult to track down as he has been feted at party after party by powerful Georgia alumni since Saturday.

HACKERS PUT MIT ATOP BCS STANDINGS

MIT, which just completed a 1–8 season and competes in NCAA Division III, is atop the new BCS standings.

The change at number one has led many to conjecture that hackers are the reason for MIT's sudden rise, being that they were unranked coming into this week, and have losses to Salve Regina University, Worcester State, and Western New England, among others. The NCAA, however, consistent in its defense of the BCS's infallibility, claims the new standings are correct.

"We use the most technologically advanced encryption software on our BCS computers," NCAA spokesman David Schapp said. "The BCS standings have taken a lot of flack over the years, but they've always proven themselves at the end of the year, and they will again this year."

Schapp said he was unaware of reports that the BCS encryption software was designed by a former MIT quarterback, J. Thomas Kilpatrick IV.

USC, formerly number one in the rankings, was displeased to hear the news.

"This absolutely sucks and doesn't seem fair," said USC had coach Pete Carroll. "But we've been on the short end of the BCS system before, so unfortunately this isn't all that surprising."

MIT players say they are working around the clock to build a solar-powered plane that will fly them to the BCS Championship Game in January.

SCHOOLS BACK OFF PREP RECRUIT
AFTER HE GETS A C-PLUS IN ALGEBRA

Nearly a dozen Division I-A football powers pursuing blue chip running back recruit Josh Williams have stated today they are rescinding scholarship offers to the high school All-American after it was discovered he received a C-plus in algebra this marking period.

"Josh is probably the greatest high school player I have ever seen and I would love to have him suit up in a Seminoles uniform," said Florida State head coach Bobby Bowden, "but Florida State is

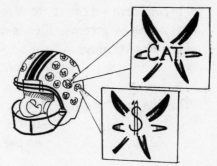

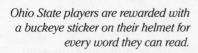

Ohio State players are rewarded with a buckeye sticker on their helmet for every word they can read.

an institution of higher learning, and we place academics far above athletic achievement here. C-plus work just won't cut it."

"A C-plus is average work," Ohio State head coach Jim Tressel, who was thought to be in the lead in the Williams sweepstakes. "We don't admit students to Ohio State who are merely average, and that includes athletes. We are very proud of the standards we have set for our program, and we will not compromise them under any circumstance."

Williams says his C-plus is due to the fact that he missed more than a week of school before Christmas due to strep throat.

"I worked as hard as I possibly could to make up the work, but I missed the pre-exam review and everything and it was tough to stay up with everyone else," said Williams. "I had a B-plus in algebra before the test, but I got a C on it and it really hurt my grade. I was hoping all the schools recruiting me would be more understanding—especially since I got a 1350 on my SAT—but they seem to take a no excuses, no second chances approach with recruits."

Virginia Tech head coach Frank Beamer says he doubts Williams, no matter how talented he is, will find any school willing to take him now.

"Maybe some junior college or something will take him, but that's a big maybe," said Beamer. "Kids like this must remember that they need to put their focus on off-the-field things like academics and community service if they want to be a part of major college football. No program that I know of is going to put up with players with poor grades or poor character just for wins and success on the field. College football is bigger than that."

"I'm confident we can contend for the national championship next year if we increase the team's payroll this off-season and sign a few top players."
—*Jim Tressel, Ohio State football coach*

"Thwhup nuhth piffft."
—*Lou Holtz, commenting on television on the USC-Notre Dame game*

"A lot of people said I could never win a Super Bowl, but today I proved them wrong. Hey, how did I get here? Where am I? Who are you people? I like cottage cheese."
—*Joe Paterno, after coaching Penn State to a victory over Northwestern*

GREAT MOMENTS IN COLLEGE FOOTBALL HISTORY

DECEMBER 29, 1978 Sixty-five-year-old Ohio State football coach Woody Hayes throws a punch at a Clemson football player during his team's loss in the Gator Bowl. Hayes was fired the next day and embarked on a successful but brief career in the ill-fated Olden Gloves boxing circuit.

NOVEMBER 20, 1982 California beats Stanford, 25–20, with a dramatic kick return in the final seconds that featured several laterals. The game will be remembered as much for the return as it will be for Stanford head coach Paul Wiggin's controversial decision to use members of the school's band on his special teams.

FEBRUARY 27, 1987 The NCAA cancels SMU's 1987 football schedule for "gross violations," including burping, passing exceptionally odorous farts, and chewing loudly without closing their mouths.

COLLEGE FOOTBALL FUN FACT

The Manning family has won just as many Heisman Trophies as your family.

SportsPickleNation Poll

Which bowl fact is most interesting?

4%   Alamo Bowl—originally called A Lame-O Bowl, the name was shortened in 1996 for marketing purposes

12%   AutoZone Liberty Bowl—the price of liberty is a $500,000 sponsorship from a discount auto parts retailer

9%   Capital One Bowl—competing teams are charged 24.99% interest on all expenses

30%   Cotton Bowl—the Cotton Bowl was much more profitable during slavery

14%   Holiday Bowl—by not calling it the Christmas Bowl, Holiday bowl organizers show they hate Jesus

11%   Motor City Bowl—each year the losing team's bus is driven to midfield, flipped over, and set on fire

7%   MPC Computers Bowl—pits the top two teams in the MPC Computer rankings, which are somehow even worse than the BCS rankings

13%   Music City Bowl—held in Nashville, the bowl's full name is the Sh—ty Music City Bowl

PEOPLE TO KNOW

BOBBY BOWDEN Bowden has forged a legendary career for himself at Florida State, accumulating the most wins in Division I-A history and leading the Seminoles to two national titles—an impressive résumé considering most of his players are forced by court order to play while wearing heavy, awkward electronic monitoring bracelets. In addition to instruction on the field, Bowden imparts Christian values to his players—at least, those values other than the Ten Commandments that outlaw lying, murder, and stealing. In recent years Bowden has turned over almost complete control of the team to his assistants, a move that came on the advice of his lawyers so it would be more difficult for him to ever be charged as an accessory.

PAUL "BEAR" BRYANT The head coach at Alabama from 1958 to 1982, Bryant is better known as the man who proudly wore the world's ugliest hat for parts of four decades. But many know him as more than an unrepentant fashion victim—he was a great football coach, winning six national titles and 323 games during his career. Bryant was revered by Alabama citizens during his tenure and many even held him in higher esteem than their local Klan Klavern leader. But Bryant himself was not a bigot, embracing the integration of black players on his team and even giving a roster spot to a mentally retarded player named Forrest Gump.

PETE CARROLL One of the top coaches to come along in college football in decades, Carroll will no doubt be an excellent NFL coach someday if he's ever given the chance. Carroll's greatest strength as a college coach is in recruiting, as he is able to somehow sell USC's facilities, beaches and co-eds to high school players. He is also regarded as a brilliant defensive mind, and that has proved out on the field as USC is yet to finish absolutely dead last nationally in team defense. *Fun Fact*: Pete Carroll thinks his 2003 USC team won the national championship. (Shhh. Don't tell him the truth.)

JOE PATERNO Known as much for his longevity as for his successes, the Penn State head coach set the mark for most career coaching victories in 2001, although Bobby Bowden has since passed him. But Paterno has an ace up his sleeve, as in recent years he has made a push for the record for most career coaching losses. His decades of achievement ensure his place among the all-time greats, but in recent years his legacy has tarnished a bit due to increased losing—which many attribute to Paterno's continued insistence that the forward pass is just a fad. The coach is beloved in the Penn State community for his tireless philanthropy. For example, he and his wife donated $250,000 and helped raise millions more for expansion of the school's library—and Penn State is currently build-

*Joe Paterno may have more than
100 career losses as a football
coach, but his glasses are
undefeated against ants.*

ing the world's largest greenhouse for its botany program exclusively with glass taken from Paterno's glasses.

KNUTE ROCKNE Born in Norway in 1888, Rockne was the first in a long line of great Norwegian football coaches. As the head coach at Notre Dame from 1918 to 1930 he achieved the greatest winning percentage in history with six national titles and a 105–12–5 record. He quit after the 1930 season when he sensed the "Win one for the Gipper!" speech he gave before each game was starting to lose its motivational powers with his players. Rockne's life was memorialized nine years after his death in the 1940 film *Knute Rockne, All-American*—a film that Hollywood released in his native land with the title *Knute Rockne, All-American (Screw You, Norwegians)*.

STEVE SPURRIER The 1966 Heisman Trophy winner as the quarterback for Florida, Spurrier coached his alma mater from 1990 to 2001, winning six SEC titles and one national championship. He then became the head coach of the Washington Redskins, where he found the going much tougher without the likes of Vanderbilt and Louisiana-Monroe on his schedule. Before the 2005 season he became the head coach at South Carolina, although most people have always thought of him as a Cock. *Fun Fact*: Spurrier thinks the greatest quarterback of all-time is Danny Wuerffel.

BOB STOOPS The Oklahoma head coach has restored the Sooner program to national prominence since taking the reins in 1999, compiling an impressive record and winning a national championship—

leading many to say he has surpassed Steve Spurrier as the greatest visored coach in football history. Stoops developed a reputation as a defensive genius with successful defensive coordinator stints at both Kansas State and Florida in the 1990s. At Florida he is greatly revered for being the first coach to introduce the team to the concept known as "defense." Stoops is married with three children, but until 2005 Texas head coach Mack Brown was legally registered as his bitch.

CHARLIE WEIS After an exhaustive search for a new football coach before the 2005 season that focused on Urban Meyer and then other coaches as a Plan B and so on, Notre Dame was forced to go with their Plan Q-2.36(b), Charlie Weis. Like an eager-to-please fat girl, however, Weis did not disappoint. He guided Notre Dame to a 9–2 record in his inaugural season and a spot in a BCS bowl. So great was his success that it forced the Catholic church to reexamine the issue of homosexuality as many American Catholic men developed intense man-crushes on the lard pile that is Weis. The former New England Patriots assistant demands absolute discipline from his players and stresses that there are no shortcuts in football or in life. *Fun Fact*: Weis underwent gastric bypass surgery in 2002 hoping to find a shortcut to weight loss.

AL-QAEDA.COM BOWL SEEKS TO SOFTEN IMAGE

Two college football programs are soon to be very grateful to Osama Bin Laden's Al-Qaeda network.

The inaugural Al-Qaeda.com Bowl will be played January 1 in Kabul. The Al-Jazeera network will televise the game live and each competing team will receive $1 million from an untraceable overseas account.

Al-Qaeda is holding the bowl in an attempt to boost its image in America from an unfriendly terrorist regime to one of a pro-American, tourist-friendly organization. The organization also hopes to boost traffic to its Web site—www.Al-Qaeda.com—to increase recruitment and promote its new sports page.

"Tourism in Afghanistan and elsewhere in the Middle East has dipped dramatically since 9/11 and we want to see more tourists here," Bin Laden said at a press conference announcing the bowl. "I can think of nothing better than having thousands of unarmed American citizens walking aimlessly around the Middle East for us to interact with."

BACKUP ECSTATIC OVER STARTER'S INJURY

As Texas State quarterback Matt Rogers was being carted off the field Saturday, minutes after receiving a concussion and a torn ACL from a brutal hit on a sack, backup quarterback Blake Mitchell could be seen joyfully jumping up and down on the sidelines, ecstatic over his good fortune.

With Rogers unable to return, Mitchell played the rest of the game with a huge smile on his face, leading Texas State to a 31–22 win over Chattanooga.

The new starter's joy did not diminish at the postgame press conference. "This is the best thing that's ever happened to me," Mitchell said, still beaming. "When I saw Matt get hit like that I got really excited, and then when he didn't get up I was just filled with happiness. The only way I was going to get to play was if he got hurt. This is fantastic. Hopefully he'll be out for the season or even have his career in jeopardy. If so, the job is mine for the rest of my career here."

BOBBY BOWDEN ROBBED,
SODOMIZED BY STARTING TAILBACK

Florida State coach Bobby Bowden was robbed and sodomized by his starting tailback on Sunday, the first time the head coach himself has been the target of a crime by one of his players.

Yet the longtime Seminole icon said he doubted the player who robbed and sodomized him was guilty, but stated that if he was, there was no way the coaching staff could keep their eyes on the players at all times. "He's a good kid. I doubt it was really him who did that to me, even though it looked a lot like him," said Bowden. "But boys will be boys, you know."

The assault occurred late Sunday evening outside the Seminoles' football offices as Bowden walked alone to his car. Bowden's starting tailback robbed the coach of his cash and credit cards before repeatedly sodomizing him over a fifteen-minute period. The player was nabbed by police three hours later after Bowden provided a physical description of the assailant; the coach refused to identify the player for police by name. An August 26 trial is scheduled.

Bowden's victimization is the latest incident in a long line of off-the-field troubles his program has experienced in the last decade. Whispers that Bowden has lost control of his football program have escalated into all-out public debate, with the coach on the defensive.

Yet Bowden denies that getting robbed and sodomized by one of his own players is an example of a loss of control.

"Okay, so let's say it was my starting tailback who did this to me," said Bowden. "I just don't see how that is a reflection on me or this program. I do not understand how you can say that if a kid goes out at two o'clock at night and gets in trouble that the coach should have stopped it. Folks, some of these kids are doing the same things I did when I was in college. The fact that it was me—the head coach of the team—who was robbed and sodomized is an entirely different matter."

Bowden said he has no plans to suspend his tailback until the case winds its way through the legal process.

"Innocent until proven guilty, right? These are kids, folks. Let's not rush to judgment here," said Bowden. "Just because I commented to the police that the assailant who robbed and sodomized me looked exactly like my starting tailback doesn't mean it was him. Anyone could get their hands on an appropriately numbered Florida State football practice jersey, have an uncanny resemblance to one of my players, call me 'Coach Bowden,' rob and sodomize me and then ask what time the team meeting is the next day, am I right, folks? So I will not suspend him until justice takes its course. And I may not even suspend him if he's convicted if he looks me in the eye and says that he is sorry."

PHIL FULMER RECEIVES YET ANOTHER PIECE OF HATE MAIL FRAUGHT WITH MISSPELLINGS

Tennessee head football coach Philip Fulmer received yet another piece of hate mail today. Like almost all the hate mail Fulmer receives, this one was full of misspellings and typos and syntax errors. It also had an Alabama postmark.

"Alabama fans are still really upset at me," said Fulmer, who ratted out the Crimson Tide to the NCAA. "That's fine if they have hard feelings, I just wish they'd take a little more time to write their hate mail. I can decipher Sanskrit better than this stuff."

Fulmer has further angered Alabama fans by having the Tennessee football office return many of the letters to their senders with a note attached saying: "Coach Fulmer regrets to inform you that he couldn't understand your illiterate ramblings, you retarded inbred."

But Alabama fans who have received their hate mail back from Fulmer say he is the one without a proper grasp of the English language. "I used several words with more than two syllables, so that was probably a problem for him," said Clyde Fisher of Montgomery. "Plus, I don't think I mentioned food in it, so he probably had trouble keeping his attention."

RIES TOP STORIES   TOP STORIES   TOP STORIES   **IN OTHER NEWS . . .**

BYU quarterback dating entire cheerleading squad . . . Player thought to be too small to play college football turns out to be too small to play college football . . . Sideline-clearing study session mars Harvard-Yale game; knowledge ensues . . . Quarterback's motivational halftime speech would have been legendary had team won . . . Sylvester Croom becomes the SEC's first black coach to get diarrhea . . . Goalposts emotionally torn down . . . Balls lightly caressed in postfumble pileup . . . Fame-seeking Stanford tuba player refuses to get off the friggin' field . . . Report: Most of hard-drive space on BCS computer filled by porn . . .

NBA

SELFISH KOBE BRYANT REFUSING TO PASS TO HIS CRAPPY TEAMMATES

Kobe Bryant's recent scoring binge may have catapulted the Los Angeles Lakers to a three-game win streak, but it's only fueled his reputation as a selfish player who never passes.

"Yeah, I hear that a lot," said Bryant. "That I need to pass and get my teammates involved more. But have you seen my teammates? Our starting point guard is someone named 'Smush,' for crying out loud. I could pass the ball every chance I get it and I'm not going to get more than four or five assists a night 'cause I'm the only guy on the team who can make a shot."

Lakers coach Phil Jackson said he pulled his star player aside last week to discuss his role on the team.

"I asked him if he would rather return this team to the play-offs and win a scoring title while building a reputation for being selfish, or improve his public persona while finishing dead last in the Western Conference," said Jackson. "He went with the former. And thank God, because if he hadn't I would have had to come up with a way to work Chris Mihm into the offense. Even I'm not that smart."

ALLEN IVERSON KEEPS IT REAL
FOR RECORD 2,548TH STRAIGHT DAY

Allen Iverson of the Denver Nuggets spent all day today keeping it real, the 2,548th straight day he has done so. The mark is thought to be a record for keeping it real for consecutive days by an athlete.

"How have I done it? I'm not sure," said Iverson. "I'm just trying to keep it real, you know?"

Iverson's string of keeping it real dates back to November 1998, when he ended a streak of 1,194 days of keeping it real at that time by watching an episode of *7th Heaven*. His previous instance of not keeping it real came in the summer of 1995 after he listened to, and enjoyed, a Bon Jovi song.

"I remember being about halfway through the episode of *7th Heaven* when I it hit me that I wasn't keeping it real by watching that show," said Iverson, "so I made a renewed commitment to keeping it real at all times." The All-Star guard says he immediately switched his television from *7th Heaven* to BET and has proceeded to keep it real since then.

Jim Brown is the previous record holder for keeping it real by an athlete. The ex-football star had kept it real consistently through the early 1990s before taking a role in the 1996 movie *Mars Attacks!*

Iverson, who grew up in Bethel, Virginia, under difficult circumstances that included scrapes with the law and a father who abandoned him, has tried to stay true to his roots, purchasing a $6 million, 14,000-square-foot home with 9.5 baths in suburban Philadelphia's ritzy Main Line area.

In addition to the home, Iverson has sought to keep it real by recording a rap album—which he ended up not releasing after receiving criticism of its lyrics—and adopting a very laissez-faire approach to practice.

"Not giving my best, or even showing up sometimes, at practice is really the key to my keeping it real in everything I do," said Iverson. "I want to be real both on and off the court. However, I do play hard in games, so if I also played hard in practice and set an example for my teammates and fans, that might not send the message that I want to get across—you know, that I don't really give a f—k and that I don't need this sh-t."

Iverson says that he has begun to sense some pressure from his supporters that he be linked to some type of criminal activity soon in order to reaffirm his credibility. It has been more than three years since Iverson has been in the police blotter.

"I understand that I probably need to get back on the police's radar in order to keep on keeping it real. I don't necessarily have to do anything, just get the police a little riled up, I guess. The only thing is, it's a bit tough to get in much trouble when you live on a huge, gated estate out on the Main Line. Maybe I'll just throw my wife, Tawanna, out of the house or something again and see if I get any ink on that. I'll do my best."

CBS DEBUTS *CSI: PORTLAND TRAILBLAZERS*

CBS debuted the latest incarnation of its *CSI* franchise last Wednesday with its new show *CSI: Portland Trailblazers*. The program will feature a team of crime scene investigators as they track the path of the Portland Trailblazers, piecing together evidence surrounding illegal activities linked to the players.

"Basing the new *CSI* in Portland, Oregon, and having it revolve around the Blazers was a natural extension of the *CSI* brand," said Les Milken, CBS president. "While the show is fictional, we want it to be as realistic as possible and having crime scene investigators on the case of the Portland Trailblazers provides that believability factor and gives it instant credibility."

CSI: Portland Trailblazers is the fourth member of the *CSI* franchise, following the original, *CSI: Miami*, and *CSI: New York*. Trailblazer forward Zach Randolph is scheduled to make guest appearances throughout the season.

LEBRON JAMES SEMEN SAMPLE TAKEN WITH FOURTH PICK IN NBA DRAFT

A Lebron James semen sample was taken fourth overall in last week's NBA draft, marking the first time in history an athlete's gametes were selected in the draft of a professional sports league. The Toronto Raptors selected the sample, claiming its enormous potential necessitated the pick.

"We actually had it second on our draft board, so we were ecstatic that it was still available when our pick came up," said Toronto Raptors general manager Bryan Colangelo. "We balanced the potential of some of the college and high school players who were out there with the potential of James's spawn in twenty years and decided we could wait it out."

NBA draft analysts immediately rated the Raptors selection of the semen as the steal of the draft. "The Raptors now not only have an opportunity to put a near duplication of Lebron James in uniform by 2025, but an entire roster of them," said ESPN's Jay Bilas. "Remember, there are millions of sperm in a tablespoon of semen, offering Toronto an amazing amount of breeding possibilities."

Raptors representatives immediately debunked a rumor that said the semen sample was obtained illegally from an NBA groupie who obtained early access to James, saying the sample was authorized and entered into the draft by its owner.

"Lebron and his representatives know good business opportunities," said Grunwald. "Now not only does he get his contract from Cleveland, but the value of the contract we'll sign his semen sample, too. Well, at least until the person that comes from it turns eighteen."

The Raptors will immediately begin searching for female eggs in which to match James's sperm, with several top WNBA players targeted as potential donors.

MAVERICKS WONDERING WHO HAS THAT GUY STANDING OVER THERE UNDER THE BASKET

The Mavericks would like to know who it is that is supposed to be covering that guy standing all alone over there right under the basket.

"I don't think it's my guy," said power forward Dirk Nowitzki. "He looks a little bit too small to be my guy. Usually I'm supposed to be guarding tall guys. So even though he's wide open, I'll just let him go because I don't think it's my assignment. I have enough trouble keeping track of my own guy."

Dallas guard Jason Terry is pretty sure the wide-open player is not his, either.

"He was mine a few seconds ago," said Terry. "But now I don't think he is. I had him until I was screened, then I switched to another man. We're switching screens, right? I thought coach told us to switch on screens last time-out. No? Then I have no idea if that's my man or not. I hope not, because he's wide open."

Swingman Jerry Stackhouse said the wide-open player who was about to score an uncontested dunk shot could very well be his man, but that's not really why he is on the court.

"They don't put me out here for defense," said Stackhouse. "I don't know who I'm guarding half the time I'm on the court. So that very well could be my man, and it very well could be not. I don't know. What I'm thinking about right now, though, is not how that guy got wide open, but the awesome turnaround jumper I want to take next time down the court. I would call it Jordanesque. Just wait until you see it. Right after this guy finishes dunking I'll have a chance to get the ball in my hands again and do it."

Center DeSagana Diop says that if he was in the game, that guy wouldn't have just completed his wide-open dunk on the Mavericks.

"I would have done everything in my power to block his shot," said Diop. "That's my role on this team. I run around maniacally trying to block shots. Sure, a lot of times I leave the guy I'm supposed to be guarding wide open as I chase a guard across the lane, but when I'm actually able to get a block, it's really awesome. I like to knock them all the way into the stands."

With his team now back on offense, head coach Avery Johnson is hopeful his team will refocus next time on the defensive end.

"We can't have lapses like that," said Johnson. "Everybody needs to know who they have. It's simple stuff. Ah, jeez . . . here we go again. A fast break for a wide-open layup."

"We're talking about practice. I mean, listen, we're sitting here talking about practice, not a recital, not an actual performance, but we're talking about practice. I know it's important, I honestly do, but we're talking about practice. We're talking about practice, man. We're talking about practice. We're talking about practice. We're not talking about a recital. We're talking about practice."

—Allen Iverson's daughter after her father told her to practice the piano

SportsPickleNation Poll

Why did Shaq and Kobe finally resolve their differences?

17% They decided to collaborate on the worst rap album of all time

14% Shaq wants to let bygones be bygones so he can focus on starting a feud with Dwyane Wade

11% Kobe sent Shaq a great recipe for sticky buns

24% David Stern reminded them that white people are uncomfortable around angry black men

6% Jeannie Buss promised she would do them both at center count during a Heat-Lakers game if they made up

16% They wanted to set a good example for pathetic egomaniacs everywhere

12% They finally realized that no one gives a crap

GREAT MOMENTS IN NBA HISTORY

JANUARY 20, 1892 Students at the International YMCA Training School in Springfield, Massachusetts, play the first organized basketball game. Unorganized basketball games had been played for centuries, however, on the AND1 Mix Tape Tour.

AUGUST 21, 1936 Wilt Chamberlain is born and begins suckling his mother's breast, an experience he always regarded as his first and most satisfying of more than 20,000 sexual encounters.

MARCH 2, 1951 The NBA holds its first NBA All-Star Game as the West defeats the East, 111–94. The game was preceded by the league's first-ever Sensible, Conservative Layup Contest, a staple at All-Star Games in the 1950s.

SEPTEMBER 14, 1991 Magic Johnson marries Earletha "Cookie" Kelly. Johnson surprised Kelly by adding the words "in HIV and in AIDS" to their vows at the last minute.

DECEMBER 21, 1993 Shaquille O'Neal's "I Know I Got Skillz" single from his debut rap album is certified Gold by the Recording Industry Association of America, dropping the value of gold in world markets to record lows.

JULY 1, 2003 Kobe, Japan, gang-rapes Eagle County, Colorado.

NBA FUN FACT

In the time it takes for you to read this sentence, five NBA players have had sex with your wife.

NBA FUN FACT

Larry Bird released a rap album in 2004 titled A Bird in Yo' Hand Is Worth a Cap in Yo' Ass. *The track list included:*

"White Chocolate"
"Comin' Atcha from Way Down Town"
"Beantown Bitches"
"Release, Rotation, Splizzash"
"Kevin McHale Yeah"
"Pass the Chronic (It's the Off-season)"
"Lakers Be Fakers"
"Mo Money, Mo Cheeks"
"Tippin' the Forty to the Boston Garden"
"Indiana Hoes Like to be French Licked"
"Haven't Ya Heard? The Greatest Be Larry Bird"

PEOPLE TO KNOW

KAREEM ABDUL-JABBAR Born Lew Alcindor in 1947, the Hall of Fame center changed his name in honor of his sporting idol, former Dolphins running back Karim Abdul-Jabbar. After dominating college basketball at UCLA in the late sixties he moved to the NBA, where he starred with the Milwaukee Bucks and Los Angeles Lakers and became the NBA's all-time leading scorer. Few people realize it, but as much as Abdul-Jabbar did to revolutionize modern center play with his patented "sky hook" and low-post moves, he did more to revolutionize modern style. Think about it—before Abdul-Jabbar came along, male-pattern baldness, short shorts on men, and sport goggles were not thought of as the epitome of "cool" as they are today. *Fun Fact*: Abdul-Jabbar's turn-ons include Islam, *Airplane!*, and pot.

CARMELO ANTHONY After a successful career as a comedian and actor, Whoopi Goldberg changed her name to Carmelo Anthony in 2003 and entered the NBA. "Anthony" grew up in Baltimore, Maryland, and still maintains close ties to the city, most notably to its burgeoning snitch-killing industry. He has been the face of the Denver Nuggets organization since being drafted by the team after one season at Syracuse, and will remain so until he becomes a free agent and signs with a franchise in a bigger market. *Fun Fact*: Carmelo Anthony's friends like to hide marijuana in his belongings to see if he can find it before he goes through airport security.

CHARLES BARKLEY A controversial figure during his playing days, Barkley accumulated numerous fines, got in fights, made outlandish statements, was sued, and even spit on a little girl. Surprisingly, though, he never ate anyone. His game more than made up for his behavior, however. Listed at six foot six but probably closer to six foot four (width, not height), Barkley was a ferocious rebounder and one of only four players in NBA history to reach 20,000 points, 10,000 rebounds, and 4,000 assists. While he never won an NBA title, he has won countless championships on the competitive eating tour. He now works as an NBA in-studio analyst for TNT, where observant viewers can actually see him gaining weight from one commercial break to the next. *Fun Fact*: In 2005

Barkley published the book *Who's Afraid of a Large Black Man?* He is currently working on a follow-up titled *Pretty Much Everyone*.

LARRY BIRD Without a doubt one of the greatest basketball players ever, the Celtics legend was All-NBA first team nine times and a three-time league MVP. He also made *People* magazine's 50 Ugliest People list thirteen times. Lacking elite athleticism, Bird made up for it with hard work and an array of near-indefensible moves. His patented move was dubbed the "Look at Me," in which he would tell the player guarding him to look at his face and then, with the defender shocked and disgusted and stifling vomit, he would dribble past him for an easy hoop. Bird's rivalry with Lakers star Magic Johnson is credited with reviving the NBA. Although Johnson got the better of him when it comes to NBA titles, winning five to Bird's three, Bird took a long-term approach to defeating Magic by regularly sending dozens of VD-ridden groupies to Johnson's hotel rooms. Bird retired after the 1992 season because he was embarrassed that his game had slipped so much that white guys had become able to guard him. *Fun Fact*: Every black person in the world thinks they could take Bird one-on-one.

LARRY BROWN If there is one thing to say about Larry Brown it's that his word is his bond. And if there are two things to say about Larry Brown it's that (1) his word is his bond, and that (2) his bond is a steaming pile of crap. The North Carolina grad and former ABA point guard is the only man to have coached teams to both NCAA and NBA titles. He is also the only man to have coached all 326 Division I basketball teams and all 30 NBA teams. The nomadic coach moved to the New York Knicks before the 2005–2006 season and immediately transformed the team upon his arrival just as was hoped, taking them from awful to downright horrible. Despite that success, Brown was let go by the team after the season—a move he said disappointed him because it showed how little loyalty there is in modern sports.

KOBE BRYANT A cautionary tale for teenage players who want to jump to the NBA, Bryant struggled mightily at the outset of his career, as it took him until his second year to become an All-Star and all the way until his fourth season to win an NBA title. Bryant grew up mostly in Italy, where his father played basketball. He is able to speak both English and Italian and can also BS fluently in each. Once the golden boy of the NBA with a squeaky clean image, Bryant's reputation was tarnished in 2003 when he was charged with sexual assault. The case was eventually dismissed when the accuser said she didn't want to proceed, a decision she made after Kobe gave her an eight-carat, $4 million, purple diamond ring. Bryant's image has slowly recovered, and he is now being used again by Nike to pitch their products—most notably the first-ever Nike Air Rape shoe, the only piece of footwear on the market designed for use while raping. *Fun Fact*: Bryant met his wife, Vanessa, in 1999 during a hunting trip to Mexico with Karl Malone.

WILT CHAMBERLAIN A descendant of Bombaata, the ancient warrior who fought alongside the great Conan the Destroyer, Chamberlain was the most dominant offensive force in basketball history. He is third in career points (31,419) and the all-time leader in rebounds (23,924), rebounding average (22.9), and chicks nailed (20,000). Chamberlain was essentially unstoppable in the low post and registered the NBA's single-game points record in 1962 by tallying a remarkable 100 points against the Knicks. (He could have scored 200 points that night, but he shot 4 of 138 from the free throw line.) Chamberlain passed away at his home in Bel-Air, California at the age of sixty-three in 1999, but his death was not discovered for several days until Trojan Condoms, Inc., reported him missing after noticing a 70 percent drop in sales.

Wilt Chamberlain had sex with your mom.

TIM DUNCAN Truly one of the biggest free spirits ever to play the game, Duncan has defined consistent excellence since entering the NBA. He was taken first overall in the 1997 NBA draft by the San Antonio Spurs, a franchise that truly needed him after suffering through one losing season out of its previous eight and had no inside presence but David Robinson. Since then Duncan has become a three-time NBA champion, two-time league MVP, and five-time World Staring Contest champion. *Fun Fact*: The Tim Duncan Foundation raises money to help treat children without personalities.

JULIUS ERVING The athletic swingman starred for the Virginia Squires, New Jersey Nets, and Philadelphia 76ers. Actually, it was just the Nets and Sixers. I threw a made-up team in there just to see if you were paying attention. Erving's aerial moves and trademark Afro—which, by the way, he grew both upstairs and downstairs—helped him become a superstar in the 1970s and early '80s when pro basketball badly needed one. Known as Dr. J, he is credited with making the dunk popular, and without it *SportsCenter* would have nothing to show during their basketball highlights. *Fun Fact*: Erving was listed at six foot seven, but he was only five feet four sans 'fro.

KEVIN GARNETT Garnett was the first player in twenty years to join the NBA straight from high school when he was drafted by the Timberwolves in 1995. Despite that, he has actually attended just as many college classes as most NBA players who played college basketball (0). His height, athleticism, and versatility make him one of the toughest players to stop in the entire league. (*Note*: The preceding sentence only holds for regular-season action. No book refunds will be accepted for postseason play.) Garnett gives liberally of his time to community and charity activities—behavior that has caused the NBA players union to threaten him with expulsion numerous times.

ALLEN IVERSON A star guard at Georgetown, Iverson turned away from a potential career in law (breaking) to enter the NBA draft early. He was taken first overall in 1996 by the Philadephia 76ers, who were smitten by his practice habits. And the tiny guard did not disappointed, winning the 2001 league MVP award and leading the NBA in scoring four times—an especially amazing feat considering how much he likes to pass the ball. Iverson's style and attitude have made him very marketable to urban youth, although he is also the loving father of four children despite refusing to attend a single Lamaze practice. *Fun Fact*: Iverson has a rare disease that causes all clear patches of his skin to be filled by dark, ink-colored markings.

PHIL JACKSON Jackson has coached teams to a record nine NBA titles, the same amount as former Celtics coach Red Auerbach and at least the same amount that anyone else in the world lucky enough to coach Michael Jordan, Scottie Pippen, Shaquille O'Neal, and Kobe Bryant in their primes would have had. Jackson is known for his triangle offense, a complicated scheme that is most simply described with this diagram:

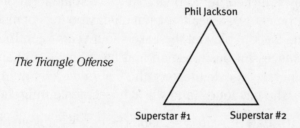

The Triangle Offense

Nicknamed "the Zen Master" due to his adherence to Eastern philosophy, Jackson published a book in 2004 about his travails with the Lakers, achieving bestseller enlightenment and showing that trashing people in a tell-all book somehow does not violate the tenets of Zen Buddhism. He is currently working on a new book, *Seriously, Kobe Bryant Is a Total Douche Bag*.

LEBRON JAMES Yet another tragic tale of a player going to the NBA too early, James scored only 25 points in his first regular-season game in 2004, and it was not until after he turned twenty years old in his second season that he was universally regarded as the league's most complete player. He won the NBA Rookie of the Year by tallying 508 votes, which edged out the number-two pick from his draft, Darko Milicic, by just 508 votes. James came out of St. Vincent-St. Mary High School full of potential and surrounded by hype—but also some controversy after it became public that his mother had given him a Hummer. Many in the media have looked at James's game and described him as the "next Magic Johnson" or the "next

Michael Jordan," although that talk has pretty much subsided as the media has become intent on uncovering the "next LeBron James," as the grizzled Cavaliers star is old news now that he's way into his early twenties. *Fun Fact*: James's opponents can take solace in knowing he won't reach his prime for another six or seven years.

MAGIC JOHNSON The Hall of Famer's given first name is Earvin, but he took on the nickname Magic as a child when he dreamed of growing up to be a porn star. Johnson burst onto the national scene in the late 1970s and early '80s as a star point guard with Michigan State and the Los Angeles Lakers, winning millions of fans and having unprotected sex with each and every one of them. Tragically, Johnson announced he had HIV in 1991 and retired from playing. But luckily, it turned out to be a totally awesome form of HIV and Johnson somehow got healthier, put on fifty pounds of muscle, and even came back to play for the Lakers four years later. Today Johnson is a successful businessman and has opened a chain of successful inner-city movie theaters, the first in the country that cater to people who talk loudly and yell at the screen during showings.

MICHAEL JORDAN Jordan is arguably the greatest athlete of all time, as long as baseball and golf are not considered athletic endeavors. Jordan dominated the NBA during most of his career, winning six championships and five MVP awards with the Chicago Bulls. His name is synonymous with Nike and the company's line of Air Jordan shoes and apparel, but he also endorsed McDonald's, Coca-Cola, and Ballpark Franks—products that any finely tuned athlete would most assuredly consume in vast quantities in order to stay in top shape. It was this level of credibility that made him the biggest marketing icon in sports history. Jordan retired and then returned several times during his career—once in 1993 to gamble on minor league baseball, and again in 1998 so he could devote time to devising a way to tarnish his legacy. And he came up with a good one: becoming a part owner and then player with the Washington freaking Wizards. Jordan struggled mightily in his two seasons in Washington but, sadly, was far and away the best player the franchise had ever seen. *Fun Fact*: A signed, mint-condition Michael Jordan rookie card can sell for more than $10,000. But not if it's signed by someone other than Michael Jordan.

TRACY McGRADY McGrady was a star Gaelic footballer before he moved with his family from Dublin as a teenager and picked up basketball. He is a relative of NBA guard Vince Carter, but McGrady comes from the side of the family that tries 60 percent of the time, while Carter's side only gives 20 percent. McGrady's career began alongside Carter with the Toronto Raptors. The pair created so much buzz in the city that they almost once made it on the front of the sports page ahead of a Maple Leafs story. After three years in Toronto he moved on to Orlando for four mostly disappointing years with the Magic. He was then traded to the Houston Rockets before the 2004–05 season where he promises to one day win a play-off series and maybe even be healthy at the same time as teammate Yao Ming for a game on two.

GEORGE MIKAN The greatest glasses'd player in basketball history outside of Kurt Rambis, Mikan was professional basketball's first big man. At six foot ten, he dominated the game in the 1940s and '50s. While many today might call his skills "Ostertagian," Mikan had an array of low post moves and his height made him almost impossible to defend during his era. He is also credited with causing the adoption of the goaltending rule, although that had more to do with Scooter "Short Stuff" McGee, a midget the Syracuse Nationals sat atop the rim to bat away opponents' shots. Thanks to medical bills, Mikan was near destitute when he passed away in 2005, but Shaquille O'Neal generously stepped forward and paid for all funeral costs under the condition it be called a Fu-neral.

YAO MING Yao had his doubters upon entering the NBA in 2002 with the Houston Rockets—mostly among those who assumed that at seven foot five he was really two Chinese guys, one on the other's shoulders, covered in some kind of draping. But he has met most expectations and become a force at the center position. He has also smashed many stereotypes since arriving in America, such as those that say all Chinese people are short and unathletic. In fact, thanks to Yao, most children of Chinese heritage are now picked second to last on playgrounds in America—just before obese girls—instead of their usual last. Yao is not without his detractors still today, though, as many say he is too nice on the court, an impression that most likely comes from his habit of offering a congratulatory high five to opposing players who dunk on him. *Fun Fact*: Yao grew up in the same town as Ichiro Suzuki and Chan Ho Park.

STEVE NASH The 2005 and 2006 NBA MVP, Nash is considered the greatest Canadian basketball player of all time, which is quite an honor considering his competition includes Bill Wennington, Todd MacCulloch, Mike Smrek, and several other players you never heard of. (Sadly, teamed just with the three players listed above, Team Canada could probably beat the crap out of the U.S. team.) Able to create separation from defenders with his body odor, Nash is a rare breed of NBA player that has interests and curiosity in things off the court. He even has a well-researched opinion on America's war in Iraq, and showed up at the 2003 All-Star weekend in a T-shirt that read "Shoot baskets, not people." He also long vowed not to wash his hair until the war is over. *Fun Fact*: Born in Johannesburg, South Africa, Nash became the latest in a long line of players of African ancestry to win the NBA MVP award.

DIRK NOWITZKI The tall, blond, muscular German came along at a perfect time for the NBA—if not sixty years too late for Hitler— breathing new life into the league by ushering in a host of dominant international players. Despite standing seven feet tall, he has an amazingly versatile game and can dribble, pass, and score from almost anywhere on the court. He is also able to allow the man he is guarding to score from almost anywhere on the court. *Fun Fact*: Nowitzki is the owner of the longest pair of lederhosen in history.

Watching Dirk Nowitzki follow through on a jumper can be frightening when you remember that he is German.

SHAQUILLE O'NEAL A true superstar, O'Neal is one of the most widely recognized athletes in the world, especially at waffle houses and all-you-can-eat buffets. Despite being born without the kind of body that would lend itself to being a dominant NBA center, Shaq's tireless work ethic has enabled him to become one of the game's all-time greats at the position. In his nearly fifteen years in the league he has almost managed to develop low post moves beyond backing over people, and he vows to one day make more than half of his free throws. O'Neal began his career with the Orlando Magic, and then moved to the Lakers, where he won three NBA titles—which he readily admits were mostly thanks to Kobe Bryant—and now plays for the Miami Heat. *Fun Fact*: O'Neal is unaware people only laugh at his horribly lame jokes because he is a seven-foot-one, 350-pound black guy.

OSCAR ROBERTSON Oscar Robertson is the retired player crotchety old people like to insist was far better than anyone who plays today. The lack of recognition he receives from today's casual fans is particularly peculiar considering he spent his NBA career in the major media markets of Cincinnati and Milwaukee. In 1962 he averaged a triple-double for the entire season, a feat that no one else has duplicated outside of rapper Ice Cube.

BILL RUSSELL The former Celtics center is the greatest defender in NBA history. Despite playing in the racially charged 1950s and '60s, Russell was lucky to avoid any negative experiences by playing in the ultratolerant and enlightened city of Boston. He is regarded as an unparalleled team player, as he won eleven championships in the thirteen seasons he played—all with Celtics squads that forced him to take the court with talentless players like Bob Cousy, Bill Sharman, K. C. Jones, Tom Heinsohn, and John Havlicek. Russell was the first black head coach of any major-league team—not counting the many black head coaches in the NHL—serving as Boston's player-coach from 1966 to 1969. *Fun Fact*: The Bill Russell terrier is a surly breed of dog that often barks at white people.

AMARE STOUDEMIRE Okay, so outside of Kobe Bryant, Kevin Garnett, LeBron James, Tracy McGrady, and Stoudemire, absolutely no teenage players are ready to play in the NBA right out of high school. Isn't that right, David Stern? Stoudemire had originally committed to play in college at the University of Memphis, but he decided to turn down Memphis coach John Calipari's big money offer and take the challenge of competing against the best players in the world, even though that would mean earning a lower salary. And he quickly established himself as a star with the Phoenix Suns, winning Rookie of the Year in 2003. He has also gone out of his way to make it clear he is in no way related to pothead guard Damon Stoudamire.

ISIAH THOMAS The former Detroit Pistons point guard and current New York Knicks president was one of the NBA's most popular players during his career, even though he carried out a very public sexual relationship with Lakers star Magic Johnson. Thomas came to the NBA from Indiana University where he majored in business administration with a minor in business destruction. He led the Pistons to two NBA titles before retiring in 1994 to pursue a career as a sports executive. As an executive he has done remarkably well, applying what he learned in college as he has almost single-handedly taken down the Raptors, Pacers, Knicks, and CBA. It is hoped he will one day be put in charge of Al-Qaeda. Or even better, the WNBA. *Fun Fact*: Isiah Thomas is a moron.

DWYANE WADE One of the NBA's bright young stars, it is frequently debated whether Wade is better than LeBron James. Most experts say Wade due to his NBA title and far superior college career. The guard forms a dynamic inside-outside combo for the Miami Heat with Shaquille O'Neal. He is already a far better all-around player than O'Neal and the key to Miami's success, but the team has let Shaq still believe that he is their best player lest he get jealous of Wade like he did when the same thing happened to him with Kobe Bryant. Wade's nicknames are Flash and D-Wade, but O'Neal is sure to give him something much stupider in the near future. *Fun Fact*: Dwyane's parents don't know how to spell.

JERRY WEST One of the greatest players and general managers in NBA history, West has been GM of the Memphis Grizzlies since 2002, where he is very, very, very, very patiently building a future NBA title contender. Or so they hope. West's previous management experience was with the Los Angeles Lakers where he helped build two different eras of Lakers dynasties. He has an unparalleled basketball mind—a mind he has protected throughout his life by a carefully parted helmet of hair. A star guard during his playing career, West's outline is used for the NBA logo. It's also used in the iPod ads.

BUDDHA SEEKS TO DISTANCE HIMSELF FROM PHIL JACKSON

At a press conference held this morning, the Buddha declared that he has never met, and has no relationship with, Los Angeles Lakers coach Phil Jackson. "I have nothing to do with Mr. Jackson, nor do I have any intention of meeting him," said Buddha.

Buddha, the enlightened figurehead of the Buddhist religion, said he decided to come public with his feelings on Jackson after seeing the coach in a new Courtyard by Marriott commercial.

"I've never really liked the guy—I mean, what kind of person plays himself off as a genius after coaching Jordan, Pippen, Shaq, and Kobe to championships? Anybody could do that," said Buddha.

While Buddha said he has never respected Jackson as a coach, he became disgusted with the man when he began presenting himself as some sort of sage of Eastern thought.

"The guy reads a couple of books on Eastern philosophy, wins a few titles, and all of a sudden he thinks he's my equal," said Buddha. "Then he writes a book [*Sacred Hoops*] and stars in a commercial, exploiting the beliefs I have championed. The dude is such a sellout."

CELTICS SOMEHOW STILL REELING FROM LEN BIAS'S DEATH

With almost no hope of making the play-offs this season, the Boston Celtics will extend a streak of futility that has extended two full decades back to their last championship in the 1985–1986 season. And there's only one reason for that, as many Celtics fans and front office employees will say—the untimely death of Len Bias, the team's 1986 first-round draft choice.

"No doubt. We're still picking up the pieces from that tragedy," said Danny Ainge, Boston's executive director of basketball operations and a player on the Celtics of the 1980s. "I can't believe that happened twenty years ago already. To me, it seems like yesterday. And I wish it was yesterday because that would give us a good excuse for sucking."

Bias died of a cocaine overdose less than forty-eight hours after the Celtics drafted him out of Maryland with the number-two overall pick in 1986. Added to a team that had just won an NBA title, Celtics fans were sure Bias, who was favorably compared to Michael Jordan, would ensure a Boston dynasty through the next decade.

"Sure, some people will say it's time we move on and that Bias would be over forty now and would be retired so we can't use his death as an excuse anymore," said former Celtics great K. C. Jones. "But people don't realize how great Bias could have been. Plus, how do we know he wouldn't still be playing? We don't. You add Len Bias in with Paul Pierce and we'd probably be title favorites this year. Okay, well, maybe not, because everyone on the Celtics right now, other than Pierce, is kind of lousy, but we'd at least be in playoff contention."

Ainge said he keeps a running tally of all the games he thinks Bias would have won for his team in case he ever needs to come up with something to save his job.

"Think of all the games over the years where we were within a point or two and had a last-second shot, only to see the likes of Antoine Walker or Rick Fox throw up an air ball," said Ainge. "And while I can't be sure, I'd bet Bias would have made every shot he ever took—so that's an additional five or six wins per year we'd have just from games with last-second shots. That's not counting all the other games we would have won behind Bias's 50 points, 20 rebounds, 20 assists, and 10 blocks a game—and those are just conservative estimates on my part. We'd easily be sitting on fifteen additional championships right now, and probably twenty in a row and going for twenty-one."

Ainge said that the Celtics will continue to lick their wounds and hope for better luck in the future.

"Until another Len Bias comes along—and since he's a once-in-a-lifetime kind of player, who knows if such a player ever will—there's not much we can do," said Ainge. "If we can make the play-offs here and there, that will be great. And you know, it's really a testament to the type of players we have in this organization that they can step on the court every night and give their best while knowing that their best player and teammate was struck down in his prime. Winning just thirty games a season is impressive considering we all have that baggage to carry around."

JASON WILLIAMS TO RID HIMSELF OF HIS SLAVE NAME

Miami Heat point guard Jason Williams announced today that he will seek to rid himself of his slave name, a name that was placed upon his ancestors by their enslavers centuries ago.

"No longer will I be called and defined by a name that was forced upon my family by the evil, ruthless white oppressors that put my family and many other black families just like it into slavery," said Williams. "As a strong and proud African-American man, I declare today that I will cast off these shackles and vestments of oppression and take on a new name, one from Africa, the birthplace of all humanity."

Williams said his early choices for an African name are Biggie Tupac or Tupac Biggie, or maybe even Slim Shady McBiggie Von Tupacsteen.

He has enlisted the services of attorneys from the Nation of Islam to help him prepare and file all of the necessary legal paperwork required to legally change one's name, and has found himself drawn to the organization as a whole.

"I hate white people," said Williams. "They're liars and snakes. They oppressed my people for hundreds of years and I had to grow up in a trailer park in West Virginia. I was the only black kid in my neighborhood. The only thing that got me through it all was the inspiration and words of strong black rappers like Vanilla Ice, Snow, and the Beastie Boys."

Williams said he wants to dedicate his career after basketball to fighting for black causes, and has found himself to be very interested in the life of Marcus Garvey and his Back to Africa movement. But Williams said that work will wait until his playing career is over.

"White America feels very threatened by a young black man having money," said Williams. "That's why I want to keep playing ball and making millions so I can rub it in their faces. Word up, homeboy."

NBA PLAYERS UNION PROPOSES USING MEDICAL MARIJUANA FOR THE TREATMENT OF ALL INJURIES

The NBA Players Association presented a one-page document to the league office this morning that proposes that all player injuries be treated with regular doses of medical marijuana.

"The benefits of medical marijuana are many, and new uses are always being discovered," read the proposal. "Today it's glaucoma and some cancers, but tomorrow it might be sprained ankles, jammed fingers, or even athlete's foot. The league should act now to make free marijuana available for all of its players. It is in the best interest of each and every player."

The proposal, which was written by team members of the Portland Trailblazers and received more than three hundred signatures from players on every team, is expected to be ruled on by the league office before the start of season.

FIFTY-EIGHT-YEAR-OLD TUSCALOOSA MACHINIST WINS NBA DRAFT LOTTERY

Leroy Mathers, a fifty-eight-year old machinist from Tuscaloosa, Alabama, won the NBA draft lottery on Thursday night when his lottery ticket matched the winning numbers. Mathers now has the opportunity to select the first pick in June's NBA draft.

"I am so excited. This is the greatest thing that has ever happened to me," said Mathers. "I bought fifteen NBA draft lottery tickets for two dollars apiece at 7-Eleven, but I didn't really think this could happen."

Mathers said he plays the NBA draft lottery every year, but this is the first time he has won. "I've never won anything in my whole life. This still hasn't sunk in. It's amazing."

Under the NBA's collective bargaining agreement, the number-one pick in the NBA draft gets a contract worth $16.8 million over four years, a sum Mathers, who works at a steel plating company, isn't sure he can afford.

"I'm going to have to start working a lot more overtime down at the plant," Mathers said. "And maybe I'll have to look into getting a loan or something. It's going be tough for a while, but I can't pass on the opportunity to take the best player available. I'm definitely not trading down, I know that."

Winning the number-one pick comes at a difficult time for Mathers. He just bought his girlfriend a new Ford F-150 extended cab, and the steel plant has cut back on available overtime. In addition, he has to pay $1,500 a month in child support for his three kids from a marriage that dissolved a few years ago.

"I'm very fortunate to win the NBA draft lottery, so I'm not going to complain about the financial burdens," said Mathers, who makes $11.75 per hour at the plant.

Add to those difficulties the fact that Mathers isn't sure what use he will have for a basketball player.

"Whoever I decide to pick will no doubt have amazing skills on the court, but that doesn't really help me at all," he said. "Hopefully, he's good around the house, too. And I guess I'll probably join the rec basketball league at work and have him play on my team. Hopefully, something will work out."

JASON KIDD THROWS AWESOME PASS OFF THE SIDE OF THE RIM

New Jersey guard Jason Kidd pulled up for what looked like a jump shot in the second quarter of the Nets victory over the Heat on Monday night, but instead flung the ball hard off the side of the rim and into the hands of teammate Vince Carter, who laid it in for two points.

"Other point guards make those shots, but not Jason," said Carter. "I think he shoots to get other people involved in the game. When he puts the ball up for a shot, you know it could come off the rim or backboard at any angle, so you have to keep your head up and be ready."

Kidd says that if it were up to him, balls that carom wildly off the basket would be assist opportunities.

"How does the official scorer know when I'm shooting the ball whether I'm trying to make the shot or pass it to a teammate in an unorthodox way?" said Kidd. "God knows I've never been able to shoot worth a crap, so I've always seen my shots as opportunities for other players to get their hands on the ball. A lot of people give me credit for hooking up with Vince and Richard Jefferson on a lot of alley-oops, but those are usually just me trying to make a three-pointer. Luckily for us, those guys know to go to the hoop when I shoot."

HOMELESS GUY STYLIN' IN RETRO JERSEY

Leroy Walter, a homeless Chicago man, has been repeatedly complimented of late by passersby on the 1969 Wilt Chamberlain Los Angeles Lakers jersey that he wears on top of his parka.

"All these kids keep coming by and complimenting me on the jersey," said Walter. "Apparently these old jerseys are really cool now. I guess I'm just lucky since I found mine near a dead prostitute in an alley about twenty-five years ago. Who knew that today it would be such a fashion statement?"

Walter says that he primarily wears his jersey in order to keep his parka from disintegrating, not for style.

"The jersey fits real tight over my coat, which is good, since for years it's been more or less full of holes and held together by duct tape," he said.

STORIES TOP STORIES   TOP STORIES TOP STORIES IN OTHER NEWS . . .

"Jordanian Jordan" finds much tougher competition outside of kingdom . . . NBA minor league to include low-grade marijuana, uglier groupies . . . Guy constantly hanging around playground either a pedophile or an NBA scout . . . NBA player to have MRI on ailing penis . . . Streetball legend also a crack pipe legend . . . Alonzo Mourning screams and flexes for thirty seconds after perfectly toasting a bagel . . . Doug Christie receives painful shock from electrified collar after straying too far from his wife . . . Celtics fans excited about acquisition of white player . . .

COLLEGE
BASKETBALL

BOB KNIGHT LIGHTLY KICKS PLAYER IN THE CROTCH

Texas Tech head basketball coach Bobby Knight has proven to be a practical sweetheart in his days in Lubbock. Run out of Indiana in 2001 for his belligerent behavior, Knight is now taking a more hands-off approach in his dealings with players at Texas Tech. The latest example came just last night in a game versus Oklahoma.

When chastising Todd Robinson during halftime for a three-second violation, Knight only lightly kicked the sophomore forward in the crotch. Most friends and acquaintances of the coach say the former, less mellow, Knight would have likely used one of the following tactics to get his point across: strangling, chair throwing, hair pulling, punching, soiled-toilet-paper showing, or racial-epithet yelling.

"I'm pleased with how Coach Knight chose to deal with my transgression," said Robinson. "I'd prefer it if he hadn't focused his attack on my genitals, but he could've kicked a lot harder. There was minimal bleeding and my left one swelled up to three or four times its regular size. I'll never stand in the lane again for more than three seconds, that's for sure."

RESTLESS STUDENTS STORM COURT
AFTER 12-POINT LOSS

Northwestern University students stormed the court after the final buzzer of last Wednesday's contest versus Illinois. The celebratory action took place even though the Wildcats lost the game by 12 points.

"We always see students from other schools running on to the court and celebrating after their teams win big games," said senior Jon Ruthie, while helping to pull down the basket. "But we don't win many games here at Northwestern, and we were bored tonight, so we decided to take any opportunity that presented itself."

Ruthie and several hundred other students whooped and hollered at center court for several minutes before being broken up by campus security. They then took to the campus streets, where they were joined by hundreds more Northwestern undergrads, and rioted into the night.

J. J. REDICK GLAD HECKLERS NEVER KNEW ABOUT HIS TINY PENIS

In an interview with ESPN on Sunday night in which J. J. Redick discussed how he has dealt with being the most hated player in college basketball during his career at Duke. He also also talked about a personal secret he's glad his hecklers were never aware of: his tiny, one-and-a-half-inch penis.

"Opposing team's fans can taunt me all they want. They can say that I suck or that I'm gay or whatever," said Redick, "but it doesn't affect me because I know it's not true. But if the people who hate me ever got wind of the fact that I have a teeny-tiny, itty-bitty little wiener, I'm sure I'd never hear the end of it—and it would hurt me to the core because it's true."

Redick says he has gone to extremes to hide his unflattering penis size throughout his career, never showering with the rest of his team and always having a towel at hand in the locker room.

"It's not that I don't trust my teammates, it's just that that kind of thing gets out and I'm sure it would somehow make it to some Maryland fans and the next thing I'd hear them yelling is 'J.J. Two Inch' or 'One J for Each Inch' or something," said Redick. "I don't know, I'm not really good at coming up with taunts, obviously. Although if they called me 'Two Inch' it would actually be kind of flattering, since I'm barely one and a half."

His newbornlike size has also caused him to take precautions in other areas, as well.

"I'm a virgin, which is another thing I wouldn't want those hecklers to know about," said Redick. "I tell myself it's because I want to wait until I'm married, but it's really because I fear having some girl that I really like pointing and laughing at my naked body."

Redick disclosed that his miniature penis doesn't even have girth going for it.

"Unfortunately, no," he said. "It kind of looks like a pinky hanging out of there. You know, if you have a really short pinky. But widthwise, it's exactly like a pinky. Almost."

The junior said he has recurring nightmares in which his shorts are pulled off during a scrum for the ball and an arena full of people see him naked from the waist down. Only they don't realize he's naked and assume he's just wearing flesh-colored underwear because his penis is too small to see.

It's ACC basketball featuring Duke. How many masturbating media members can you spot in the crowd?

"That's why I tie my shorts really tight before each game," said Redick. "I'd die if that happened or if anyone outside of this room ever heard about any of this."

Redick also showed a sensitive side of himself in the interview, explaining his love for writing poetry and even going as far as sharing some verses of his own.

One such poem, called "My Almost 1.5 Incher," was broadcast by ESPN in its entirety:

My penis is very small
Yet I stand tall
Knocking down threes
Though I have to use tweezers when I pees
Rising above to hit another jumper
My opponents unaware that I'm hung like Thumper
Starring in the NBA is my next jump
Then I'll be able to afford a top-of-the-line Swedish penis pump

SportsPickleNation Poll

What is the best mascot in college sports?

10%	Austin Peay's Mr. Peay Pants
17%	George Washington's Sambo the Fightin' Slave
11%	Harvard's Arrogant Prick
13%	Hawaii's Big Gay Rainbow
11%	Morehead State's Guy Who Wants Morehead
5%	Princeton's Mascot Who Was Rejected by Harvard and Yale
7%	Texas's Lethal Injection Larry
26%	USC's Smokin' Hot Chick

COLLEGE BASKETBALL FUN FACT

More than two hundred people are arrested each year for practicing Bracketology without a license.

"I regret to inform you that the South bracket has seceded from the NCAA Tournament." —*NCAA president Myles Brand*

"Rock, choke, Jayhawk!"
—*Kansas fans' NCAA Tournament cheer*

"I am a leader who happens to coach basketball. When [my players] get into the workplace, they're armed with not just a jump shot or a dribble. I want you armed for life. Especially because Duke players tend to suck in the NBA, so they need other career options."
—*Mike Krzyzewski in his American Express ad*

GREAT MOMENTS IN COLLEGE BASKETBALL HISTORY

JANUARY 27, 1894 The University of Chicago defeats the Chicago YMCA Training School, 19–11, in the first basketball game involving a college team. Despite the victory, Chicago's RPI rating dropped significantly due to playing the lightly regarded YMCA squad.

MARCH 29, 1982 North Carolina freshman Michael Jordan hits a sixteen-foot jump shot with just fifteen seconds left to give the Tar Heels the NCAA championship over Georgetown. Sadly, it would be the seminal moment of Jordan's disappointing career, as the coming years saw him suffer a knee injury, get linked to gambling, fail in professional baseball, flounder with the lowly Washington Wizards, commit adultery, and suffer through marital problems.

APRIL 2, 1984 Georgetown defeats Houston, 84–75, to win the NCAA basketball championship. Houston's loss was blamed on their players being severely hungover due to a late-night frat party the evening before at Phi Slamma Jamma.

JANUARY 13, 1986 The NCAA adopts the controversial Proposal 48, which set standards for Division I freshman eligibility. Under the new guidelines, athletes had to at least be able to count to forty-eight in order to be eligible to play college athletics.

MAY 6, 2006 North Carolina State hires Sidney Lowe as the new head coach of its men's basketball team. Lowe agreed to take the job after he was offered Duke and North Carolina season tickets.

PEOPLE TO KNOW

JIM CALHOUN Jim Calhoun has won two national championships during his time at the University of Connecticut, in 1999 and 2004. However, the coach sees those as the lowest points of his career because it left him with nothing to yell at his players about, although he did ridicule them for the way they cut down the nets each time. In 2003 Calhoun announced he had been diagnosed with prostate cancer, which he told his players was caused by their inability to limit turnovers and hit the offensive glass. The cancer was removed by doctors, however, which really pissed him off. UConn has produced numerous NBA players since Calhoun came to the program in 1986, including stars such as Ray Allen and Richard Hamilton. But no matter if his former players go on to the NBA or not, they all credit Calhoun with completely destroying the joy they found in playing basketball prior to enrolling at UConn.

BOB KNIGHT Bob Knight is a polarizing figure in college basketball, pitting those who respect despicable human beings who choke and kick people, throw chairs, and shove used toilet paper in players' faces, and those who don't respect despicable human beings who choke and kick people, throw chairs, and shove used toilet paper in players' faces. Regardless of where one falls in his or her opinion of Knight, most everyone can agree that his style is better suited to a past era. (The best era being the Middle Ages.) His greatest successes came at Indiana, where he led the Hoosiers to three NCAA titles. A legend in Bloomington almost from the moment he set foot on campus in 1971, Knight was fired after the 2000 season when his act had begun to grow tired, meaning it took the school nearly thirty years to realize what the rest of the country

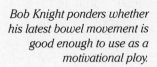

Bob Knight ponders whether his latest bowel movement is good enough to use as a motivational ploy.

knew from the beginning: Bobby Knight is an enormous dick. To-day he is the head coach at Texas Tech in Lubbock, where summer temperatures can exceed 100 degrees—heat that should prepare Knight nicely for his inevitable stint in hell. *Fun Fact*: Most believe that Knight, a former head coach at Army, is somehow responsible for the Abu-Ghraib prison abuses.

MIKE KRZYZEWSKI Dubbed "Coach K" due to his difficult-to-pronounce last name, the Duke coach's first name is just as confusing—spelled like "Mike," it's actually pronounced "Phony." Throughout his tenure with the Blue Devils, the Hall of Famer has guided Duke to numerous Final Fours and three national championships, building a reputation as one of the brightest and most respected minds in the sport's history—all the while maintaining an open and very controversial homosexual relationship with broadcaster Dick Vitale. (He has also been linked to CBS's Billy Packer and numerous referees.) Coach K is so popular on the Duke campus that students have dubbed an area where they camp out for tickets "Krzyzewskiville." During the off-season, this community of tents is used to provide charity housing for the many former Duke players who have failed in the NBA. In his spare time, Krzyzewski enjoys spending time with his family, doing charity work, thinking of new ways to use expletives, and competing in Hitler look-alike contests.

RICK PITINO The former head man at Kentucky, where he won a national title, Pitino came to Louisville in 2001 after three-and-a-half wildly successful years as the president and head coach of the Boston Celtics. His arrival in Louisville caused many in the state to call him a traitor, but he smoothed things over by assuring the Kentucky faithful that he would always be a Wildcat at heart by never masturbating to anyone other than Ashley Judd. Pitino had big shoes to fill following legendary Louisville coach Denny Crum—or a big toupee to fill in Crum's case—but the Cardinals have thrived under his guidance, so much so that it's inevitable some NBA team will be dumb enough to offer Pitino a job again.

DEAN SMITH The North Carolina head coach from 1961 to 1997, Smith retired with the most victories in NCAA history with 879. (Tennessee women's coach Pat Summitt surpassed his record in 2005, but comparing Smith's mark to Summitt's is comparing apples to vomit.) Smith was an unparalleled basketball mind and is credited with numerous innovations, including the four-corners offense and the foul-line huddle, but the most ingenious being the practice of somehow signing three of four high school All-Americans every freaking year. His leadership engendered an almost cultish devotion among former assistants and players. Actually, scratch "almost," because it's downright creepy. Today North Carolina plays its games inside the Dean Smith Center, an arena constructed inside Smith's enormous nose.

JOHN WOODEN Nicknamed the "Wizard of Westwood" and the "Indiana Rubber Man" due to his love of witchcraft and condoms, Wooden is such a relic of a bygone age that during his years as coach of UCLA he didn't even pay his players or encourage boosters to give recruits' parents jobs. Imagine that! But despite eschewing those common practices of modern coaching, Wooden was still able to be successful somehow and built the greatest dynasty in college basketball history, winning ten national titles with the Bruins. In his retirement years, Wooden has stayed healthy through the use of medical marijuana, hitting the chronic at least twice a day with former players Bill Walton and Kareem Abdul-Jabbar.

BRACKETOLOGIST COMPLETES MOCK BRACKET FOR 2048 NCAA TOURNAMENT

ESPN resident bracketologist Joe Lunardi released today his first projection for the seedings in the 2048 NCAA Tournament. He sees Duke, Arkansas, Stanford, and the University of Berlin as the number-one seeds in 2048.

"Duke is safe bet for being a top seed in '48, and Arkansas and Stanford are programs that are dominant in cycles, and they'll be on the upswing again in forty years," said Lunardi. "Berlin is sort of a dark horse, but I project that in twenty-five years the NCAA will go global and welcome international members, and U of B is a smart choice for a number-one seed in the Syracuse bracket."

Lunardi said he put out his projections for the 2007 through 2048 tournaments for the same reason he puts out mock brackets every week for this year's tournament.

"Basically, I'm just trying to justify getting a paycheck every week," he said. "I'm fully aware that trying to predict the seedings for the NCAA Tournament weeks out is total and complete crap, yet apparently there is a market for it, and so it's no more ridiculous for me to do it for years into the future. In fact, right now I'm working on seedings for the 4050 tournament. There will be 640 seeds, most of them from other galaxies, and the Final Four will be held on the Planet Vektron. Honestly, I can't believe I get paid for this, but I'm going to ride this train as long as I can."

BRUCE PEARL REPORTS TENNESSEE'S ENTIRE SIDE OF THE BRACKET FOR NCAA VIOLATIONS

Tennessee head basketball coach Bruce Pearl ratted out all thirty-one teams on the Volunteers' side of the NCAA Tournament bracket today, a bold step he hopes will ease his team's path to the championship game April 2 in Atlanta.

"Our first game is Thursday afternoon against Winthrop," said Pearl, "but if everything goes to plan, we'll win by forfeit because they won't even show up due to being suspended by the NCAA."

Pearl sent NCAA president Myles Brand an e-mail this morning detailing "grievous violations" committed by every team in the

Washington, D.C., and Minneapolis regions, from boosters giving re-cruits money to more outlandish claims, such as players being given gifts of unicorns and magical flying carpets.

"Admittedly, some of the claims in my report are a bit absurd," said Pearl, "but it was hard to make up thirty-one different fictional charges, so I started to run out of ideas by the end. Hopefully the NCAA will buy it all. But even if not, I'm hoping that by the time they realize everything is a bunch of bull, all of the teams will have been suspended and we'll be playing in the national championship game."

Pearl, of course, has a proud history of being a rat. As an assistant coach at Iowa in 1989 he lost out on a prized recruit to Illinois and proceeded to try to get the Illinois program busted on recruiting charges—going as far as to secretly record phone conversations with the recruit—but the allegations were never upheld.

"When I fail at something, it's my natural instinct to whine and cry and blame other people and make stuff up to protect my self," said Pearl. "That's just how I operate. And now I'm in charge of the most undeserving, if not the worst, number-two seed in NCAA Tournament history. We have no possible chance of success in this tournament by playing it straight. So that's why I'm reverting to old form and trying to help myself out by ratting on other people. It's the only shot I've got."

COACH ENCOURAGING HIS BAD PLAYERS TO DECLARE EARLY FOR THE NBA DRAFT

Penn State men's basketball coach Ed DeChellis is reportedly en-couraging his many lousy players to declare early for the NBA draft.

The Nittany Lions, without a winning season since the 1990s, do not have any open scholarships, even though several top junior college players have inquired about transferring to the university. DeChellis denies he is urging his players to leave school, but several team members say he has talked to them about the possibility.

"Coach told me I had the ability to play on the next level and that it's time I provide for my family," said Mark Davis, a six-foot junior guard who averaged 2.9 points last year on 32 percent shooting from the field.

Jameel Hollaford, a freshman center, said DeChellis told him he shouldn't risk losing his promising NBA career to injury by returning for his final three seasons. Hollaford missed twenty-seven games last season due to exercise-induced asthma and weight problems. "He made a lot of sense," Hollaford said. "He said I've accomplished all I could on this level and that it's time to move on."

MAN PUTTING MORE EFFORT INTO RUNNING OFFICE POOL THAN HE EVER HAS INTO HIS ACTUAL JOB

With only three days between Sunday evening's announcement of the NCAA Tournament brackets and the beginning of action on Thursday, Jeff Reiss has been working tirelessly in order to set up his company's tournament pool—at work almost two hours early on Monday and staying late every day so far this week. In short, he's working much harder on organizing and running the office pool than he ever has at his actual job.

"I've noticed a definite hop in his step this week," said Nicole Smith, who works in the cubicle beside Reiss. "He really seems to want to be here. He's running around, very alert and busy. Usually he just sits slumped in front of his computer with a glazed look on his face, not really seeming to be doing anything at all."

Reiss, an assistant software programmer, arrived at work on Monday morning just after 7:00 A.M. to send out a company-wide e-mail about the tournament pool. He then set to making copies of the bracket and left one on the desks of all his fellow employees. Only then did he go online and begin researching his own tournament picks, which lasted the rest of the day, interspersed with answering any office pool questions his coworkers e-mailed him.

Yesterday he split his day between tracking down fellow employees to remind them of the Thursday noon deadline and doing more research for his picks. He plans more of the same for today.

"Thursday is when my work day will get really hectic," said Reiss. "First, I need to make sure I have all of the brackets and all of the money. Then, once the games start, I'll be monitoring all of them online, and then making updates to the brackets. Then I have to send out a company-wide updates at the end of the day, in addition to answering individual queries. I have a lot of long days ahead of me, I'm afraid. That's why I've postponed all of my client and vendor meetings and calls until mid-April."

Friday will be just as busy as Thursday for Reiss. And then comes the Round of 32 over the weekend.

"Official company policy is that we are not supposed to work on weekends, but when a project needs to get done, it needs to get done," said Reiss. "That's how this weekend will be. I'm going to be up working really late on Sunday and then back in here early Monday morning to update all the brackets, because I know people are going to want to know where they stand when they get to work on Monday."

Reiss's hard work hasn't gone unnoticed by his superiors.

"This is the kind of work we've wanted out of Jeff all along," said Gary Conner, the company vice president who oversees the programming department. "He's been here for three years now, and this is the first time we've ever seen him show any excitement or dedication to anything. It's a breath of fresh air. If this keeps up throughout the whole tournament, we're thinking of calling him in to tell him that if he would only put forward a tenth of the effort to his job as he does to running the tournament pool, he'd get a promotion."

STORIES TOP STORIES   TOP STORIES TOP STORIES **IN OTHER NEWS . . .**

Latest Bin Laden tape declares death to infidels, Carolina over Duke by 10 . . . That skank from sales somehow wins tourney office pool again . . . Dean Smith wows onlookers by drinking water while Roy Williams talks . . . Cancer 84, Coaches 72 . . . Krzyzewski inspires class of fourth-graders with expletive-filled motivational speech . . . John Wooden arrested for masterminding six-state drug and prostitution ring . . . Jewco transfer refuses to practice on Yom Kippur . . . Highly touted recruit happens to find $20,000 and an Escalade in his driveway . . .

NHL

ICING EXPLAINED WELL INTO THIRD PERIOD

Jim Thyer spent the most of a date at a St. Louis Blues game last Thursday night explaining hockey's icing rule to his girlfriend, Tara McMichael.

"The Blues were called for icing early in the first period and Tara didn't understand so I tried to explain the rule," Jim said. "But I couldn't remember everything myself so I had to check the program."

McMichael felt she understood the rule by the end of the first pe-

Icing is delicious.

riod, but early in the second period when the Blues dumped the puck into the offensive zone and were not called for icing, Thyer had to clarify the rule.

"I had forgotten to explain that if a team dumps the puck in and then gets to it before their opponent, they aren't called for icing," he said. "But that really got Tara confused."

Both Thyer and McMichael decided after the game that they will not go to hockey games on dates anymore.

LADY BYNG WINNER PROBABLY GAY

Joe Thomas, the Tampa Bay Lightning wing who won the NHL's award for gentlemanly play—the Lady Byng Trophy—at the league's awards banquet Thursday night, is probably gay, his teammates and fellow players assume.

"It was such a big surprise to find out about Joe," said teammate Roger Martin. "I mean the award for gentlemanly play in hockey, the Lady Byng, how gay is that?"

"To my knowledge, nobody in the league knew he was gay," said Vezina winner Geoff Williams of the New Jersey Devils. "On the ice he's tough and gritty—not at all gay. But it really opens your eyes, you know? Maybe some gay men don't really fit all of the stereotypes."

Thomas said he was pleased to accept the award, but that he worries about the impact it could have on his career.

"I have nothing against being gay, but I don't want everybody thinking I am just because I won the Lady Byng," he said. "And since Thursday night nobody will listen to me when I tell them that I'm not. I'm going to have to start fighting a lot next year and take tons of penalty minutes."

NHL MAXES OUT ITS DISCOVER CARD

Commissioner Gary Bettman announced today that the NHL, already strapped financially, has maxed out its Discover Card.

The credit card's $8,000 limit was exceeded by the NHL in less than six weeks. With an annual APR of 24.99 percent, Bettman said the league will likely be saddled with the debt for several years.

"We can only afford to make the minimum monthly payments right now," Bettman said. "It might take us a while to dig ourselves out of this one."

Bettman said that the high-interest Discover Card was the only credit card that the league qualified for and therefore was the only account used in making recent purchases.

"Our Visa and MasterCard accounts were closed by debt collectors more than a year ago," he said. "One of the league's best hopes for maintaining financial solvency was to use our Discover Card responsibly, but that hasn't happened, unfortunately."

Bettman claims he has put in a call to the 800 number of a debt consolidator, AmeriDebt, in hopes of getting the league's skyrocketing monthly credit payments under control.

"I called last night but the automatic operator said I'd have to wait approximately fifteen minutes for the next available customer service representative and I didn't really feel like waiting," Bettman said. "I'll probably give them another call tonight."

The league has also reportedly considered taking out home equity loans on the thirty NHL arenas.

"We're entirely confident we can get out of this debt," Bettman said. "We've just been going through a tough time lately. I'm sure we will make more money down the road, and if we only start saving a little bit more each month, in no time we'll be in the black."

FIRST ALL-BLACK HOCKEY TEAM INSPIRING, AWFUL

The first hockey team with an all-black starting lineup took the ice last night in Cape Breton Quebec, inspiring all those in attendance on the way to a 23–1 loss to Victoriaville in Quebec Major Junior Hockey League action.

The decision by Cape Breton head coach Buck Gillette to start an all-black lineup was motivated by the movie *Glory Road*, the story of the 1966 Don Haskins-coached Texas Western squad that won the NCAA championship with an all-black starting five.

"I learned all about that legendary Texas Western team and I was inspired to see that happen with hockey here in Canada," said Gillette. "So I scoured the Cape Breton area for any black players. I already had one black kid on my team who is actually pretty decent—a right wing—but it was difficult finding anyone else for the other five positions."

Gillette struggled to find enough young black men with an interest in hockey, so he turned to anyone at all he could find, including three recruits who can't skate.

"I was hoping the significance of the whole thing would overcome all that and lead the team to a historic victory," said Gillette.

Unfortunately, it didn't work out that way.

"I've never gone from inspired to humiliated so fast," said Will Goulet, the all-black team's goalie. "I knew we were in trouble when our center fell on his back before the ref even dropped the puck for the opening face-off, or whatever that's called at the beginning of hockey games."

No matter the outcome, Gillette is hopeful he has been a part of an important moment in hockey history.

"I hope so," he said, "but part of me fears I may have set the sport back several decades."

> *"I think that part of the reason the TV ratings are so low in the U.S. for the Stanley Cup finals is that by the time the finals come around all the play-off beards make it look like you're watching al-Qaeda on Ice."*
> —*Gary Bettman, NHL commissioner*

GREAT MOMENTS IN HOCKEY HISTORY

JANUARY 15, 1841 Lord Frederick Stanley, the man for whom the Stanley Cup is named, is born. Stanley's parents were so excited they took turns running around the hospital screaming and wildly shaking the child over their heads.

JANUARY 28, 1943 Chicago Blackhawks forward Doug Bentley, with the help of four assists from his brother, Max, sets an NHL record with five points in a single period. The opposing team's goalie was Bentley's sister, Charlene.

FEBRUARY 12, 1949 Canada beats Denmark, 47–0, in the world hockey championship tournament, the highest score in the history of the sport. The Danes blamed the loss on the fact that several of their best players had to leave the game when their wooden skate blades broke.

MAY 16, 2003 The Mighty Ducks advance to their first Stanley Cup finals in franchise history, essentially sealing Emilio Estevez's selection as coach of the year.

MARCH 8, 2004 Vancouver's Todd Bertuzzi nearly kills Colorado's Steve Moore with a brutal hit from behind that fractures Moore's neck and leaves him hospitalized, at the same time providing the NHL with an awesome new clip to add to its next Heavy Hitters DVD release.

FEBRUARY 16, 2005 After a prolonged lockout, the NHL officially cancels its 2004–05 season, effectively placing the entire population of Canada on Prozac.

TERMS TO KNOW

PULLING THE GOALIE A slang term used for a crude activity most often done when a player is alone in the postgame shower. Also often referred to as "stick handling," and—if another party is involved—it can include a "wraparound."

SportsPickleNation Poll

What is the most interesting fact about the Stanley Cup?

29%   Every engraving of "Gretzky" is followed by "is a huge wuss"

15%   It's taller than Theo Fleury

14%   It prefers the name "Stan" to "Stanley"

14%   The hollow center contains the remains of Eric Lindros's career

28%   It hates Canadians

NHL FUN FACT

Miroslav Satan knows what his last name means in English. So shut up about it already.

PEOPLE TO KNOW

RAY BOURQUE The Boston Bruins legend holds virtually every NHL career record for defenseman, including most goals, most assists, and most points. He also owns the all-time record for most consecutive seasons playing for a crappy team. Bourque logged twenty-one seasons in Boston before forcing a trade in 2000 to the Colorado Avalanche in hopes of finally winning a Stanley Cup. When the Avs won a season later he returned to Boston with the Cup in tow and received a hero's welcome at City Hall before 20,000 screaming fans—an event even the most self-loathing Boston fan would have to admit is pretty pathetic.

MARTIN BRODEUR The most accomplished goaltender in the game today, Brodeur has minded the net for the New Jersey Devils since winning the Calder Trophy in 1994—or, as the year is called in New Jersey: When Bon Jovi Released "Always." Stuck playing in the wide-open, offense-first Devils attack, Brodeur is often forced to turn away 40, sometimes 50 shots (a month). In addition to guiding New Jersey to three Stanley Cups, he also backstopped Canada to victories at the 2002 Olympics and the 2004 World Cup of Hockey, and has even scored a play-off goal—putting a shot past Montreal goalie Blindy McCataract in the 1997 playoffs.

SIDNEY CROSBY Sidney Crosby is the greatest thing to happen to hockey ever. Or at least he'd better be, as he has been dubbed "the Next One" since his early teens. The NHL is banking on him being more of "the Next One" variety of a Mario Lemieux than the crap Eric Lindros, Alexander Daigle variety. Crosby was drafted number one overall by Pittsburgh in 2005, which was a perfect fit, as he could both play and learn alongside Lemieux and use his bilingual skills to mesh with Pittsburgh's vibrant French-speaking community.

Crosby met all expectations as a rookie, becoming the first player under the age of nineteen in league history to score 100 points in a season. Unfortunately for the Penguins, he was involved in every goal they scored in the 2005–06 campaign. *Fun Fact*: Sidney's mother isn't sure if his father is Crosby, Stills, or Nash.

PETER FORSBERG The Flyers center is regarded by many as the best player in the NHL. And even if not, he is definitely a dominant force in the twelve or thirteen games he manages to make it through each year without getting hurt. Forsberg played for the Quebec Nordiques/Colorado Avalanche for nine years until he signed with the Flyers in 2005. He was actually originally Philadelphia property, but the Flyers made the extremely brilliant move of trading him to Quebec in 1992 along with Ron Hextall, Steve Duchesne, Kerry Huffman, Chris Simon, Mike Ricci, two first-round draft picks, and $15 million for Eric Lindros and a neurologist to be named later. Despite his success in the NHL, Forsberg has often said he will cut his career short in North America so he can return home to Sweden to play hockey and raise a family of alcoholic, suicidal socialists.

WAYNE GRETZKY Born in Brantford, Ontario, in 1961, Gretzky was immediately dubbed "the Next Gretzky." The Hall of Famer is widely regarded as the greatest hockey player of all time, and owns numerous NHL records, including most career points, most goals, most assists, and most fights fled from while screaming like a little girl. In fact, to this day, if visitors to the NHL Hall of Fame in Toronto stare at Gretzky's bust for too long, they are attacked from behind by Marty McSorley and Dave Semenko. Nonsports fans best know Gretzky as the husband of silver screen legend Janet Jones, who won a Best Supporting Actress Oscar in 1988 for her work in *Police Academy 5: Assignment Miami Beach*. Jones brought great embarrassment to the Gretzky family in 2006 when she was linked to a gambling ring run by ex-NHL player Rick Tocchet. Even worse, she had bet most of the family's savings on Canada's hockey team to win a medal at the Torino Olympics.

GORDIE HOWE Mr. Hockey is as dominant a player as the NHL has ever seen. And Gordie Howe was nearly as good. Howe played twenty-five seasons with the Detroit Red Wings, from 1946 to 1971, setting the world record for most times hit by a thrown octopus. He then made two comebacks, one from 1973 to 1980 that saw him retire at age fifty-one as a member of the Hartford Whalers, and another in 1997 at age sixty-nine with the minor league Detroit Vipers to become the only player to have played in six different decades—proving he wouldn't let respect for the game get in the way of becoming a stupid, meaningless historical footnote. Howe once held nearly every career scoring record, but they have since been obliterated by Wayne Gretzky (although Howe has vowed to return to the NHL and retake the marks if the league allows him to outfit a walker with skate blades).

BOBBY HULL The greatest left wing ever, Hull is a legendary Chicago Blackhawk. (*Note*: The Chicago Blackhawks were a once competitive NHL franchise that folded in the late 1990s.) Hull starred in a golden age of the NHL, as fans could come out to watch his 120 mph slapshot rip the flesh clean off the faces of maskless goaltenders—something the pussified goalies of today only have to experience in their worst nightmares. Hull bolted the Blackhawks in 1972 to join the upstart Winnipeg Jets of the World Hockey Association, only returning to the NHL in 1979 when the WHA folded. He played his final season in 1980 at age forty-one with the Hartford Whalers alongside fifty-one-year-old Gordie Howe, forming the legendary Urologist's Line.

JAROME IGINLA One of the top talents in the game today, Iginla is also probably the best black player in NHL history. (Some might say that Hall of Fame goaltender Grant Fuhr is, but he's not really fooling anyone by claiming he's black.) Iginla has become one of the NHL's most marketable stars since captaining the Calgary Flames to the brink of the Stanley Cup in 2004. The NHL hopes he can help grow the popularity of hockey among a younger, urban demographic—although Iginla has so far resisted pressure from the league to wear sagging hockey pants, tricked-out skates, and his helmet cocked sideways on his head. Regardless, playing in a large market like Calgary should make him a household name in no time.

JAROMIR JAGR Jagr burst onto the hockey scene in 1990 with a style that could best be described as: "Business up front, party in the back." A force in the offensive zone if a bit lax on defense, the mulleted right wing became an NHL superstar while helping the Penguins to back-to-back Stanley Cups in his first and second seasons. He thrived in Pittsburgh for eleven years, winning six scoring titles and a Hart Trophy. But perhaps more important, he completely defeated the stereotype of European players as soft and temperamental. Despite that, the Penguins traded him in 2001 to the Capitals, who then shipped him to the Rangers two years later. He scored 123 points in the 2005–2006 season following a disappointing 2004–2005 campaign in which he was held without a point.

MARIO LEMIEUX Perhaps the greatest talent the sport has ever seen, Lemieux was a superstar immediately upon his arrival in the NHL in 1984. In addition to winning numerous scoring titles, he brought Pittsburgh its first Stanley Cup titles in 1991 and 1992. Hoping to better market its star, the NHL then started allowing constant clutching and grabbing by defenders, thinking TV viewers would better be able to spot Lemieux on the ice if two or three opponents were hanging on to him at all times. Unfortunately, that ill-conceived idea and health concerns hindered Lemieux through much of his career. He has fought Hodgkin's disease, which he treated with radiation, and chronic back problems, which he oddly treats with thirty-six holes of daily golf. From 2000 to 2005 he served as player-owner of the Penguins—a role that left him in quite an unenviable position during the 2004–2005 lockout, as he often was not on speaking terms with himself.

MARK MESSIER Messier is regarded as hockey's greatest leader. And who could argue? He guided the Edmonton Oilers to five Stanley Cups and only had the likes of Wayne Gretzky, Jari Kurri, Paul Coffey, Kevin Lowe, Steve Smith, Grant Fuhr, Bill Ranford, Glenn Anderson, Craig MacTavish, and Esa Tikkanen to work with. In 1994 he captained the New York Rangers to their first Cup in fifty-four years in dramatic fashion and, with his reputation cemented, figured no one would mind if he underachieved for the next decade. *Fun Fact*: Messier's last name is French for: "more messy."

BOBBY ORR The Hall of Fame defenseman was the best ever at his position. Able to jump forward and score a goal or fall back and head off a rush, he could do it all. Unfortunately, his career was hindered by frequent injuries—injuries mainly caused by his habit of leaping wildly onto the ice headfirst after every goal he scored. Despite that, his career accomplishments are nearly endless. The Bruins legend is the only defenseman to ever lead the league in scoring, and he won eight Norris Trophies, three Hart Trophies, and two Stanley Cups. He even has his name on Canada's Walk of Fame. *Fun Fact*: Canada's Walk of Fame is four feet long, and is really more of a Stand of Fame.

ALEXANDER OVECHKIN The exciting Russian was the number-one overall draft pick by the Washington Capitals in the 2004 NHL draft and his selection immediately invigorated the Caps fan base, boosting their number of diehard supporters from seven all the way up to eleven or maybe even twelve. During a breakout season in 2005–06, Ovechkin built a reputation for netting awe-inspiring goals, some of which almost made it onto sports highlights shows in the United States. *Fun Fact*: Ovechkin doesn't distribute the puck much for being one of those "share everything" Commie pinkos.

MAURICE RICHARD Both dead *and* Canadian, Richard is a member of one of hockey's greatest families. Nicknamed "the Rocket," his younger and smaller brother was Hall of Famer Henri "the Pocket Rocket" Richard. And their younger, still smaller, and much wimpier brother was "the Pocket Pussy" Harold Richard. The Rocket is the first player in NHL history to score 50 goals in one season, doing it in just 50 games, and played on eight Cup-winning Canadiens teams. His name is linked to the second darkest moment in Montreal sports history when, in 1955, after Richard was suspended by the league for injuring an opponent, thousands of city residents rioted through the night. (The darkest moment in Montreal sports history being, of course, whenever the design for Olympic Stadium was approved.)

PATRICK ROY Roy is one of the originators of the butterfly goal-tending style, in which the goaltender attempts to make saves by dropping to his knees and extending his legs in opposite directions. In Roy's case, this style also included being a huge prick. A Montreal Canadiens icon, he demanded to be traded from the Habs in 1995 after being left in the game for the first nine goals of a 12–1 loss—apparently because he didn't want to play on a team with a goalie bad enough to allow nine goals in less than two periods. Montreal shipped him to Colorado, where he won two of his four Stanley Cups. Roy retired from hockey after the 2003 season to dedicate his time to the Patrick Roy Foundation, a charity organization that works to help children throughout the world mispronounce the letter *r*.

COLUMBUS BLUE JACKETS FAN COMPLAINS OVEREXPANSION IS THE CAUSE OF NHL'S ILLS

Dave Lewis, a self-proclaimed die-hard Columbus Blue Jackets fan, opined to all who would listen at a downtown Columbus sports bar yesterday that overexpansion is to blame for the NHL's many financial ills.

"Look, the NHL has teams in Tampa Bay and Miami and Atlanta and Nashville and San Jose—the league never should have expanded that much. It's spread too thin," said Lewis. "Even Minnesota, which is a big hockey state, shouldn't have been given an expansion franchise."

Lewis said he thinks the league should contract to approximately twenty teams, or the number it had before the expansion era was ushered in the with San Jose Sharks in 1991.

"I think all of these new expansion teams should be contracted and their players should be dispersed in a draft," said Lewis. "But Columbus should definitely keep its franchise because I think the team is really starting to grow a strong fan base here. Plus I have season tickets."

GOALIE'S PADS LOOK SUSPICIOUSLY LIKE A SOFA

Opposing players and fans were very intrigued to see that the leg pads worn by Anaheim goaltender Jean-Sébastien Giguère during Sunday's game looked suspiciously like a sofa.

"There's no way those pads were within the league specifications," said Rangers wing Brad Isbister. "I may be wrong, but I'm pretty sure he was just standing behind a couch that he had Velcroed to his shins. That was totally cheating. There was almost no opening to shoot on net."

The comments by Isbister and other Rangers were just the latest charges that Giguère uses illegal pads, an accusation the Anaheim goalie vehemently denies. "Any time a goalie is playing well you hear rumors that their pads are too big," said Giguère. "It's just typical talk from frustrated offensive players who can't score on you."

But very few believe Giguère's denials. "Whatever—I don't believe him," said Scott Stevens of the New Jersey Devils, who played the Ducks in the 2003 Stanley Cup Finals. "He said the same stuff when we played him for the Cup but in one of the games against us he didn't even try to disguise it. He was just standing there in net, leaning on some ugly, old, bright orange couch that looked like it was pulled out of somebody's den in 1974."

JESSE JACKSON PROTESTS NHL'S RECORD ON MINORITY HIRING

Jesse Jackson has found a new cause.

"The National Hockey League's track record of hiring minority coaches is atrocious, abysmal, appalling, abominable, and iniquitous," Jackson said at a press conference last week. "Think of all the great African-American and African-Canadian players there have been throughout the league's history. The NHL has gotten to where it is today on their backs, yet there is not one minority head coach or general manager."

Jackson called on all people of color to boycott the league's games until NHL commissioner Gary Bettman addresses the minority hiring policy.

Despite Jackson's boycott request, NHL attendance has re-

The NHL increased scoring after the lockout by requiring each team to have one amputee defenseman on the ice at all times.

mained steady to higher and has even seen a marked increase in several southern cities over the past week.

ES TOP STORIES   TOP STORIES TOP STORIES IN OTHER NEWS . . .

Hockey news the lead story again on Canadian sports network . . . Vast right-wing conspiracy leaves left wings scoreless . . . Cross Czech gets in fight in Prague bar . . . Excitement contained in neutral zone trap . . . Team you didn't even know existed in second round of NHL play-offs . . .

BOXING

"BEST POUND-FOR-POUND" TITLE DOING LITTLE FOR 58-POUND MIDGET

Little Mickey Tittle is universally regarded by boxing experts as the greatest pound-for-pound fighter in the world. But the fact that Tittle is a three-foot-eight, fifty-eight-pound midget has severely restricted his boxing career.

"The poor guy can't find anyone to fight in his weight class," said Ed Myers, a longtime boxing writer. "He's relegated to fighting other midgets or picking fights with grade-schoolers."

Countless boxing experts attest to Tittle's unparalleled hand speed, foot movement, power, and knowledge of the sport.

"If you combine the best attributes of Ali, Marciano, Joe Louis, and Julio Cesar Chavez and put that guy up against Tittle, it's not even close," said Myers. "Tittle—albeit a full-sized Tittle—would destroy that guy."

Tittle has been involved in professionally sanctioned bouts, fighting in the junior flyweight class. He fought Luis Ibisco in 2001 and Rosario Ibáñez in 2003. But in each match the pint-sized brawler was disqualified for repeatedly hitting below the belt.

"No matter what I did I couldn't get my punches to land above the belt," said Tittle. "I was jumping, standing on their feet—I did everything. It was the most disappointing moment of my career."

The disqualifications had serious repercussions for Ibisco and Ibáñez, as well. Tittle's power-packed uppercuts repeatedly landed square on the men's genitals, putting both in the hospital for months and leaving Ibáñez impotent and sterile.

"Imagine Mike Tyson teeing off on your crotch, then magnify it a thousand times," said Ibisco. "That little dude packs a wallop."

It was those crotch wallops that got Tittle suspended from professional boxing. Each major governing body in the sport banned Tittle after his 2003 defeat.

"Some people said the decision was discriminatory to little people," said IBF chairman Vincent Ruff. "But the simple fact was that Tittle was hurting people and it was all for naught—he couldn't even land regulation punches. We had to protect our fighters."

Today, several years after being banned from the sport he loves and would dominate if only two feet taller, Tittle is found boxing in carnivals and sideshows throughout the country.

"Sometimes I get sad about my lot in life, but these carnivals and exhibitions make me a living and I get to do what I love to do," Tittle recently said between rounds of a match against a wild boar. "God only knows why he didn't make me taller."

FEMALE BOXER PLAGUED BY GLASS RACK

While blessed with one of the most athletic builds and powerful punches in all of women's boxing, Christi Mitchell has struggled with one thing since beginning her fight career five years ago—her pair of glass jugs.

"Christi has it all—speed, power, stamina—and a great mind for boxing, as well," said her trainer, Mickey Arista. "But unfortunately she wasn't born with a sturdy rack. If she lets those ta-ta's take a couple good shots, she goes down."

Mitchell's latest loss—which dropped her to a disappointing 22–7 for her career—came Saturday night in Atlantic City when she was KO'd in the sixth round in a fight against lightly regarded Lisa Lowry (19–16–2).

"There almost no way that woman had any business being in a ring with Christi," said Arista, "but she stuck to the playbook that people have developed for fighting her—hit a tit, move, hit the other tit, move again—and came out on top. I don't want to admit this, but it's gotten to the point where we may have to accept the fact that Christi's fun bags are going to prevent her from ever winning a title."

Lowry said she was confident entering the fight with Mitchell due to the game plan provided by her trainer.

"Every day that I was training and sparring in the weeks leading up to the bout my trainer kept stressing the three Hs—Hit Her Hooters," said Lowry. "He even stenciled three Hs on each of my gloves to help me remember. And it really struck me how well the strategy was working when we I got tied up with Christi in the fourth round and she whispered in my ear and begged me to please stop hitting her hooters. But I didn't, and by the end of the sixth round she was down for good, clutching at her sensitive boobies."

Mitchell—wearing a giant, ice-filled bra after the bout—admits she struggles when getting knocked in the knockers, but doubts she has it any worse than any of her other competitors.

"I can't imagine any female boxer likes getting punched there. It really freaking hurts," she said. "That's really what women's boxing is all about—come out aggressive and knock someone out before they get a chance to crush your cans. I just need to regroup for my next fight and be prepared to turn the tables and bash some bazoombas of my own."

MALNOURISHED LATINO BOY HAS GREAT POTENTIAL AS A FLYWEIGHT BOXER

Little José Cantó, an eight-year-old Mexican boy removed from his parents by government social workers yesterday due to reports of abuse and malnourishment, is thought to have a great future as a flyweight boxer.

"I've seen some prospects in my day, but I don't think I've seen a child with a bigger upside than José," said Felipe Rodríguez, a long-time Guadalajara boxing trainer familiar with the boy. "With how stunted his growth is, there's no way he'll ever get much bigger than 110 pounds or so. He has a very bright future."

The boy hasn't stated whether or not he wants to be the next in a long line of lightweight Latino boxers—not that he has many other options—and, in fact, has not spoken at all outside of reportedly telling those who rescued him: "I am very, very hungry."

It's that hunger that many believe will fuel the sickly child to greatness.

"All the great ones have that burning feeling in the pit of their stomach," said Rodríguez. "Sure, in the cases of José and many other flyweight boxers it's more intense hunger pains from years of starvation than the desire to dominate their opponent in the ring, but you have to take what you can get."

Rodríguez says the determining factor in Cantó becoming a successful flyweight boxer is whether or not he is too frail and malnourished to ever build up enough stamina to box.

"It's a fine line for kids his age between the right amount of malnourishment and too much," said Rodríguez. "But it looks like he came out on the right side, so his parents can be proud of the job they did. And if he can tap the rage and resentment he probably has inside over his lot in life and unleash it in the ring, he could be one of the great flyweights of all time. He's that messed up. But if not, I suppose he could always be a jockey."

"I can be knocked out by any man alive."   *—Roy Jones Jr.*

A SPORTSPICKLE.COM INSIDE LOOK AT . . . WEIGHT CLASSES

Boxing weight classes help keep the sport safe by grouping fighters with others of a similar weight. The ranges within classes vary anywhere from 15 pounds (cruiserweight: 176 to 190 pounds) down to just 3 pounds (junior flyweight: 106 to 108 pounds), where a midsize bowel movement can cause a boxer to drop an entire weight class or more. There are seventeen different weight classes in boxing, from heavyweight at 190 pounds and over to the 100 pounds-and-under division reserved for anorexics, called the still-too-fat weight class. The heavyweight division is the most popular, primarily because Americans relate more to fatties.

BOXING FUN FACT

Former heavyweight Jack Dempsey was known to barge into bars and declare: "I can't sing and I can't dance, but I can lick any man in this house." This boast went over particularly well at gay bars.

GREAT MOMENTS IN BOXING HISTORY

SEPTEMBER 22, 1927 Gene Tunney wins a ten-round decision over Jack Dempsey in the celebrated "long-count fight." The long count was just the latest on the résumé of longtime boxing referee "Stuttering" Tom McGee.

MARCH 6, 1976 Seventeen-year-old Wilfred Benítez wins a fifteen-round decision over champion Antonio Cervantes to win the world junior welterweight title. Benítez was the youngest boxer in a professional title fight since Joe Louis knocked out six-year-old Petey "Soft Neck" O'Reilly just seven seconds into the first round of a 1943 bout, breaking the child's neck and paralyzing him for life.

MAY 8, 1984 The Soviet Union announces it will not participate in the 1984 Summer Olympics Games in Los Angeles, dashing the Olympic dreams of young Soviet heavyweight Ivan Drago.

NOVEMBER 5, 1994 Forty-five-year-old George Foreman knocks out Michael Moorer to become the oldest heavyweight champion in boxing history. Moorer struggles to land legal, above-the-belt punches during the bout because the middle-aged Foreman wore his trunks hiked up all the way to his chest.

PEOPLE TO KNOW

MUHAMMAD ALI Born Seymour Reilly in 1942, Ali changed his name to Cassius Clay in 1958 when he joined the Nation of Alliteration. He then changed that to Muhammad Ali upon joining the Nation of Islam in 1964. Few people initially accepted Ali taking on the new name, especially after some reported he boasted that he would: "Float like a butterfly, jihad like a bee." And Ali further became a polarizing figure when he refused to go to Vietman in 1967, reasoning that the average Viet Cong was well below his weight class. But as his career progressed, the graceful heavyweight became perhaps the most beloved athlete of all time. Even in losing, Ali was likable—and highly quotable. After getting his jaw broken in a loss to Ken Norton in 1973, Ali unveiled one of his patented rhymes. But it was unique for Ali in its humility: "He hit me with his paw, broke my jaw, and now I'm eating through a straw." Despite suffering with Parkinson's disease today, Ali remains as popular as ever. In fact, in 1996—some twenty years past his prime—he was asked to light the Olympic torch at the Atlanta Games, marking one of the last times in U.S. history the general public would feel comfortable allowing a Muslim to have access to an open flame.

OSCAR DE LA HOYA One of the most marketable and talented boxers in history, De La Hoya's interests extend well beyond the ring to acting, fashion, real estate, and singing. In 2000 he released a CD that was nominated for a Latin Grammy, but the effort was mocked within boxing, and *Ring* magazine panned the album, calling it "Gayer than Emile Griffith after five cosmopolitans." Also in 2000 De La Hoya married Latin pop star Millie Corretjer, providing Corretjer full-time protection in case her fan club president ever tries to go Selena on her.

ROBERTO DURÁN Born in Panama in 1951, Durán is the only boxer in history to fight in five different decades. He got the nickname "Manos de Piedra"—or Hands of Stone—at age fourteen when he knocked out a mule with one punch. A reputation for mule brutality haunted Durán throughout his career, but he always insisted the mule had asked him to knock it out upon learning it was sterile. Despite holding world titles at four different weights, Durán may be best remembered for his November 1980 loss to Sugar Ray Leonard, in which he quit in the eighth round, saying: *"No más"*—an outcome that was celebrated wildly throughout the mule community.

EVANDER HOLYFIELD Regarded as one of the grittiest fighters in history, Holyfield's strength was also his weakness, as he often endured brutal beatings on the way to becoming the only four-time heavyweight champion. Unfortunately, Holyfield continued boxing into his early forties, and signs of severe brain damage have already made themselves apparent. Most notably, the fact that Holyfield actually agreed to appear on the ABC reality show *Dancing with the Stars* in the summer of 2005. And not only did Holyfield not win the dance competition, but he had a large chunk of his ear bitten off by his partner, who he had enraged with an accidental head butt while tangoing.

JACK JOHNSON Born poor in 1878 in Galveston, Texas, Johnson was the second of six children of former slaves, and had only five years of formal schooling. But despite his posh upbringing, Johnson turned to the brutal sport of boxing by age fifteen. He became the first black heavyweight champion of the world in 1908 when he defeated Tommy Burns of Australia. Johnson further endeared himself to white America by marrying three white women during his life. In fact, Johnson was so beloved by the powers-that-be that he was given a no-expenses-paid trip around the world from 1913 to 1920, thanks to trumped-up charges that forced him to flee the country.

SUGAR RAY LEONARD Leonard won titles in four different weight classes—from junior middleweight all the way up to light heavy-weight—between 1981 and 1988, a time of rapid weight gain in which he was known better as "Diabetic Ray" than "Sugar Ray." Leonard retired six different times during his career, causing many major dailies to hire Sugar Ray Leonard retirement beat reporters.

LENNOX LEWIS Despite dominating the heavyweight division for much of the 1990s and early 2000s, Lewis never was feared or respected to the same degree as past great heavyweights, primarily because no one in world history has ever been scared or intimidated by a guy with an English accent. Lewis retired in 2004 after Mike Tyson ate his children.

JOE LOUIS Considered to be the greatest puncher of all time, Louis's legacy will probably be that of causing World War II. Louis lost to German Max Schmelling in June of 1936, confirming Adolf Hitler's ideas that the Aryan race was superior. Louis beat Schmelling in a 1938 rematch, but by then it was too late—Hitler's plans had already been set in motion. So thanks a lot, Joe Louis.

ROCKY MARCIANO Born Rocco Marchegiano in 1923, the boxer went by Rocky Marciano because it sounded much, much less ethic. Nicknamed the "Big Bopper," Marciano is the only heavy-weight champion to retire undefeated, but he died tragically in 1969 in a plane crash that also killed musicians Ritchie Valens and Buddy Holly.

SUGAR RAY ROBINSON The greatest "Sugar Ray" of all time—yes, even greater than the band fronted by Mark McGrath, if you can be-lieve it. Robinson registered 109 knockouts during his career, and is thought by many to be the greatest boxer ever. As his career wound down, Robinson famously began hanging out with the Rat Pack, perfecting a bit where he would playfully punch Sammy Davis Jr., popping his eye right out of his head.

JOHN L. SULLIVAN Driven by rage he held inside from being mocked as a child for his middle name, Labia—which was from his mother's side—Sullivan was arrested several times as a youth for fighting. He eventually directed that anger into organized fighting and became the last bare-knuckle boxing champion. He was also the last bare-ass boxing champion, but that was due less to his skills as a fighter than it was to his well-documented drinking problem.

MIKE TYSON Born in Brooklyn's tough Brownsville section, Tyson was very poor and spent his youth being passed in and out of vari-ous juvenile detention centers. This upbringing left him without much money, guidance, or support, but did leave him with—strangely enough—the voice of a woman. Tyson was rescued from reform school by legendary trainer Cus D'Amato, but D'Amato died of a heart attack in 1985, forcing Tyson to use Apollo Creed as his trainer for his much-anticipated title fight that year with Clubber Lang (played by Mr. T). Tyson's dominance came to an end in 1990 when he shockingly lost to Buster Douglas, an unknown fighter who only got his shot at the champ by submitting a secret code—007-373-5963—to Tyson's popular video game. While primarily thought of as a brutal and ferocious puncher during his career, Tyson could also be a skilled technician when utilizing his patented "Rape-a-Dope" style, which resulted in a three-year prison sentence. After leaving jail in 1995, Tyson experienced further troubles and went

Strapped for cash, Mike Tyson begins selling long-term advertising space on his face.

broke, thanks to years of having to live (multimillion-dollar) paycheck to (multimillion-dollar) paycheck. His boxing suffered, too, and he famously bit off a chunk of Evander Holyfield's ear in a fight. On the bright side, he surprisingly has never murdered anyone.

BRAWL BREAKS OUT AT JENNY CRAIG WEIGH-IN

Homemakers Margie Weeks and Linda Watson exchanged punches yesterday when a brawl erupted during a weigh-in at a Jenny Craig Weight Loss Center outside of Dayton, Ohio.

"I wonder what is written on these cards," thought Destiny. "I hope it doesn't say: 'I'm a stupid, illiterate bimbo.' "

Weeks claims she heard Watson make a snide comment about her size after she weighed in at 213 pounds. She lunged at Watson and the women whaled on each other for several seconds until they were broken apart.

"Margie thinks I said something rude, but all I said was 'I wish I were that slim,'" said Watson.

But Weeks says Watson was being sarcastic. "I could hear the tone in her voice. It wasn't a compliment."

MUHAMMAD ALI BOBBLE-HEAD DOLL SEEN AS INAPPROPRIATE

Bobble-head dolls of Muhammad Ali have become a bestseller at sports memorabilia shops and on Internet auction sites. Fans are snatching up the shaky-headed dolls of the past champ and current Parkinson's disease sufferer in record numbers.

"I just like to watch him stand there shaking and quivering in complete silence with a glassy look on his face," said Garry Lyght, owner of Lyght's Sports Memorabilia in Lexington, Kentucky. "There's something about the doll that really makes people think of him, even more so than with bobble-head dolls of other athletes. I don't know what it is, but the resemblance is uncanny."

The Ali doll retails at $19.95 but has been sold on the Internet for as much as $95. BobbleCo, the manufacturer of most sports bobble-head dolls, says it has struggled to keep up with demand for the doll. The company has managed to develop other Ali bobble-heads, however.

"The Muhammad Ali Sleeping Bobble-Head Doll is also a big seller here," Lyght said. "It shakes for a couple of seconds, but then the eyes close and it stops. Then it'll snooze for a little, open its eyes and start shaking again. I've had a few people bring it back because they've thought it was broken, but that's the way the Sleeping version is supposed to work."

But while the Ali dolls continue to set bobble-head sales records, some find the dolls inappropriate. "The man has a disease," said Linda McWilliams, a Parkinson's specialist at New York's Samaritan Hospital. "These dolls are making light of a serious condition. It shouldn't be a source for amusement."

Lyght and others don't think the dolls are insensitive. "I don't see it," Lyght said. "I think it's sick to even think of that. People said the same thing a few years ago about the Mahmoud Abdul-Rouf bobble-head doll, just because it would shake and curse uncontrollably. All we're striving for is authenticity."

STORIES TOP STORIES   TOP STORIES TOP STORIES IN OTHER NEWS . . .

Man tells wife he meant to order boxing on pay-per-view, not the porno he was watching . . . Muhammad Ali impersonator asleep . . . Brawl at prefight weigh-in likely to be more exciting than the actual fight . . . Boring boxing match ends without a death . . . Boxing match marred by postfight fight . . .

GOLF

NEW DRIVER BOASTS LARGER SWEET SPOT, PROVIDES FALSE SENSE THAT YOU'LL ALL OF A SUDDEN STOP SUCKING AT GOLF

Taylor Made's new R7 Quad titanium driver offers advanced club-head weighting, superthin wall casting technology and, at 400 cubic centimeters, one of the largest clubheads and sweet spots on the market. And all for less than $500.

But the club's biggest selling point is the false sense it provides golfers that if they buy it, they'll suddenly and magically stop sucking at golf.

"I plunked down five-hundred bucks for an R7 last August because I thought if I had the best driver out there I'd have to stop hitting 120-yard duck hooks all the time," said Matt Franklin of Birmingham, Alabama. "It turns out that it's just that my swing sucks and that better clubs don't help. Now I just hit one hundred and forty yard duck hooks, only they all go out of bounds now instead of just some of them."

Jon Gonzalez of Santa Fe, New Mexico, said he experienced the same disappointing result when he bought the R7 driver last summer.

"I'm starting to think that the whole golf equipment industry is some sort of racket," said Gonzalez. "Can they really be making any significant improvements from one line to the next? I have a friend who has 38 putters, yet he can't make a single putt outside of three feet. Maybe if I would have used the $4,000 I've spent on equipment over the last three years on some lessons I wouldn't still stink at golf. Or maybe I just need to get some new wedges first and see if that helps before I waste time on lessons."

JOHN DALY LOVABLE, CONSIDERING HE'S NOT BLACK

John Daly, the overweight, substance-abusing professional golfer who has been married four times, is still a fan favorite on the PGA Tour, despite having only a handful of wins in his Tour career. Also, he's white.

"I love John Daly. He's my favorite player," said Jake Welch, a Daly fan. "He's overweight, has women troubles, drinks a bit too much booze—he's an everyman. But, oh yeah, if he was black I'd definitely hate him."

Jack McClintock, the editor of *Golf Gazette,* agrees. "Daly is one of golf's most beloved players even though he's rarely even in contention. But put some melanin in him and he'd be a total punk thug—a Portland Trail Blazer with a golf club. He's everything that's wrong with sports, except, of course, he's white."

Golf insiders say Daly's alcoholism and four marriages—including the one to his current wife, Sherrie, who was indicted on laundering drug money—as well as his weight problem, and poor play matter very little to a public that loves the big blond's self-effacing manner and grip-it-and-rip-it approach on and off the course.

"Daly's whiteness actually makes all of those negatives positives for him," said McClintock. "It's really quite an interesting phenomenon."

Daly, like many black football and basketball players, even has recorded an album. But Daly's is a country album, with songs such as "All My Exes Wear Rolexes," not rap or hip-hop. "Rap is horrendous. We didn't need another athlete with no musical talent yelling into a mike," said Welch. "But John's album is just about having fun."

Even Tiger Woods, professional golf's poster child, has noticed the benefit of the doubt Daly receives as a white guy.

"John is an everyday reminder for me that I can't screw up in my personal life," said Woods. "Can you imagine if I did all the stuff he has done? People would look at me like I was some kind of gangbanger. That's why I just try to keep my mouth shut and smile a lot."

SportsPickleNation Poll

Which golfer has the brightest future as a rapper?

12%   T. Woody

26%   Ol Dirty Jesper

13%   D-Love3

21%   Shegeki Maruyama Yo Mama

28%   Gary Playa

SportsPickleNation Poll

What is your favorite part about the Masters?

31%   The Champions Dinner of fried chicken and collard greens (or other race-appropriate food)

22%   The azaleas. I FRIGGIN' LOVE AZALEAS!

18%   It means my favorite tournament, the MCI Heritage, is only one week away

29%   It's a tradition of mine to watch the Masters every year; in fact, it's a tradition unlike any other

"Do you want to know what else is a tradition unlike any other? Me having my sex with my hot Swedish wife every night. So I could honestly give a crap if I win the Masters or not."

—Tiger Woods

GOLF FUN FACT

Sorry, but you're never going to consistently break 80.

GOLF FUN FACT

In 1967 Martha Burk appeared as the centerfold in Golf Digest*'s one and only swimsuit edition.*

GREAT MOMENTS IN GOLF HISTORY

DECEMBER 12, 1899 George Grant patents the wooden golf tee. The safety, and popularity, of golf immediately skyrocketed, as golfers no longer had to use holders when teeing off.

NOVEMBER 9, 1961 Facing heavy pressure, the PGA eliminates its "caucasians only" rule. The PGA changed it to a more inclusive "Caucasians only, please."

JUNE 13, 1991 A spectator is killed by lightning at the U.S. Open Golf Tournament. PGA officials determined the fan's fallen body was an immovable hazard, forcing golfers to play off of, through, and over him throughout the tournament.

APRIL 13, 2003 Canadian golfer Mike Weir wins the Masters. Following the victory, Fuzzy Zoeller tells reporters: "Tell him not to serve Canadian bacon next year. Or Molson. Or whatever it is they eat."

COURSES TO KNOW

AUGUSTA NATIONAL Home of the prestigious Masters Tournament, Augusta National is also home to some of the world's most prestigious sausage parties, as no woman has ever been offered membership in the club. More of a tradition than an official policy, the club's stance on the issue is nonetheless reinforced by the numerous and prominent GIRLS HAVE COOTIES signs that are found through-

*Every year Augusta National holds
one of the nation's best sausage
parties. Girls have cooties!*

out the grounds. Probably the best-known course in the United States due to its hosting of a televised major championship every year, many characteristics of the tract are easily identifiable to even casual golf fans. For instance, most anyone can talk about the "Eisenhower Tree" along the seventeenth hole—so named because former member and president Dwight D. Eisenhower would commonly stand behind it to take a leak during a round—or Rae's Creek, which runs in front of the twelfth green and is convenient for pushing Tiger Woods's wife into if she's wearing a white shirt. Opened in 1932 under the guidance of Bobby Jones, the course design has been tweaked often since then, including numerous "Tiger proofings" in recent years. The most recent addition is bushes along the ninth fairway that spell out "Blow me, Martha Burk!" when seen from above.

PEBBLE BEACH Host to four U.S. Opens and a PGA Championship, Pebble Beach is unlike most other major championship courses in that the general public has a chance to get on and play. Yes, Pebble Beach is a public course and—for the low, low price of $425, plus a cart fee—anyone can play there. The course is renowned for its natural beauty—the rugged coastline, crashing surf, towering cliffs and . . . you're still hung up on the $425, aren't you? Yeah, that's right, $425 for a freaking round of golf. Screw you, Pebble Beach. *Fun Fact*: Golfers can purchase a hot dog at the turn for just $28.50!

ST. ANDREWS Regarded as the home of golf, the club's full name is the Royal and Ancient Golf Club of St. Andrews, but many refer to it simply as the R&A. Interestingly, the town of St. Andrews's finest gentlemen's club—the T&A—is located just across the street from the clubhouse. The Old Course at St. Andrews is the oldest golf course in the world and has hosted dozens of Open Championships. Play began there in 1552 when Callum the Mud Farmer defeated Kieran the Drunk, 3-and-2 to win the Clarett Jug.

PEOPLE TO KNOW

BEN HOGAN The most accurate ball striker of all time, Hogan spent countless hours at the driving range during his career, causing him to be despised by range tractor drivers due to their repeated plunkings. One year after he won ten tournaments in 1948, Hogan's career was derailed when he was seriously injured after his car was hit by a bus. But Hogan courageously returned eleven months later and took second at the Los Angeles Open, losing in a play-off to Sam Snead when he was run over by a golf cart while lining up a short putt for the win. The nine-time major winner authored the preeminent golf instruction book, *Five Lessons, Modern Fundamentals on Golf,* which laid out five essential elements in constructing an effective and repeatable golf swing. The book's five chapters are: (1) The Grip, (2) Stance and Posture, (3) The First Part of the Swing, (4) The Second Part of the Swing, and (5) Don't Get Hit by a Bus.

BOBBY JONES The greatest golfer of the early twentieth century, Jones learned to play golf as a child in the brutal Georgia heat with a cut-down, hickory-shafted club and an old ball. And he appreciated every minute of it, okay? Some days he even played in six feet of snow on courses that were uphill from the first to eighteenth holes, and you know what? He was just happy to be out there. And he never, ever rode in a cart. And back then, golfers had to work at their games, okay? Sure they have to work at them now, too, but that's not the point. The point is that you are a no-good, pathetic, multiple-club-using pussy. Now that that's established, you should also know that Jones was a renaissance man, with bachelor's degrees from Georgia Tech and Harvard and a law degree from Emory

Phil Mickelson models his green jacket.

University. And he is the only golfer to win the Grand Slam. But he did it while retaining amateur status, proving that despite all the academic degrees he was a bit of a moron.

PHIL MICKELSON Easily one of the most talented players in the modern game, Mickelson was plagued for years by the inability to win a major. Finally, at the age of thirty-three in 2004, he broke through to win the Masters. And not only did he win, but the green jacket really complemented his cleavage. The victory by a golfer with bosoms took some heat off Augusta National, as well, as it came one year after Martha Burk's very public protest over the club's males-only membership rules. In addition to his on-course success, Mickelson is a loving husband and devoted father to three children, having breast-fed all of them from birth. *Fun Fact*: Phil Mickelson has big tits.

JACK NICKLAUS Nicknamed the "Golden Bare" for his blond hair and his proclivity to prance around naked in the locker room, Nicklaus is mostly remembered as golf's biggest loser due to his nineteen second-place finishes in majors. Pathetic. But not many realize he actually won a few major titles during his career. In fact, he has the second-most PGA titles in history with seventy-three, which is even more impressive considering he did it while battling Arnold Palmer, Gary Player, Tom Watson, Lee Trevino, and extremely tight pants. *Fun Fact*: Nicklaus's voice caused many to opine that he really belonged on the LPGA Tour.

ARNOLD PALMER As beloved a golfer as there ever was, the seven-time major winner is credited for making televised golf popular with the American public. In fact, Nielsen research showed that in tournaments Palmer participated in, viewers stayed awake an average of four minutes longer than in those he did not. Today Palmer is still extremely popular and continues to be a go-to pitchman for brands ranging from Cooper Tires to Sears. This is thought to be because now more than ever the public can identify with Palmer, since most people have a handicap in the twenties just like he does. *Fun Fact:* J. Edgar Hoover had an FBI file in the 1950s on Arnie's Army.

VIJAY SINGH It is a point that is tirelessly debated, but there are some who say Singh is the greatest Fijian golfer of the last twenty years. While that's likely unwarranted praise, his three career major titles are nevertheless impressive. A tireless worker, Singh often takes his family to the driving range on vacation. But despite all the hard work, Singh has never been able to master the putter. In fact, he hasn't beaten his son at mini golf since the boy turned three. While he focuses little of his attention off the course, his debut album—*Vijay Singhs,* a collection of sugary dance grooves—has been at No. 1 on the Fijian pop charts since its release last year.

SAM SNEAD Growing up in backwoods Virginia during the Depression, Snead taught himself to play golf using clubs carved from trees by his father, and balls carved from his dog by the local veterinarian. He became a legend for his folksy nature by playing tournaments in bare feet and a straw hat. ("Folksy" because the word "redneck" wasn't common in the early half of the twentieth century.) In 1979 at age sixty-seven Snead—the winner of seven career majors—became the youngest professional golfer to shoot his age, besting Earl "Oldy" Olmstead who had done it at age one hundred in the 1962 Western Open. Many have attempted to duplicate Snead's silky-smooth swing, but only the likes of Lee Trevino and Jim Furyk have ever come even remotely close.

TIGER WOODS Woods was trained from birth to be a champion golfer by his father, Earl, who once famously declared that his son would be bigger than Gandhi. And already he is, with four green jackets to Gandhi's pathetic total of zero. (Where you at now, Gandhi? Maybe if you would've eaten something you could have been strong enough to win a major, biatch!) Woods was thought to be the next Jack Nicklaus since his teens—especially after Harold Miner, Grant Hill, and Jerry Stackhouse fell short of their potential— and has delivered on that promise, winning all four majors at least once already. His success and single-minded determination have turned him into an international superstar and marketing machine— although that probably has more to do with his charismatic, bubbly personality and propensity to speak from the heart and not like some programmed, corporate robot. *Fun Fact*: Tiger's wife wants me.

HEAVY HOUSEWORK LOAD PREVENTING MARTHA BURK FROM PROTESTING THIS YEAR'S MASTERS

Reports that women's rights advocate Martha Burk will not protest this April's Masters were confirmed this morning when Burk said she cannot commit the time due to "having too much housework to do right now."

"My dedication to women's equality in general, and breaking the exclusionary culture of the Augusta National Golf Club in particular, remains as strong as ever," said Burk, chairwoman of the National Council of Women's Organizations. "However, with all of the rabble-rousing I've done in past years, I have hardly been home and I've gotten way behind on laundry and ironing, and my husband is getting rightly angry that I haven't cooked him dinner in ages. Whether I like it or not, sometimes my traditional roles as a wife and mother and in keeping my husband happy come first. I have no problem accepting that."

Despite intense media coverage of Burk's past protests of Augusta National, the club made no concessions to her demands. Yet Burk said she may still target the club again in the future.

"If I can get caught up on my housework in time for next year I'll be there, I can guarantee you that," said Burk. "Maybe I'll cook a lot of stuff in advance and freeze it so my husband can eat while I'm away. And I can get one of my friends to clean and do his laundry and stuff while I'm protesting. That should work."

SERGIO GARCIA WINS PRESTIGIOUS
BEST-PLAYER-NEVER-TO-WIN-A-MAJOR AWARD

PGA Tour star Sergio Garcia was awarded the prestigious Best-Player-Never-to-Win-a-Major Award at last night's PGA Tour awards dinner in New York. The award is voted on by players and media.

Sergio Garcia, who lost in the past to Phil Mickelson and David Duval, was a near-unanimous selection this year. "What an honor," gushed Garcia. "I think I have a good chance to defend this award next year."

The seven-hour dinner included awards for every PGA professional, including Tour player David Gossett for "245th Best Player Never to Win a Major."

STORIES TOP STORIES   TOP STORIES TOP STORIES **IN OTHER NEWS . . .**

Knowing pin position somehow vital for 28-handicapper . . . Retired golfer looking forward to spending more time in the office . . . Payne Stewart still getting made fun of in heaven for his stupid outfits . . . Fred Funk faked on nasty dunk . . . Good walk spoiled . . . Black America exalts latest victory by half-Thai, three-eighths-black golfer . . . God chunks 1-iron . . . David Duval excited to shoot 3-under his handicap of 15 . . .

HORSE RACING

INJURED JOCKEY PUT DOWN

Luis Mercado, the jockey for Kentucky Derby favorite Swift Tide, was put down this morning after injuring his ankle during a practice run yesterday. The horse's trainer killed Mercado with a single shot to the back of the head.

"It's a sad day for all of us," said Robert Winthrop, Swift Tide's trainer. "We had made a major investment in Mercado and hoped for big things. You never want to see something like this happen, but it was the humane thing to do."

Mercado is thought to be the first injured jockey to be killed in horse racing history. He sprained his ankle when he dismounted Swift Tide awkwardly after taking some practice laps at Churchill Downs.

"When it occurred, it didn't seem to bad—Luis just walked it off," said Winthrop, "but as the day progressed, it got more tender and started to swell up. By this morning we realized what was going to have to happen."

Despite Winthrop's insistence that Mercado was resigned to his fate, the jockey's friends and family say they were surprised to hear of his death.

"I talked to Luis last night and everything seemed fine," said his brother, Manuel Mercado. "I'm pretty sure he would have told me if he knew he was going to be put down. All he said was that he had turned his ankle and hoped it didn't hurt on Saturday for the race. It didn't seem like a big deal to him."

"We always encouraged Luis to go after his dreams as a jockey," said Conchita Mercado, Luis's mother. "Never did we think he was an injury away from being shot. It's a very sad day for all of us."

Mercado's fellow jockeys were equally shocked by the news.

"Euthanizing always seems like such a harsh decision, but even more so when it's done to a jockey," said Gary Milton, the jockey for Lanyard. "I understand that he couldn't race anymore, but I wish they could have found an alternative. I think Luis would have happily accepted being put out to stud or something with a light, short woman to produce future jockeys. Anything would be better than this."

SportsPickleNation Poll

Which horse is least likely to win the Triple Crown?

8%	Smell My Poo Trail, Loser
11%	I'm In This for the Breeding
8%	GetThisMidgetOffMyBack
10%	Break-a-Leg
16%	Seattle Slow
10%	Farty Jones
11%	Glue Gun
11%	Fatty McGimpsteen
9%	Sir Lose-a-Lot
6%	Half Horsepower

"If you all don't mind, I'd prefer to be put out to stud immediately. I see no reason to wait."
—Afleet Alex, to his trainer and owner, after winning the Preakness Stakes

SportsPickleNation Poll

What is the most interesting fact about the Kentucky Derby?

29% If you buy a mint julep for one of those old ladies with the big hats, they are required to have sex with you in the in-field

8% All jockeys are outfitted free of charge by OshKosh B'Gosh

7% More than 50,000 Kentucky residents drive their homes to the Derby each year

17% Pedophiliac zoophiles view the Derby as the best place to see hot three-year-old horses

19% All injured horses are beaten to death with bats provided by the nearby Louisville Slugger company

20% Yum! Brands, the owner of KFC, just became the official sponsor of the Derby as part of their plan to unveil new Horsemeat Snackers

"Oompa loompa doompadee doo."
—Mike Smith, Giacomo's jockey,
on his thoughts on winning
the Kentucky Derby

GREAT MOMENTS IN HORSE RACING HISTORY

MAY 23, 1901 H. Spencer rides Commando to victory at the Belmont Stakes. Spencer was the last jockey permitted to ride without underwear.

MAY 6, 1933 Broker's Tip and Head Play engage in the dirtiest stretch duel in Kentucky Derby history as jockeys Don Meade and Herb Fisher resort to whipping each other. The jockeys' actions were all the more disturbing considering both were wearing ass-less chaps.

JANUARY 16, 1936 The first photo-finish camera is installed at Hialeah Racetrack in Hialeah, Florida. While a good idea in principle, due to the camera technology of the time, horses had to pause and hold their pose for ten minutes at the finish line while their image was captured on the camera's photoreflective paper.

HORSES TO KNOW

CITATION Winner of the Triple Crown in 1948, Citation was the only thoroughbred to achieve the feat for twenty-five years, until Secretariat came along in 1973. And Citation took advantage of his status during that period, pulling some of the best tail from Saratoga Springs to Santa Anita Park on the way to siring dozens of offspring. In 1951 he became the first racehorse to reach $1 million in career earnings but, sadly, he blew the entire sum on shoes. *Fun Fact*: Citation was ridden by legendary jockey Eddie Arcaro. But never in a race.

MAN O' WAR The most accomplished Irish thoroughbred of all-time, O' War lost only one race in his illustrious career. Many rank him the top champion in horse racing history, while others give the nod to Secretariat. Still others, mostly children, say Black Beauty was the greatest ever. Man O' War was an enormous animal, carry-

Barbaro reading his get-well letters.

ing nearly thirty pounds more than many of his rivals yet, interestingly, he was hung like a horsefly. He passed away in 1947 after living a remarkably long thirty years, which in horse years is . . . well, it's still thirty years.

NATIVE DANCER Despite being owned by the wealthy Vanderbilt family, Native Dancer was not raised with a silver spoon in his mouth. Instead, he was made to sleep and eat outside, and was often fed nothing other than oats and hay. Even worse, he was forced to start racing for money at just two years of age. Given the nickname "Gray Ghost" because people apparently found his given name to be too formal, he burst onto the scene as America was falling in love with the television. And as he raced to victories in the 1953 Preakness and Belmont Stakes, he became the sport's first matinee idol—so much so that he parlayed his fame into a starring role on the hit 1960s TV show *Mister Ed. Fun Fact*: British pop singer Elton John's 1971 hit "Tiny Dancer" was originally titled "Native Dancer" and touched on John's fantasy of taking it from a horse.

SEABISCUIT An undersized, lazy, bowlegged horse owned by a man with a history of failed business ventures, trained by a reclusive near mute, and ridden by an overweight, gimpy, half-blind jockey, Seabiscuit's story was one many Americans could identify with in the late 1930s . . . making one wonder what kind of pathetic, self-hating losers the country was full of back then. Seabiscuit's first successes came on the West Coast circuit, and as his victories mounted the public demanded he take on the dominant thoroughbred of the time, War Admiral. In the "Match of the Century," the two finally met in November 1938. Seabiscuit came out on top, landing a brutal combination in the final round that opened a large gash over War Admiral's left eye and sent him whinnying grotesquely to the canvas for a knockout. *Fun Fact*: Seabiscuit wore a saddle by Vera Wang to the 2004 Academy Awards.

SECRETARIAT In 1973 Secretariat became the first Triple Crown winner since the Yaz in 1967. His victory at the Belmont Stakes was so dominant that he won by a stunning thirty-one lengths—although others placed more importance on the girth. Listed by ESPN as the thirty-fifth-greatest athlete of the twentieth century, Secretariat ranked just in front of Oscar Robertson and just behind this one cheetah that was running really fast on one episode of *Mutual of Omaha's Wild Kingdom* in 1981. A key to Secretariat's success was his massive heart, which was three times the size of regular horse's heart and allowed him to pump far more blood during a race. He died of a massive heart attack in 1989. *Fun Fact*: Secretariat's Day is celebrated in late April each year.

OTHERS TO KNOW: John Elway, Bill Walton, Jerry Seinfeld, Sarah Jessica Parker

KENTUCKY DERBY BEGINS WITH CEREMONIAL FIRST CRAP

The Kentucky Derby will begin on Saturday, as always, with a ceremonial first crap. Past Derby winners will be brought back to take a dump on the finish line minutes before the starting gun is fired.

"What says horse racing more than the Kentucky Derby?" said event organizer Willard McIntyre. "And what says horses more than steaming piles of fresh crap? We felt the two would go perfect together."

Thirteen past Derby winners will be in attendance at the cere-

Please enjoy this life-size poster of Hall of Fame jockey Bill Shoemaker.

mony, from the 1983 Derby winner, Sunny's Halo, to more recent winners like Monarchos and Funny Cide. After the mass dumping, the champion horses' respective jockeys will scoop the poo from the track and spread it in the infield.

McIntyre says the fifteen participating horses have been on strict, synchronized diets for the past month. Every meal and every bowel movement has been scheduled right up until the ceremony. With only three days until the Derby, the horses bowel movements are within two minutes of one another, McIntyre said.

"We'll feed them an extra-large oat bag the night before at about 7:30 P.M.," he said. "Then it's a laxative two hours before race time."

If all goes well and the horse crappings are synchronized, Kentucky Derby organizers hope the event will become a tradition. "The sight of fifteen fresh piles of horse crap, steam rising majestically to the heavens, the stench wafting into the crowd . . . it will be breathtaking," said Derby chairperson Elizabeth Dugan.

SEVERAL MARES ACCUSE FORMER DERBY WINNER OF RAPE

Former Kentucky Derby and Preakness Stakes winner Smarty Jones learned today that several mares have accused him of rape. The allegations claim Jones has had sex with three female horses for months against their will. The mares were reportedly brought to Jones's stall by their owners.

"If this is true, it's a horrific story," said Roger Cossack, ESPN's legal analyst. "Smarty Jones is being accused of serial and systematic rape that was enabled by numerous parties. It's a black mark on horse racing and the entire sports world."

"This case exposes a dark secret of the horse racing and horse breeding industry," said Dale Ramsey, editor of the *Equine Racing Times*. "Young females are being traded and sold for sex at an alarming rate. It is a practice that must come to an end."

Jones is expected to be present at a press conference scheduled for this afternoon that will address the accusations. Parties close to Jones will admit to his having sex with the mares, but maintain that the horse thought the sex was consensual.

Funny Cide wistfully eyeing the jar containing his decaying testi-cles . . . Horse doesn't seem to be understanding that he just won a very important race . . . Camel jockeys now referred to as jockeys who race camels . . . Horse racing jockeys working hard to finish making Christmas toys . . . Horse trainer struggling to explain how he contracted equine herpes . . .

SUMMER OLYMPIC SPORTS

SWIMMING PHENOM RETIRES DUE TO EMBARRASSINGLY SMALL SWIMSUIT BULGE

Landon Phillips, a nineteen-year-old U.S. swimming phenom expected to star at the upcoming Summer Olympics, quit the sport yesterday due to embarrassment over the lack of a prominent swimsuit bulge, his coach reported.

"Landon is tired of the pointing, the snickers, the immature 'the water a little cold today?' comments—and rightly so," said Leslie Robinson, Phillips's longtime coach. "People have made him feel horrible about himself, and in doing so we have lost one of the greatest young swimmers this country has ever had."

Robinson said she is making Phillips's embarrassment over his small penis public in hopes it will prevent future swimmers from being ridiculed in the same way. "People thought it was okay to stare at him, to make comments that they thought he couldn't hear. And because our society is so hung up on size, a great swimming talent has vowed to never enter the pool again. It's a tragedy," she said.

Phillips himself refused to comment on his reasons for quitting the sport, only to confirm that he has retired and that he "would prefer if Coach Robinson would stop saying what she's been saying. Not that it's true or anything, but it could make me feel more self-conscious and she's letting millions of people think that I'm hung like a small boy. Again—not that it's true. Really, it's not. But that's the impression that she's giving and I wish she would stop."

Robinson said she has long known that Philips was very uncomfortable with how he looked in his swimsuit. "In the tight suits that swimmers wear, it was easy to notice that he was quite small down there," she said. "And when he would get out of the cold pool it was even worse—he didn't even look like a male from the waist down. And he knew everybody noticed."

"Not that I would ever look or anything," said U.S. teammate Darryl Lake, "but I have sort of noticed that there wasn't much. I felt bad for the guy, but it did make me look a whole lot better standing next to him, you know? He'll be missed."

An early indication that Phillips's inadequacies would affect his swimming career came two years ago when he quit the backstroke, his best event. "He hated the backstroke," said Robinson. "It horrified him that his crotch was facing up just millimeters below the water for everyone to stare at. He told me he didn't want to do it anymore because he wanted to focus in other events, but I suspected the real reason."

Phillips was expected to challenge for five medals at the 2008 Olympics, but now the U.S. team is stuck without one of its top swimmers.

"We all tried to convince him to stay, but if he's that self-conscious about it, the Olympics, with hundreds of millions of people watching, is no place for him to be," said Lake. "We hope he gets through his issues. Maybe he can get an operation or respond to one of those spam e-mails about penis enlargement. We just want him to have a normal life."

Robinson doesn't see any way Phillips will come back. "He can't take it anymore," she said. "He's horribly embarrassed. He asked me if he could compete in a pair of baggy surf shorts, but their weight and absorbency would slow him down too much to be competitive. Instead we'll just wish him the best and express our condolences about his tiny penis and balls."

NYPD ARRESTS FOUR BLACK MEN SEEN FLEEING START OF NEW YORK CITY MARATHON

New York City police arrested four black men seen fleeing the start of the New York City Marathon on Sunday.

Police were unable to apprehend the suspects until they stopped running just over two hours later near the marathon's finish line in Central Park. All four men, Kenyan foreign nationals, were taken into custody and were discovered to have winners' checks on their persons.

"We knew there was something going on when they sprinted away from the crowd after the starter's pistol was fired," said NYPD lieutenant Mark Alameda. "It speaks to the perseverance of our uniformed men and women that they were able to track these guys for more than twenty-six miles."

NOBODY TOLD MAN THAT RUNNING A MARATHON COULD MAKE HIS NIPPLES BLEED

First-time marathoner Mike Riley claims that nobody told him that running a marathon could make his nipples bleed.

"If anyone had mentioned that to me before, you can bet I wouldn't have run," said Riley, moments after completing the 26.2-mile Marathon for Cancer course Sunday in Seattle, an experience that left his nipples severely chafed and bloody. "I volunteered to do this for charity, and now I'm in the type of pain that no human being should have to experience."

Riley said that his nipples never bled in any of his premarathon training runs, all of which were less than sixteen miles. "Apparently, once you run more than sixteen miles or so, the constant friction of your shirt rubbing against your nipples gets them all chafed and bloody," he said. "Now they tell me I could have put tape over my nipples and prevented this from happening, but it's a bit too late to tell me that now, don't you think?"

The Seattle financial advisor raised more than $850 dollars for cancer by participating in the marathon, but says he would have donated all of that and more himself if he could have not run and prevented his nipples from such abuse. "This girl in my office came around months ago trying to get people to participate in the marathon and I thought, 'Why not, it's for a good cause and it will help me get in shape,'" said Riley. "But I don't remember anywhere on the application there being a disclaimer saying the tips of one's nipples could be rubbed off."

Riley claims he didn't notice his nipples were bleeding until approximately mile 18. "I saw this guy pass me with blood stains all over his shirt from his nipples to his waist and I was absolutely disgusted. I almost threw up," he said. "Then I noticed people along the side of the course were pointing at me with looks of utter revulsion. I looked down, and to my horror, saw that my own nipples were bleeding. It was all I could do to keep running and not pass out."

Riley said the psychological battle that marathoners face is one of the hardest parts of the race, but even more so when their nipples are bleeding.

"All kinds of crazy stuff starts going through your head, like: 'Oh my God, have they been rubbed completely off?' or 'Is my shirt ruined?' or 'Is the tip of my penis also bloody and rubbed off only I can't see the blood because I'm wearing dark shorts and when I have to go to the bathroom after the race there isn't going to be anything there, just a big, gaping hole into my bladder?' or 'Am I keeping up with my split times?' It's not pleasant."

However, Riley admitted that his panic over his bleeding nipples made the latter quarter of the race go by rather quickly. "I was so worried I would be permanently scarred that the running became secondary to me," he said. "Before I knew it the race was over."

Even though Riley was assured by other runners after the race that his wounds would heal up nicely in a week or so, he said he is going to visit a doctor just to be safe.

"I think I might have it a little worse than some of the other bleeders," he said. "The problem is that I didn't change immediately after the race and my nipple scabs dried to my shirt, so when I pulled off my shirt, big chunks of nipple came with it. Boy, was that painful. I can only imagine what it's going to feel like when I get in the shower tonight."

"I'm a disgrace to my country. I'm going to go kill myself."
—Joseph Museki of Kenya, after allowing a non-Kenyan
to finish ahead of him in the New York City Marathon

GREAT MOMENTS IN SUMMER OLYMPICS HISTORY

JUNE 24, 1894 Olympic organizers decide to hold the Olympic Games every four years. The decision was made with a 5–4 vote

SportsPickleNation Poll

If you had an Olympic gold medal, what would you do with it?

12%   Wear it with an open-neck shirt and nestle it deep within my chest hair

18%   Fashion it into a totally blinging eye patch

32%   Trade it for steroids so you could win not one, but two gold medals in the next Olympics

38%   Swing it back and forth and try to hypnotize hot chicks

SUMMER OLYMPICS FUN FACT

Studies show that the rhythmic gymnastics method is not an effective means of birth control.

that the previous time span of 1,598 years between Olympics was too long.

MARCH 25, 1896 The first modern Olympics begin in Athens, Greece. The first postmodern Olympics began on the same day at an Athens coffee shop, in which competitors pondered the irony of athletics having importance in society.

APRIL 6, 1896 James Connolly wins the first gold medal of the modern Olympics, winning the hop, step, and jump. Connolly, who many thought was gay, also went on to win the leap, skip, and sashay, as well as the traipse, prance, and saunter.

JUNE 29, 1956 Charles Dumas high-jumps 7 feet, ⅝ inch at the U.S. Olympic trials in Los Angeles, becoming the first high jumper to clear seven feet. Dumas's jump did not receive as much publicity in

SportsPickleNation Poll

What is the most memorable event in Summer Olympics history?

8%   1968: John Carlos and Tommie Smith anger millions with their actions on the medals stand when each raises an arm in the air for the filming of a Sure deodorant commercial. (Carlos was "Sure"; Smith "unSure.")

14%   1972: Terrorists strike by peeing in the Olympic pool

15%   1976: Nadia Comaneci poses in *Perfect 10* magazine

11%   1984: Mary Decker takes a fall in a futile attempt to draw a penalty shot

33%   1984: U.S. wins 174 medals to the Soviet Union's 0, proving democracy is superior to communism

19%   1988: Martin Short wins first-ever gold medal in men's synchronized swimming

8%   1996: That rent-a-cop clears his name in the bombing of Atlanta's Olympic Park. But everyone still finds out that he lives with his mom. Ha! What a loser.

SUMMER OLYMPICS FUN FACT

It's is Michael Phelps's dream to one day swim in a pool full of beer.

Europe, however, as few cared that no one had cleared 2.1336 meters before.

SEPTEMBER 27, 2000 The United States Olympic baseball team beats the heavily favored Cuban team to win gold in Sydney. The key to the U.S. team's victory came during the seventh-inning stretch when it acquired the entire Cuban team via defection.

TERMS TO KNOW

CLEAN AND JERK The primary lift in weightlifting, the clean and jerk is practiced most by teenage boys in the shower, especially when they're thinking about the snatch.

PEOPLE TO KNOW

ROGER BANNISTER Bannister is a former British track star who in 1955 became the first man to run the mile in less than four minutes. But, of course, Bannister is just one of many great British track and field athletes from the past, including . . . uh, well, surely there's been one or two others. Following his track career, Bannister went to medical school and became a neurologist. Sadly, his competitive streak saw him kill dozens of patients as he sought to complete brain surgery in less than four minutes.

FLORENCE GRIFFITH JOYNER Nicknamed "Flo-Jo," Griffith Joyner was a dominant American track star in the 1980s. She may be best remembered for her stylish outfits and for setting the women's world record in the 100 meters in 1988 with a time of 10.49 seconds—although many claim it was unfair that Griffith Joyner's fingernails broke the tape a full second before the rest of her body. Tragically, she passed away in her sleep in 1998 at age thirty-eight. Her funeral was attended by hundreds, and rapper Sir Mix-a-Lot gave a stirring eulogy in which he remarked: "I'll keep my women like Flo-Jo."

BRUCE JENNER Jenner gained fame by winning gold in the decathlon at the 1976 Olympics. However, he later proved that his best sport was not a track and field event, but competitive face-lifting. In fact, when he appeared on the cover of the Wheaties box, one in ten thousand lucky buyers found a discarded Jenner nose inside. Since retiring from competition Jenner has become a motivational speaker, infomercial pitchman, and author, penning four books. His latest—*Here's Another Book by Someone the Public Stopped Caring About Two Decades Ago*—hits stores later this year.

A SPORTSPICKLE.COM INSIDE LOOK AT . . . THE OLYMPIC FLAME

The Olympic Flame is meant to symbolize purity, the endeavor for perfection and the struggle for victory. But the Olympic Flame has often not upheld those ideals. Instead, it has a troubled past that includes arson, substance abuse, sexual experimentation, and anti-Semitism.

Every Olympiad the Olympic Flame winds its way through the host country, bringing hope and inspiration to those it passes. But the Flame acknowledges it has a checkered past.

Flame was first hired for the ancient games, held in Olympia. Those games hit their peak in the fourth century B.C. But as the ancient games began to lose their hold on the people, Flame fell into a deep depression.

"I reacted violently," Flame said. "I was staying lit every day and no one seemed to care anymore."

Flame's rage caused him to set fire to Rome in A.D. 68. The shock of the fire caused Emperor Nero to turn mad and fiddle while the city burned.

When Theodosius the Great declared an end to the Olympic Games in A.D. 394, Flame was unemployed and his life quickly spiraled out of control.

"I started with heavy substance abuse," Flame says. "I'd take gasoline, sometimes even kerosene, and I just blew up at everyone. I even experimented for a time with water, and that almost killed me."

Flame turned to violence again in 1666, setting fire to London. The Great Fire of London burned for five days and destroyed 13,000 structures. In 1871, Flame's rage came to the United States where he started the Great Chicago Fire.

Twenty-five years later, Flame was employed again as the Olympics were revived in Athens, Greece. "It was such a relief to bring hope to people again," Flame says. "I thought I had put my dark past behind me."

It hadn't.

The 1936 Berlin Olympics featured the Olympic Flame more prominently than any of the other modern games had. Overwhelmed by the Germans' graciousness, Flame became fascinated by Adolf Hitler and the Nazi movement.

"I was very impressionable at that time," Flame says. "And I began hanging around with the wrong crowd and got indoctrinated by their views."

When pogroms exploded in Berlin in November 1938, Flame lit the fires that led to Kristallnacht. "I'm not proud of that," Flame says.

Seeing the destruction that Kristallnacht caused, Flame mended his ways once and for all. It entered counseling and several twelve-step programs. Flame also says that now that there are Olympics every two years, it is able to stay busy. "I can finally say that I am rehabilitated," Flame says.

MICHAEL JOHNSON Johnson developed his world-class speed as a child by fleeing from neighborhood bullies who wished to beat him up for wearing gold shoes. He is the world record holder in the 200 meters and 400 meters and in 1996 became the only man to win both events in the same Olympic Games. While Johnson was well known in the United States, he never achieved the same level of fame as he had internationally, most likely because his erect running style meant most of his races weren't televised in the United States due to decency laws.

JACKIE JOYNER-KERSEE Joyner-Kersee is often mentioned with Babe Didrikson Zaharias as the greatest female athlete of all time. Born poor in East St. Louis, Illinois, in 1962, Joyner-Kersee followed the path many do to escape poverty and took up heptathloning. She became the first woman to score 7,000 points in the event at the 1986 Goodwill Games, and went on to win five Olympics medals during her career. Even more impressively, Joyner-Kersee achieved all that despite suffering from asthma—an accomplishment that ruined a valued gym class excuse for millions of nerds across the country. *Fun Fact*: Joyner-Kersee's husband, Bob Kersee, was also her coach, and he wisely inserted two-a-day sex training in her workout program.

CARL LEWIS Lewis is thought of as the greatest track and field athlete in history. He won ten Olympic medals during his career, nine of which were gold. (Nice job on the silver, loser.) One of his gold medals was won under controversy, however. At the 1988 Olympics, Canada's Ben Johnson beat Lewis in the 100 meter finals, but raised steroids suspicions with a time of 4.82 seconds. Once Johnson tested positive, the gold was awarded to Lewis. Despite his remarkable success, Lewis never was fully accepted by the American public, mainly because of his cocky demeanor, but also because of his habit of lodging the baton in his rectum during relays.

JESSE OWENS Owens is famed for striking a blow to Hitler's theory of Aryan superiority by edging the Führer in the 100 meter finals at the 1936 Berlin Olympics. Owens's success at the 1936 Games and Hitler's refusal to shake his hand was highly publicized in the United States, where the public was angered to learn that Germany would dare copy them by treating a black man poorly. Upon his return home, Owens struggled to make ends meet and had to resort to racing against horses in order to make money. Sadly, the horses also refused to shake his hand.

MICHAEL PHELPS A successful swimmer since he was a young boy, Phelps has never had a body hair that hasn't been immediately

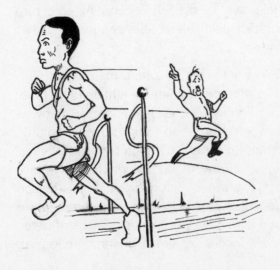

Jesse Owens struck a blow against the idea of Aryan supremacy by defeating Adolf Hitler in the 100 meter dash at the 1936 Berlin Olympics.

waxed off upon sprouting. He exploded into the public consciousness at the 2004 Athens Olympics, which NBC promoted as "The
Michael Phelps Show." Phelps failed to reach his goal of eight gold
medals, which would have bested Mark Spitz's record, but he did
manage six gold medals and two bronze. (He later traded his
bronze medals for a case of Miller High Life.) *Fun Fact*: Phelps is
working with Speedo to design a swimsuit that covers nothing but
the base of his nut sack.

MARY LOU RETTON At the 1984 Los Angeles Olympics, Retton became the first gymnast from outside Eastern Europe to win the
Olympic all-around title. And, therefore, was also the first gymnast
without pit hair and an overwhelming smell of boiled cabbage to
win the Olympic all-around. She gained instant fame for her performance and became the first woman to appear on the cover of the
Wheaties box, as well as the first person to appear on the box life-
size. Retton retired after the '84 Games and is now married with
four daughters—daughters that all have a striking resemblance to
Bela Karoli. *Fun Fact*: Retton saves money by traveling in her husband's carry-on luggage.

MARK SPITZ Spitz won a remarkable seven gold medals at the 1972
Olympics, and is widely considered to be the best Jew with water
since Moses. His performance at the Munich Games is all the more
impressive considering that his huge, porn-star-like 'stache created
significant drag in the water. Spitz retired after the '72 Olympics, but
did attempt to qualify for the 1992 Barcelona Olympics at age forty-
one. While he failed in his attempt, he did win the award for Biggest
Midlife Crisis of 1992.

JIM THORPE Few know him by his Indian name, Wa-Tho-Huk—
which is Indian for "Jim Thorpe"—but Thorpe was not only the
greatest Native American athlete ever, but perhaps the greatest athlete ever from any race. Thorpe won Olympic gold in 1912 in the
pentathlon and decathlon, but the medals were taken away after it
was discovered he had once played semipro baseball. The International Olympic Committee finally returned them in 1983, however,
after Thorpe's family mounted a media campaign accusing them of
being Indian givers. In addition to track and field, Thorpe also
played professional baseball and football, a combo that influenced

future multisport stars like Bo Jackson and Deion Sanders. Unfortunately, this may have also influenced Michael Jordan.

GUY WHO JUST REALLY HAD TO PEE
WINS RACEWALKING MEDAL

Ben Hafer of Austrialia cut more than twenty-five minutes off his best-ever time on Friday to win the men's 20-kilometer walk final at the world championships. Hafer credited his victory to having to pee really badly.

"I drank too much water before the race, thinking it was going to be hotter than it was, I guess," said Hafer, "and at about five kilometers it hit my bladder full-on. I was like: 'holy crap—I've got to get to a bathroom and fast.' "

In forty-third place at the five-kilometer mark, Hafer quickly gained ground on the pack, moving to twentieth at ten kilometers, eighth by fifteen kilometers, and then won going away at the finish, setting a world record with a time of 1 hour, 15 minutes flat.

"To be honest, I didn't even realize how well I was doing until I walked through the finish line, into the bathroom, and started peeing," said Hafer. "All I could think about was getting to the bathroom as soon as humanly possible. Halfway through my leak I thought: 'Hey, I wonder if I won that thing?' I came back out to the track after I had finished up and sure enough, they were waiting for me with a gold medal."

Andre Salora of Spain, who was favored to win the race, said he knew he was in trouble when he heard Hafer come up behind him at eighteen kilometers.

"You could hear him from about a hundred meters behind you," said Salora. "He was just muttering: 'Omigod, omigod, omigod, omigod, please don't let me piss my pants, please don't let me piss my pants, please don't let me piss my pants, omigod, omigod, omigod,' over and over and over. I set my personal best a couple of years ago after eating Indian for lunch, so I know what a motivator getting to the bathroom can be."

Salora said Hafer continued muttering after he passed him. "He went by me like I was standing still," said Salora. "I glanced at him when he passed and he had a crazed look in his eyes like he was possessed or something. I don't think he thought he was going to make it in time."

"I'd say that I'd drink lots of liquids before every race from now on," said Hafer. "But the discomfort I was in is definitely not worth it. Had I not broken the world record I'd have urine all down the front of me right now. It was that much of an emergency."

KENYAN POLICY OF PLACING ALL SCHOOLS 26.2 MILES FROM VILLAGES REALLY PAYING OFF

Robert Cheruiyot won the Boston Marathon on Monday, giving Kenya its twelfth victory in the race in the past thirteen years. The win is just the latest example that the Kenyan government's two-decades-old policy of placing all schools 26.2 miles from villages is reaping dividends. Cheruiyot is the eighth Kenyan to win the race since his country began its domination of the Boston Marathon in 1991. The Kenyan government instituted the school distance policy, named Provision 26.2, in 1980.

Monday's race was just Cheruiyot's second officially recognized marathon in his career, but the twenty-four-year-old ran a marathon distance each way to school every day during his twelve years in the Kenyan educational system.

"Today wasn't even my best time," Cheruiyot said of his winning mark of 2 hours, 10 minutes, 11 seconds. "I once overslept in the tenth grade and made it to school in time for the opening bell by running two hours, six minutes flat. I was burning that day 'cause I had a test I couldn't be late for."

Benjamin Chepchumba, Kenya's minister of athletics and the author of Provision 26.2, said the measure has been successful even beyond his greatest hopes.

"Provision 26.2 was enacted to give the Kenyan people a sense of pride," said Chepchumba. "We had no international identity back then. But now we are known as a nation full of really skinny people who can run very fast for long distances. That is something we can all be proud of."

But despite the success of Kenyan marathoners, all Kenyans are not happy with Provision 26.2. Joyce Okayo, a mother of four who lives in Nairobi, the country's capital and largest city, said the extreme distance to school has been nothing but a headache for her children.

"We live in a major city, yet the closest school is 26.2 miles outside of it," Okayo said. "My kids don't want to be famous runners, they just want to get an education, yet they have to run a marathon every day to get to school. Bussing is not even offered. And in the time it takes them to run to school and back, there are only a couple of hours left for actual schooling. It's ridiculous."

Chepchumba admits that Provision 26.2 is not without some problems, but says the benefits it brings far outweigh the negatives.

"Look at Monday's results," he said. "The top five runners were Kenyan. Nine of the top eleven were Kenyan. Once we move our schools within that 26.2 mile radius we won't have such fantastic placings anymore. We can't have the best of both worlds."

STORIES TOP STORIES   TOP STORIES TOP STORIES   IN OTHER NEWS . . .

Reports of 200-meter butterfly spreads panic through swimming venue . . . Photo finish shows sprinter has big nose . . . Textbook cannonball receives measly 1.3 from judges . . . World-record javelin throw lands in stands, kills three . . . Top U.S. finisher in marathon accused of blood doping with Kenyan blood . . . Eight horses drown in water polo match . . . Relay runner runs right into fart left by team anchor . . . Cell phone on Greco roaming . . .

Water polo matches conclude when all of the horses have drowned.

WINTER OLYMPIC SPORTS

MALE FIGURE SKATER TESTS POSITIVE FOR HIGH LEVELS OF ESTROGEN

The figure skating world was rocked this week when a prominent male figure skater tested positive for high levels of estrogen, the hormone found in the female body that is responsible for development of female sex organs. The offender, American skater Blaine Myles, is suspected of having used the hormone to maintain a lithe, artistic frame and promote general fabulousness, a much-desired attribute among male skaters.

A doping scandal in such a high-profile sport comes at an inopportune time for the International Olympic Committee, which is seeking to crack down on drug usage and blood doping among athletes. However, many figure skating insiders think the positive test is only the first of many in the sport that will be made public in the coming months.

"We are disappointed to hear about the positive estrogen test by a male figure skater," said Dick Pound, the IOC's antidoping czar. "Admittedly, men's figure skating was not a sport we thought would have a doping problem, but looking back there are countless signs of estrogen abuse by male skaters throughout the years."

Myles was subjected to a random test before last week's U.S. Figure Skating Championships. He was likely nabbed under the IOC's new testing measures, which look not only for illegal substances that are traditionally abused, such as anabolic steroids, but any and all chemical irregularities.

"Myles's blood was highly estrogenic," said Dr. Allan Smiley, who administered the test. "His body had more than eight times the amount of estrogen in it than does the body of a typical teenage girl experiencing puberty. Also, we were only able to detect trace amounts of testosterone. In fact, at first we thought we might have gotten his sample mixed with that of a menstruating eighteen-year-old girl."

Dr. Smiley also found that Myles was found to be wearing large amounts of perfume. Additionally, his skin was highly moisturized and had a faint scent of mangoes and papaya. "The perfume and moisturizer stuff isn't illegal under IOC rules. It's just kind of peculiar for a man," he said.

Gregory was pulled from the competition after his test results came back positive. Word of his infraction spread quickly among the other competitors and left many on edge.

"If Blaine's test came back positive, then we're all going down," said a skater who wished to remain anonymous. "Blaine is one of the more manly skaters we have. He is very conservative with the amount of sequins and tassels he wears on his tights, and his facial makeup is subtle, refined, and rarely tarty. In short, he's a total and complete dreamboat. You should just see his little tushie wiggle when he does the footwork part of his routine . . . but anyway, where was I? Oh! . . . No, I don't think he took estrogen supplements."

Under IOC rules, Myles is banned from all international competition for a year. The skater is appealing the test results, claim-

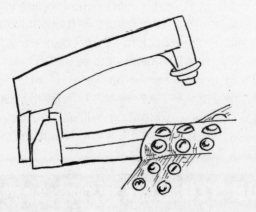

The Bedazzler and the sequin: two things that make a figure skater great.

ing he has never taken estrogen supplements. The outcome of his appeal will likely determine the fates of his fellow male figure skaters.

"It all depends on whether or not the IOC budges and increases the minimum limit of estrogen it will allow in a male athlete," said Dara Turner, a skating writer for *The New York Times*. "Even if Myles is able to prove he didn't estrogen dope, he—like all of the other skaters—is still going to test at estrogen levels that are off the charts. These guys are just, you know . . . come on, you know . . . just, uh . . . different than most guys. They're not pumping themselves full of estrogen to cheat and get a performance edge, they're just quite, uh . . . womanly. The IOC needs to realize that and increase the estrogen limit or it's going to find itself completely out of male figure skaters."

As for Dr. Smiley, he claims it is not his job to set IOC policy or to interpret the rules, only to enforce them. "Sure, maybe they aren't taking estrogen supplements. Maybe they are born that way, but I doubt it," he said. "Something strange is definitely going on with these male figure skaters."

STUDY: OTHER COUNTRIES' NATIONAL ANTHEMS STUPID

A study of American Olympians released today found that 98 percent find other countries' national anthems stupid. Two percent think they are just boring.

"U.S. Olympians by a huge margin dislike having to listen to the national anthems of other nations," said Nancy Grazban, a USOC staffer who conducted the research. "In fact, they hate it, and many would rather pour boiling water directly into their eardrums than have to listen to any more of the pathetic dirges that supposedly honor these overseas craplands."

U.S. skiing star Bode Miller said his intense dislike of foreign anthems drives his desire to succeed. "Losing means you get subjected to the musical suck that is foreign anthems," said Miller. "I try to win simply because I don't want to have to mock reverence for some country's retarded ditty. Just more 'Oh say can you see' for me, please."

Figure skater Michelle Kwan said she is confused about why other countries even have national anthems.

"I mean, what is that they have to be so proud about anyway?" asked Kwan. "Oooh—you won some naval battle back in the 1700s against some other dumb little country nobody cares about anymore. What have you done for me lately? U-S-A, baby. U-S-A."

Sasha Cohen echoed Kwan's sentiments. "Until these other countries become as great as we are, I say they just keep their songs to themselves. They'd be better off just standing silently and thinking about what they need to do to be like us. I can't tell you how much I wanted to jab a knife into my ears when we had to listen to Russia's anthem when Irina Slutskaya won the world championship. Ooh—Russia. There's a really great friggin' country. Poverty rocks."

"The anthem I hate the most is Japan's," said Miller. "It's all da-da-da-da-dum-dum-dee-dum-dum. I'm standing there thinking: 'Seriously, you people couldn't come up with something better than this?' And the Japanese guy was tearing up. I guess because his anthem sucked so bad."

Winter Olympics Fun Fact

The most frequently played songs during men's figure skating routines are:

23%	"It's Raining Men"—Weather Girls
11%	"In the Navy"—The Village People
9%	"Let's Hear It for the Boy"—Deniece Williams
7%	"Closer"—Nine Inch Nails
5%	Anything by Elton John
0.0002%	"Can You Control Yo Hoe"—Snoop Dogg (featuring Soopafly)

WINTER OLYMPICS FUN FACT

Pairs figure skating began during the Great Depression as a means of giving employment to lousy singles figure skaters.

"Could we add 'drunker' to the end?"
—Bode Miller, on the Olympic slogan
"Faster, higher, stronger"

GREAT MOMENTS IN WINTER OLYMPICS HISTORY

FEBRUARY 3, 1951 Dick Button wins the U.S. figure skating title for the sixth time. Thanks to his success on the ice Button was approached with the opportunity to star in the classic adult films *Finger on the Dick Button* and *Help Me Undo My Dick Button,* among many others.

OCTOBER 14, 1986 The International Olympic Committee votes to stagger the Summer and Winter Olympic Games. The decision was made so that the IOC would have a more consistent cash flow, with bribes coming in every two years instead of every four.

MARCH 27, 1988 Katarina Witt of East Germany wins the world figure skating championship. Witt received an average score of 5.6 for artistry, 5.8 for technical merits, and a perfect 10 for breasts.

PEOPLE TO KNOW

BONNIE BLAIR Like every little girl, Bonnie Blair dreamed of being a champion speed skater from an early age. But unlike most, she achieved that dream, winning five gold medals in a career that spanned four Olympics. Humble, friendly and down-to-earth, many remember watching Blair compete on television as dozens of friends and family—apparently all unemployed—from her hometown of Champaign, Illinois, cheered her on from the stands at all of her races. Her supportive throng was shocked, however, when Blair was named Sportswoman of the Year in 1994 by *Sports Illustrated* only to appear wearing nothing but a single skate shoelace over her nipples and vagina in the magazine's skankiest swimsuit spread ever. *Fun Fact*: Blair's nickname growing up was "Thunder Thighs."

PEGGY FLEMING Fleming swept the figure skating world championship from 1966 to 1968, and also took home gold at the 1968 Winter Olympics in Grenoble. Fleming's victory gave the United States its only gold at the '68 Games, as most of her contemporaries were back home having drug-fueled orgies and didn't want to harsh their buzz by competing in the Olympics. In 1998 Fleming announced she had breast cancer, an affliction she later defeated. The announcement was shocking to the millions around the world who thought Katarina Witt was the only figure skater in history with breasts.

DOROTHY HAMILL Hamill won figure-skating gold medals at the world championships and the Innsbruck Games in 1976, establishing herself as the best skater of her generation. Unfortunately, Hamill's success and popularity caused millions of females to ruin their appearance by copying her ugly-ass bob hairdo. Hamill developed a new skating move during her career, a sit-spin dubbed the "Hamill camel." Coincidentally, when she performed the move one could plainly see the "Hamill cameltoe," which is likely the reason she also had a fairly strong male following.

SCOTT HAMILTON A strapping five foot three, Hamilton turned down numerous big money offers from NHL teams to be a defenseman and instead forged a career as one of the greatest figure skaters of all time. He won four national titles, four world championships, and an Olympic gold in 1984, becoming the first American male to win gold since 1960. And—you may want to sit down for this—he's not even gay. No, seriously. Really. In all honesty. He says he's not. *Fun Fact*: Nah, he's probably gay—what with the figure skating and everything.

ERIC HEIDEN The speed skater won five gold medals at the 1980 Games in Lake Placid, four in speed skating and one as the lightning-fast left wing who scored a hat trick in the U.S. ice hockey team's historic 3–2 win over the Soviet Union. His gold medal take at the Games is the most-ever by an individual at a Winter Olympics, more than even legendary Great Britain ski jumper Eddie "the Eagle" Edwards tallied at the 1988 Calgary Games. Heiden's accomplishments are held in much higher esteem in Europe than in his native America, as speed skating is quite popular in Europe. *Fun Fact*: Europeans like boring sports.

SONJA HENIE The most dominant figure skater in history, the Norwegian-born Henie won ten consecutive world titles and took gold in the 1928, 1932, and 1936 Olympics. She was the first skater to use choreography and also is credited with introducing short skirts—which sounds great until you consider she was a European woman of the early twentieth century. While disgusting, yes, her long, flowing, blond leg hair made her movements appear all the more graceful. After the 1936 Olympics, Henie became a full-time entertainer, performing in ice shows and movies. She also fronted the first-ever skate band, Puke Nazis.

DAN JANSEN The greatest male speed skater of his era, Jansen was thought of more as a failure than a champion for much of his career, as frequent falls and poor performances left him without an Olympic medal. But in the final race of his career, the 1000-meter at the 1994 Olympics, he finally broke through and took gold. Unfortunately, he reverted to old form when he fell off the medal stand during the playing of the national anthem. Since his retirement from competition, Jansen has served as a speed skating commentator for television—which, as you can imagine, keeps him quite busy.

FRANZ KLAMMER The most dominant downhill skier of all time, Klammer had many nicknames—"Kaiser Franz," "the Austrian Astronaut," and "the Klammer Express"—proving both that he was immensely popular and that skiing fans come up with some really lame nicknames. His defining moment came at the 1976 Winter Olympics in Innsbruck when, cheered on by his home fans, he took the downhill gold in the final run of the competition. After his skiing career ended he focused on bodybuilding and for a time hosted a show on NBC with his friend Hans.

JEAN-CLAUDE KILLY The handsome Frenchman swept the Alpine skiing events at the 1968 Winter Games in his home country, becoming an object of female lust along the way (although only to females completely unaware of the permanent shrinkage that plagues a man who spends much of his life on a cold, snowy mountain). After retirement from competition, Killy briefly acted and raced cars, and since 1995 has been a member of the IOC. He is not expected to advance very far in the organization, however, due to his unwillingness to accept bribes.

JOHANN OLAV KOSS Koss won three speed-skating gold medals, all in world record time, at the 1994 Winter Games in his native Norway. His Olympic career did not begin quite as successfully, however. He was hospitalized with gallstones a week before the 1992 Albertville Games started and finished only seventh in the 5,000 meter, his best event. But he was able to win the 1,500 meter when his gallstones spilled out onto the ice and his competitors stumbled over them and fell. Since retiring, Koss has worked with the humanitarian Olympic Aid project and UNICEF, and has personally donated more than 5,000 speed skates to starving African children. *Fun Fact*: Koss endeared himself to his fellow Norwegians by always racing in a Viking helmet.

BODE MILLER Miller grew up in the forests of New Hampshire without electricity or running water and was homeschooled by his parents. And when the hippies took their eye off of him to get high, do some pottery, or write rambling, illogical letters to CEOs of large corporations, Miller skied. The practice paid off, too, as he won two silver medals at the 2002 Olympics and the overall World Cup title in 2005. The 2006 Olympics in Turin, Italy, were supposed to be a coronation of Miller's greatness. It didn't turn out that way, however, as Miller instead decided to go on a two-week bender. Not only did his medal-less performance disappoint the U.S. Ski Team and the American public, but his many corporate sponsors, as well—including Nike, which converted JoinBode.com into an online support group for losers following the conclusion of the 2006 Games. *Fun Fact*: Miller often skies while wearing a beer helmet.

ALBERTO TOMBA A legendary ladies' man, Tomba's late-night, playboy-lifestyle exploits went a long way toward dispelling the stereotype that all Italian men are shy and introverted around women.

But he was more than a charmer. He was also a great athlete. Tomba is the first skier to win a medal in three different Olympic Games, and first to win back-to-back Olympic gold medals in giant slalom. That came at the 1992 Albertville Games, when he won the event with such ease he actually had sex with two Brazilian models *during* his final run.

TONYA HARDING HAS LEGS BROKEN OF WOMAN WHO BOUGHT THE LAST BAG OF CHEETOS AT WAL-MART

Former figure skater Tonya Harding had the legs broken today of a woman who bought the last bag of Cheetos at a Portland, Oregon, Wal-Mart last night. Harding said the woman grabbed the bag from the shelf moments before she was going to reach for it. The former Olympian's friend, Gary Lewis, followed the woman home from the store and beat her with a pipe, at Harding's behest, early this morning while she slept.

"I really wanted those Cheetos," said Harding. "The store was all out of pork rinds and orange soda, so I was in no mood to have the Cheetos be gone, too. And that woman just wouldn't listen to me when I told her how much I wanted them, so she had it coming."

If Harding is charged with a crime in relation to the attack, it could stall her fledgling boxing career.

Winning a shiny Olympic medal is totally worth not having a childhood.

"I've had to deal with stuff like this before and I've always stayed strong," said Harding. "I just wish my idiot boyfriend had stolen the Cheetos out of that woman's house after he broke her legs. The whole point was that I wanted Cheetos."

FATHER CONCERNED HIS SON ASKED FOR FIGURE SKATES FOR CHRISTMAS

James Hunter is very concerned that his twelve-year-old son, Danny, has asked for a pair of figure skates for Christmas.

"Danny has a perfectly good pair of hockey skates," said Hunter. "I don't see why he needs figure skates. I didn't raise my boy to prance around on figure skates."

While Mr. Hunter is opposed to getting his son the white patent leather figure skates he so desperately wants, his wife, Sandra, wants to fulfill Danny's Christmas wish.

"He'll look cute in a pair of white figure skates," Sandra said.

"A boy his age doesn't need to look cute, Sandra," countered James. "What he needs is to stop acting like a girl. I'm worried about him."

STORIES TOP STORIES   TOP STORIES TOP STORIES **IN OTHER NEWS . . .**

Luge bronze medalist not being offered as many endorsements as he had hoped . . . Medal-less Olympian stuck at crappy job at Home Depot . . . Ski jumper worried his skill might not be applicable to life after the Olympics . . . Athlete maimed in car accident eagerly eyeing Special Olympics . . . NBC just now beginning to air the 2002 Olympics on tape delay . . . Sources: Sasha Cohen a saucy little minx . . .

AUTO RACING

ZERO CAR PILEUP MARS NASCAR RACE

Sunday's UAW-DaimlerChrysler 400 was marred when none of the cars were involved in any dramatic, fiery crashes. Despite the setback the race was completed.

"It's always disappointing for NASCAR and the fans when there is no huge pileup or massive explosion," said Mike Helton, NASCAR president. "Fortunately, we go crashless very rarely and thank God for that, because without huge wrecks, NASCAR is just a bunch of guys driving in circles."

With several laps remaining in the race, the stands at the Las Vegas Motor Speedway were nearly half empty. Said Terry Martin, a fan who was pulling out of the parking lot when the checkered flag was raised: "I sure as heck wasn't going to stick around if nobody was going to blow up or nothing."

IRL LAUNCHES MARKETING PLAN THAT WILL LET EVERYONE BONE DANICA PATRICK

As the Indy Racing League looks to continue to capitalize on the frenzy surrounding Danica Patrick, IRL executives announced today the launch of a marketing plan that will let everyone bone the young, shapely Patrick if they promise to be fans of the circuit.

"We're riding high right now and we don't want to lose this opportunity to stay in the spotlight and cut into the popularity of NASCAR," said IRL president Brian Barnhart. "It was a bold move to bring in a woman driver in Danica Patrick, and we need another bold move to take the next step. That's what this is."

And Barnhart says Patrick is completely on-board with the plan.

"Danica has been very up front about the fact that she has no problems with using her body and her sexuality to advance her career and the stature of the IRL," he said, "because she knows she is more than just T and A. She has the ability to back up the attention on the track. Her suggestive photo spreads in *FHM* and other publications may have raised some eyebrows, but she put to rest any doubts about her abilities through her performances on the track. We view this new marketing effort as just an extension of what she has done in the past, responsibly using her sex appeal for the gain of the circuit."

"I'm not foolish enough to think that I'm only getting attention because I'm a good driver," said Patrick. "I know it's partly because people find me attractive, and I'm fine with taking advantage of that. I've done it before and I'll do it again. We need to strike while the iron is hot in order to get the message out that the IRL is the greatest racing circuit in the world. If I need to do a bunch of people, so be it. I'm sure my husband will understand. It's for our financial well-being."

IRL's marketing plan will not make Patrick an easy lay for just anyone, however. There are numerous requirements that prospective suitors must meet in order to get thirty minutes with the driver.

"We're not willing to exploit Danica's sexuality without being very conscientious," said Barnhart.

IRL will start taking reservations for Patrick on the Web site Do-Danica.com beginning tomorrow. Applications will only be accepted by those who agree to attend one IRL race per season, watch ten on television, and—here's the kicker—vow to never again attend or watch a NASCAR race or purchase any NASCAR-related merchandise. Patrick will begin having sex with approved candidates following Saturday night's Bombardier Learjet 500 at the Texas Motor Speedway.

"Danica Patrick is marketing gold for the IRL," said Barnhart. "And we're going to use her any way we can. Thankfully she's a world-class athlete with lots of stamina."

SportsPickleNation Poll

What do you think will be the most popular exhibit at the NASCAR Hall of Fame?

12%   Mustaches of the Busch Series

9%   100 Ways Jeff Gordon Is Gay: A Patchwork Quilt

26%   Tony Stewart's Greatest Knock-Outs

20%   The AC Delco Home Depot Coca-Cola Pfizer Boudreaux's Butt Paste Office Depot Budweiser M&Ms Hall of Sponsors

2%   Breast Flashing: The Female Fans of NASCAR (warning: most are fatties)

31%   Dale Earnhardt Sr. Shrine/Masturbatorium

"I want to ram Tony Stewart really hard from behind."
—Jeff Gordon, after being crashed out of the MBNA 400 by Stewart

GREAT MOMENTS IN RACING HISTORY

OCTOBER 5, 1919 Enzo Ferrari appears in his first auto race and places fourth. Ferrari's cousin, Fredo Kia, finished dead last.

RACING FUN FACT

The NFL's Super Bowl is often referred to as the "Daytona 500 of Football."

RACING FUN FACT

Ninety-eight percent of male NASCAR fans have consulted a urologist about Dick Trickle.

RACING FUN FACT

Magic Johnson, the basketball Hall of Famer, who claims to be a longtime racing fan, was named the cochairman of NASCAR's newly created Executive Steering Committee for Diversity in 2004. Johnson immediately made a huge impact in his position, increasing NASCAR's minority viewership 400 percent by forcing his wife and three children to watch races with him.

MAY 19, 1991 Willy T. Ribbs becomes the first black driver to qualify for the Indianapolis 500. Ribbs was also the first driver to qualify with a car that had hydraulics, ground effects, tinted windows, spinning rims, and a $3,000 stereo system.

TERMS TO KNOW

POLE POSITION The term describing the first starting position in a race, which is awarded to the fastest driver during qualifying. Also the area in a strip club where many NASCAR drivers have first laid eyes on their wives.

PEOPLE TO KNOW

BOBBY ALLISON Born in Miami in 1937, Allison stayed true to the South Beach party lifestyle by becoming a stock car driver. Forbidden to race by his parents, he competed for a time under the name "Bob Sunderman" until they found out. His 84 career NASCAR wins

A SPORTSPICKLE.COM INSIDE LOOK AT . . . NAVIGATING A NASCAR TRACK

As anyone who has ever seen a NASCAR race can attest, it's difficult to follow the many twists and turns of the circuit's complicated track designs. And imagine how hard it is for the drivers to do it at triple digit speeds. To alleviate this problem, most NASCAR teams have turned to technology for help. The Web site MapQuest.com is a favorite tool drivers use to help them follow complex track layouts. For example, the following are the MapQuest directions drivers use to stay on course during the Daytona 500:

1. *Start out going forward (distance: 3,800 feet)*
2. *Turn left (distance: 3,000 feet)*
3. *Go straight again (distance: 3,000 feet)*
4. *Turn left again (distance: 3,000 feet)*
5. *Go straight again*
6. *Repeat Steps 1 through 5 a few hundred times*

Drag racers also frequently use MapQuest:

1. *Start out going straight (distance: 0.25 miles)*
2. *Stop.*

place him third all-time, behind Richard Petty and Bob Sunderman. He is the oldest driver to win NASCAR's Daytona 500, doing so in 1988 at age forty-nine. Other drivers said Allison's peculiar driving style during the race—going much slower than normal speeds, swerving wildly, and leaving his turn signal on throughout the race—caught them by surprise and contributed to his win. For his part, Allison said he drove so fast because he wanted to finish in time to catch the early-bird special at Shoney's.

MARIO ANDRETTI Thought of by many as the epitome of the American dream, Andretti was born in Italy (yes, he has Italian roots; shocking, I know) during the early months of World War II, emigrated with his family to the United States in the mid-fifties, and be-

A SPORTSPICKLE.COM INSIDE LOOK AT . . . WHAT NASCAR FLAGS MEAN

Most everyone knows what a checkered flag or a yellow flag means. But what about the other flags you see being waved from time to time at NASCAR races?

Only fifty miles to South of the Border.

Deaf child at play around next corner.

Reminder: No right turns.

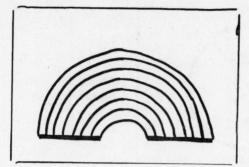

Jeff Gordon is in the lead.

Check it out! Boobs being flashed in the infield!

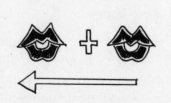

Holy crap! Now two chicks are making out!

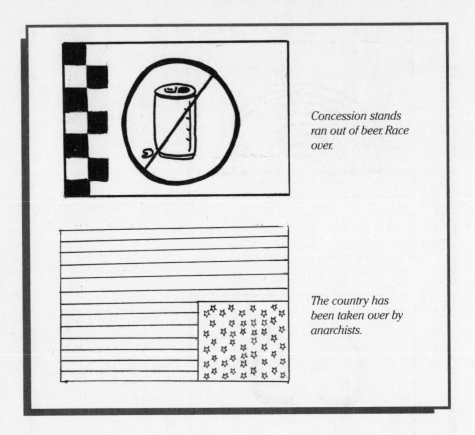

Concession stands ran out of beer. Race over.

The country has been taken over by anarchists.

came one of the greatest race car drivers of all time, winning the Indy 500, Daytona 500, and Formula 1 world title. Only in America! (Of course, he just as easily could have become a champion driver in racing-mad Italy, but that kind of hurts the story.) *Fun Fact*: Andretti often claims that no food from the Old Country can hold a candle to what is offered at the Olive Garden.

DALE EARNHARDT Earnhardt was a driver who transcended NASCAR. Even those who don't follow racing can recall at some point in their life seeing a broken-down Chevy along the road with a number 3 bumper sticker, or have seen their neighborhood property values plummet when a new neighbor moved in and flew an "Intimidator" flag from the front porch. Earnhardt's career on the track began in his late teens when he told his father: "All I want to do is race, Daddy." Little did anyone know that those eight words would result in one of the greatest racing careers of all time, along with an Earnhardt brand name that produced some of the crappiest merchandise and collectibles the world has ever seen—memorabilia that today grace the insides of trailer homes from New Hampshire to New Mexico. Earnhardt was killed in an accident at the 2001 Daytona 500, an incident that Earnhardt fans believe to be the worst tragedy that occurred on American soil that year.

DALE EARNHARDT JR. Earnhardt Jr., along with his brother Kerry, prove that nepotism has no place in NASCAR. (In the South it's called the Good Ol' Boy Network). Just months after his father passed away in 2001 at Daytona, Junior won on the same track in a race many thought was fixed, if only because snipers stationed around the speedway shot out the tires of anyone who tried to pass him. In 2004 Earnhardt Jr. proved his status as an elite driver, however, by winning the Daytona 500, but later that year he was burned in an accident at California's Infineon Raceway—his charred skin emanating an odor that witnesses likened to the smell of burnt cracker. He recovered quickly, though, and his career resumed on a course that may one day see his name and number on more crappy collectibles than even his legendary father's. *Fun Fact*: Earnhardt Jr., whose number 8 car is sponsored by Budweiser, has never been offered an honorary membership from MADD.

A. J. FOYT Foyt won his first race at the age of eighteen in a midget race in his hometown of Houston, but was stripped of the title when he stepped out of his car to receive his trophy and it was discovered he was five foot ten. Undeterred, he went on to become the only driver in history to win the Indy 500, Daytona 500, and the 24 Hours of Le Mans. (He set a record at the Le Mans by finishing in 23 hours, 56 minutes, and 38 seconds.) After retiring in 1993, Foyt parlayed his track winnings into a successful business career, including a seat on the board of directors of Service Corporation International, the nation's largest funeral business, where he lobbies against improvements in racing safety in order to keep the company flush with bodies.

JEFF GORDON Despite his undeniable talent, Gordon is more hated than black people by a large contingent of NASCAR fans. Many male fans also believe that Gordon is a homosexual—and these are dudes

A SPORTSPICKLE.COM INSIDE LOOK AT . . . NASCAR DRIVER UNIFORMS

The jumpsuits NASCAR drivers wear are just as important as their cars.

Two-way mirror—we can see him, but he can't see us.

Beer helmet (domestic beer only)

Flame retardant suit (to prevent sponsor logos from getting burned)

Zippered sponsor logos; zippered so they can be quickly replaced if a new sponsor deal is finalized during a pit stop

Confederate flag underwear

Circular mark on back pocket from carrying Skoal container

Gloves, in case any minorities want to shake hands

Lead shoes

who know them some gayness thanks to their proclivity to cover their cars, homes, and bodies with various paraphernalia bearing the name and image of their favorite driver. But Gordon's polarizing presence among die-hard NASCAR fans has done nothing to hurt his popularity as a corporate spokesman. The four-time circuit champion endorses Pepsi, Frito-Lay, the color pink, and brunch.

RICK MEARS One of only three men to win the Indy 500 four times, Mears career almost ended in 1984 when a crash broke both of his feet, prompting him to say: "I wouldn't know what to do if I couldn't drive. I've got methanol in my blood." Alerted to his condition, doctors were then able to treat his severe methanol poisoning along with his feet. Mears didn't return to racing full-time until 1986 due to his injuries and getting caught up in the drama that was *Knight Rider,* but went on to win his third and fourth Indy 500s in 1988 and 1991.

DANICA PATRICK In 2005 Patrick became the fourth woman to race in the Indy 500 and the first to ever lead the race. She ultimately finished fourth, though, disappointing many around the country who watched, personal lubricant at the ready, in hopes of seeing her doused with milk as the race champion. Patrick's attraction to fast cars has caused many to opine that she is overcompensating for a small penis, but, true or not, she has proven she belongs, displaying skills on a par with the best in the IRL circuit as well as an uncanny willingness to stop and ask for directions when she gets lost.

RICHARD PETTY The winner of more NASCAR races than any other driver, Petty also is the first stock car driver to win more than $1 million in his career—although he foolishly blew most of that on mustache maintenance costs and an extensive wardrobe of cowboy hats and sunglasses. Known as "the King" by NASCAR fans, among non-NASCAR fans he is better known as "That One Guy Who Is a Country Singer or Maybe an Old NASCAR Driver or Something. You Know, the One Who Always Wears a Hat and Sunglasses. Jeez—I Can't Remember His Name. Is It Merle Haggard? Wait, No. That's Not It. Ah, Never Mind."

MICHAEL SCHUMACHER The most successful F1 driver ever, Schumacher took heat early in his career for what appeared to be a habit of trying to crash his rivals in important races. But in true German form, Schumacher claimed innocence and said he was just following the orders of superiors. A member of Team Ferrari, Schumacher won five consecutive F1 titles, 2000 to 2004, an accomplishment that went a long way toward changing Ferrari's decades-old reputation for inferior craftsmanship.

TONY STEWART Known as much for his fiery temper as his driving ability, Stewart was forced into anger management counseling in 2002. He was quickly discharged and said to be cured, however, after threatening to kill his therapist during his first session. Despite his bad boy image, the 2002 NASCAR champion has raised millions for critically ill children through the Tony Stewart Foundation and his annual "Don't Make Me Punch You" donations drive. *Fun Fact*:

NASCAR cars have netting in the driver's-side window to protect drivers from Tony Stewart's punches.

The netting in the driver's-side window of a stock car is to protect the driver from an attack by Tony Stewart.

AL UNSER SR. The most accomplished driver from racing's premier family, Unser Sr. won the Indy 500 four times during his career. In fact, six different Unsers have competed at Indy and have totaled nine victories in the race since 1968, an accomplishment most credit to the family's tradition of giving their children a Lamborghini on their fifth birthday. *Fun Fact*: Unser Sr.'s son Al Jr. is the only driver to be pulled over by police and charged with DUI during an Indy 500.

DALE EARNHARDT RETURNS TO CALL
NASCAR FANS TO HEAVEN

The heavens roared with the sound of a 750-horsepower engine and the skies broke yesterday afternoon, ushering in a choir of angels which Dale Earnhardt quickly drafted past as he sped down to the earth below.

And so the day NASCAR fans had waited and prayed for since the Intimidator was called home on the fateful day at Daytona in 2001 had arrived—Dale Sr. returned to call NASCAR fans to heaven.

Within minutes, millions of people from all over the country— but primarily the South—were taken up to spend eternity in heaven with their Lord and Savior, Dale Earnhardt Sr. Cars were instantly left without drivers, wives without husbands, Wal-Marts without employees and customers.

"It was the most amazing thing I've ever witnessed," said Rich McCabe, a Jeff Gordon fan from Raleigh, North Carolina (Jeff Gordon fans seem to have been left behind). "I heard a loud roaring like hundreds of engines revving and also some faint Merle Haggard music, and then people all around me just started shooting up into the sky. The only thing to prove they were ever here was a stream of chew spit or maybe a tipped-over Budweiser can."

James Lincoln, whose job transferred him and his family to Jacksonville, Florida, from Boston a year ago, said he had heard of people talking about a Dale Sr.–led rapture. But not being a NASCAR fan, Lincoln dismissed it as crazy talk by die-hards, even though

Dale Earnhardt will one day return to call NASCAR fans to heaven.

coworkers and neighbors regularly invited him to races and told him about all the excitement the circuit had to offer.

"They spoke of heaven as a place where streets paved with black-top are banked between 8 and 14 degrees and all of them turn left—and where domestic beer flows like water," he said. "In heaven they were to do nothing all day but sing the praises of Dale Sr. and talk about racin'. Supposedly it had all been prophesied some-where in one of those countless Dale Earnhardt tribute books that are all over the place down here. I don't know which one."

Lincoln, like tens of millions of other non-NASCAR fans through-out the country, are left to wonder whether they are damned to an eternity in hell because of their denial of Dale Earnhardt and stock car racing.

"I don't want to go to hell, but I can't help it if I honestly don't like NASCAR," said Lincoln. "I suppose I can see what it does for some people, but I really don't care for it. If that's my fate, I suppose there's not much I can do to prevent it."

SENIOR NASCAR CIRCUIT DEBUTS IN FORT LAUDERDALE

The Senior NASCAR circuit will debut this Saturday with a two-mile race at a CVS pharmacy parking lot in Fort Lauderdale.

Organizers of the circuit hope the Senior NASCAR will be as pop-ular as the Senior PGA Tour, where PGA professionals over age fifty play. The Senior NASCAR will differ from the Senior PGA in that it will not admit professional drivers and that the entry age is seventy-five.

"We think the Senior NASCAR will be a huge success," said Mike Schilling, president of SNASCAR. "Watching old people drive is very entertaining."

The circuit will be based in Florida in order to tap the large pool of senior drivers in the state. Races will be conducted in the parking lots of shopping centers. All tracks will be oval tracks around the shopping centers.

While the first driver to finish will have the best chance of win-ning, competitors can have time deducted from their race by re-membering to switch off their turn signal.

INDY DRIVERS NOT SURE THREE WEEKS OF PRACTICE ENOUGH TO PREPARE THEM FOR COMPLEX OVAL TRACK

With only five days until the Indy 500, drivers competing in the race say they're unsure if the month they've spent practicing at the track will sufficiently prepare them for the many twists and turns found throughout the 500-mile course.

"It's tricky, I'll tell you that," said Dan Wheldon. "There's no amount of practice that can prepare you for the Indy 500. It's such a complex layout. I've tried to memorize the track, but I can't get past the twenty-third or twenty-fourth mile. After that I just have to go on instinct."

Danica Patrick says she is getting closer and closer to having a good feel for the design.

"I've got about 85 percent of it down," she said. "It's straightaway, left turn, left turn, straightaway, left turn, and then after that I'm still unclear. Hopefully my spotters will be able to help me out over that latter portion, because I don't think a few more days of practice are going to be enough for me to get it all down. If it were up to me and the other drivers, we'd start practicing and qualifying here in January. Three weeks is not enough."

IES TOP STORIES   TOP STORIES   TOP STORIES   **IN OTHER NEWS . . .**

F1 racer killed by F1 tornado in ironic storm . . . Pit crew quickly applies driver's antiperspirant . . . Flame-retardant suit keeps flames off of retard . . . NASCAR driver reportedly likes to fish . . . Bill Lester edges Danica Patrick in first-ever Token Diversity 500 . . . Carl Edwards's car does backflips in totally awesome crash . . . Sucky Busch drivers tired of having their suckiness exposed by good NASCAR drivers . . .

SOCCER

AMERICANS EAGERLY ANTICIPATING WHEN THEY'LL BEGIN TO LOVE SOCCER

Although the vast majority of Americans above age ten still don't like soccer all that much, more and more are looking forward to the day when they will.

The success of the United States men's and women's teams, the popularity of youth soccer, and the ever-shrinking global community and its passion for soccer (or football) have caused many to opine that the game will soon explode here.

"We're increasingly told how exciting soccer is and about all that we're missing," said Ed Craft, a Phoenix engineer. "I can't wait for the day that I'm finally able to realize how great the sport really is."

Garry Wescock, a window washer from Chicago, echoed the sentiments of Craft and many others. "I don't really like soccer at all right now," said Wescock. "But the media assure me that I soon will, so I'll just have to wait it out and let soccer fever infect me whenever it is ready."

Several communities around the country have invited soccer experts to conduct seminars about the history, rules, and intricacies of the game. "Many of us thought that maybe we didn't love soccer because we didn't understand it," said Michelle Ogbie, the mayor of Bakersfield, California, and the organizer of a seminar called, "Soccer Fever—Catch It!" "But after the seminar we realized that we do understand it, but just don't like it . . . that is, yet."

Perhaps the main reason soccer has never really caught on here in the homophobic United States is because the World Cup trophy looks like a penis.

SOCCER LINKED TO POVERTY, DISEASE

A thirty-year study released today by the World Health Organization links soccer to poverty, famine, and disease. The results of the study show that the game is very popular in countries with poor and unhealthy populaces and thrives in third-world countries.

"The results of this study are shocking, but the culprit was pretty much staring us in the face for all these years," said Dr. Gro Brundtland, director-general of WHO. "Soccer is the clear cause of many of the world's ills."

The study showed that countries where soccer is the dominant sport almost exclusively have the greatest economic and public health problems.

"The only thing that has saved much of Europe is that there are other popular sports there that dilute the effect of soccer," said Brundtland. "But in many African countries, the destructive effects of soccer have been able to spread unchecked."

The WHO's presentation of its study results was accompanied by a slide show, including pictures of starving children clutching soccer balls on their deathbeds, and groups of malnourished children playing games with balls made out of rags and string.

"It is horribly sad what the game has done to these people," said Brundtland. "They have put soccer above everything else, and it has destroyed their lives."

Brundtland asked the United Nations to take immediate action to free third-world countries from soccer's grasp.

"I can't comment on the World Health Organization's findings right now," UN secretary-general Ban Ki-moon said in a brief statement. "But if the results are true—and all signs suggest they are—we will take immediate action against soccer."

The WHO will present to the United Nations next week an outline of actions to take to end soccer's many ill effects in third-world nations. The plan includes introducing other sports to some countries, completely eradicating soccer in others, and stemming the growth of the game in prospering countries where it has yet to gain a hold, such as the United States and Canada.

LACK OF YELLOW CARD MIRACULOUSLY HEALS SOCCER PLAYER'S BROKEN LEG

Moments after a slide tackle dropped him to the ground and left him writhing in pain with what seemed to be a broken femur or some other serious injury, Paraguayan midfielder Christian Riveros popped up and continued playing after referee Hans Kimmel failed to produce a yellow card.

"It's amazing. I see it all the time in matches," said Kimmel, a longtime referee. "I seem to have the power to heal serious injuries simply by deciding whether the felled player was taken down legally or illegally. I can't explain it, but I guess you could call me a miracle worker."

Riveros said at first he thought he was going to die when he was lightly bumped from behind by an English midfielder in the first half of Saturday's match.

"I felt my soul leaving my body. 'Surely I am going to perish,' I thought to myself," said Riveros. "But as my soul was ascending up to the heavens, I looked down on my body and saw that the referee wasn't going to make a booking, so I decided to go back into my body, get up, continue playing as though nothing had happened and then try to draw a card later in the game by blatantly taking another fall."

ENTIRE MLS CROWD DEPORTED

An INS raid at the Major League Soccer championship game on Sunday in Carson, California, resulted in the entire crowd of 25,797 spectators getting deported.

"We have long been aware that a lot of illegals attend soccer matches in this country, but even we were surprised to find that not even a single legal U.S. citizen was at the game," said John Everett, director of the Immigration and Naturalization Service. "I guess it goes to show you that soccer still hasn't really caught on too much here in America."

INS officials made their way through the crowd during halftime and had all 25,000-plus driven away in buses to a detention center before the second half was five minutes old. The illegal aliens will be sent back to Mexico or their South American country of origin by the end of the week.

Kansas City Wizards coach Bob Gansler said the absence of a crowd in the second half made it difficult for his team to overcome DC United's 3–1 lead.

"We got a goal to get within one, but it's hard to keep the momentum going when the crowds are completely out of it," said Gansler. "We can never understand what they're chanting anyway, though, because it's all in Spanish. But any noise at all helps when you're trying to dig out of a hole."

The deportation of the entire crowd at the league's premier event was seen as a blow to the MLS, which has struggled to develop a fan base throughout its ten-year history.

"Sure, this hurts," said commissioner Don Garber. "We knew we had developed a pretty big following in the Hispanic community, but we figured at least some of them were citizens, or at least had green cards or work visas. Unfortunately that doesn't seem to be the case."

SOCCER FUN FACT

The United States' upset victory over England in 1950 is its greatest accomplishment in World Cup history. Here are other great U.S. moments at the World Cup:

SOCCER FUN FACT

Brazil has won the most World Cups with five, followed by Italy with four, Germany with three, and Argentina and Uruguay with two, proving that the more body odor a nation's people have, the more likely it is that they'll win a World Cup.

"I probably shouldn't be telling you this, but the rest of the world calls it fútbol just because it pisses off Americans."

—*Pele*

GREAT MOMENTS IN SOCCER HISTORY

DECEMBER 25, 1914 British and German troops observe an unofficial truce on the Western Front during World War I and play soccer together. The British team won 28–0, easily weaving its way through the goose-stepping German defense.

PEOPLE TO KNOW

FREDDY ADU Born in 1989(ish), Adu is thought to be the future of American soccer, which many would say is akin to someone being viewed as the future of the Haitian space program. A native of Ghana, Adu and his family came to the United States in search of a better life only to see Freddy get forced into child labor at the hands of a professional soccer league. In 2003 Adu signed deals with both the MLS and Nike which netted him more than $2 million, but he foolishly blew it all on video games, candy, and comic books within months. *Fun Fact*: Pop star Michael Jackson is the founder of the official Freddy Adu fan club.

FRANZ BECKENBAUER Born in 1945 into the carefree paradise that was postwar Germany, Beckenbauer was able to focus his energies on recreation and became one of the greatest soccer players ever. Attacking yet efficient, he was beloved in Europe due to being the first German in history not to use those traits in a military invasion.

The only man to have won a World Cup both as a player and a manager, he is currently writing a screenplay for a movie called *Bend It Like Beckenbauer*, in which a British Sikh girl dreams of becoming a middle-aged German man.

DAVID BECKHAM The most famous sports personality in the world, Beckham is known as much for being the only physically attractive British person in all of history as he is for his abilities on the pitch. The midfielder is married to former Spice Girl Victoria Adams, whom he first saw in a music video and became determined to meet. (Interestingly enough, unlike most people who have seen a Spice Girls video, Beckham wanted to meet her not so he could kill her and rid the world of Spice Girls music, but so he could ask her for a date.) The couple named their first child after the place he was conceived: Brooklyn. Their second and third children are named Bathroom and Grandma's Couch, respectively. *Fun Fact*: Thanks to write-in votes from soccer moms, Beckham received 22 percent of the vote in the 2004 U.S. presidential election.

JOHAN CRUYFF Cruyff was known during his career for making Yogi Berra-esque comments that almost defied logic while being brilliant at the same time. Among them: "To win, you have to score more goals than your opponent"; "Chance is logical"; and the most famous and befuddling: "Soccer is never boring." The Dutch forward was a master and proponent of Total Football, in which all players on the pitch are equal and can be seamlessly replaced by one another, a system that was enthusiastically adopted by the Soviet national team.

DIEGO MARADONA Born outside of Buenos Aires in 1960, Maradona began his playing career with Los Cebollitos—The Little Onions—charting a life path that would be dedicated to soccer and food. Perhaps the most talented player ever, Maradona is remembered for leading his country to the 1986 World Cup, including a dramatic quarterfinal victory over England which allowed his country to advance in the tournament and regain the Falkland Islands. His first of two tallies in that match was the infamous "Hand of God" goal, in which a clear Maradona hand ball was ignored by the referee. After the match Maradona said that God had intervened in the play and God admitted as much, stressing that he goes above and beyond to help gluttonous, adulterous cokeheads whenever possible. Maradona left the game in 1997, but he loved the sport so much he dedicated his retirement to forming his body into the shape of a soccer ball.

PELE Born Edson Arantes do Nascimento in 1940 in Brazil, his nickname is Portuguese for "the only soccer player most Americans have heard of." After leading Brazil to the 1958 World Cup at age seventeen—his first of a record three world titles—Pele was given big money offers from European club teams, but Brazilian president Janio Quadros retained his rights by declaring Pele a "national treasure" that was "second only to naked Brazilian chicks." From 1975 to 1977 Pele ended his career playing for the New York Cosmos of the North American Soccer League, exponentially boosting league-wide attendance from a couple to a few. *Fun Fact*: Pele was so well known around the globe during his career that even Vietnamese prostitutes were known to say his name in hopes of luring English-speaking business: "Pay lay?"

RONALDO The latest Brazilian great to follow in Pele's footsteps, Ronaldo has also kept the tradition of one-name soccer stars alive, a tradition that was tarnished in the past by the likes of Clumsi, Retardo, Cher, Labia, and Eczema. The Real Madrid forward is often confused by casual fans with fellow soccer stars Ronaldinho and Cristiano Ronaldo, leading to rumors he might change his moniker to the untaken, if less cool sounding, Ronald. Ronaldo is the all-time leading scorer in World Cup history with . . . let's see here . . . 15. Fifteen?! That's kind of pathetic.

ZINEDINE ZIDANE Zidane led France to its first victory on home soil (athletically or militarily) at the 1998 World Cup. The midfielder is viewed as boring both on and off the field and admits he is shy, a trait he says comes from a lack of confidence he developed from always being called last during grade school roll call. Despite his many talents, Zidane was virtually unknown in the United States for a long time because he never "snogged" a Spice Girl. However, that all changed in 2006 when he was thrown out of the World Cup final for head-butting an opponent who said something mean about his sister. *Fun Fact*: Zidane's sister is a whore.

ETHIOPIAN SOCCER COACH
DOUSED WITH COOLER OF DUST

Mengistu Kebede, head coach of the Sumale Tigers of the Ethiopian Soccer League, was doused with a cooler full of dust in the waning moments of his team's championship victory on Sunday. The dust shower was modeled after the American football custom of dousing the winning coach with Gatorade.

Several of Kebede's players snuck up behind him as time expired and dumped the cooler over his head. "Boy, is that warm and dry!" Kebede exclaimed as the dust poured down on him.

One of the Tigers admitted that he contemplated pouring his water bottle over his coach's head to more closely simulate the Gatorade shower, but thought it would be better to conserve the bottle's precious contents.

FRIGGIN' EXCHANGE STUDENT
NOT EVEN GOOD AT SOCCER

Jan Hummel, a German exchange student at Los Palos High School in California, has shown very little interest in athletics in his three weeks at the school, and isn't even good at soccer.

"It's a huge disappointment," said Kip Davis, Los Palos boys' varsity soccer coach. "We've never had a foreign kid who hasn't at least been good enough at soccer to be a serviceable backup on the team. And usually they're our best players."

Without its annual foreign recruit the Los Palos boys' team has struggled to a 3–4 record so far this season, the first the squad has been without at least one player from overseas since 1984.

"I just want to come to U.S., learn better English and get ready for my further studies," said Hummel. "I do not really like to play the game you here call soccer. I do not mean to disappoint my new school, but it is a thing I must do."

Hummel claims he never played soccer, even while growing up in Germany.

"I don't buy it," said Coach Davis. "I looked in on his gym class the other day and they were playing soccer. He's not a superstar, but he's definitely better than some of the kids I have playing and he would contribute. He should be on the team."

But Hummel maintains he never played. "Honestly, I do not lie about this," he said. "I watched some soccer as I grow up as a boy on television, but I never play it."

Coach Davis has scheduled a meeting to review Los Palos's exchange student program with the school's principal next week.

"If we're going to have these foreign kids come over here, give them a place to stay, feed them, and give them an education, the least they can do is play soccer for us," said Coach Davis. "There's no benefit to our school if they aren't contributing to us in some way. I don't want to see this happen again next year. This kid is abusing the system."

ORANGE SLICES INTEGRAL TO YOUTH SOCCER TEAM'S SECOND-HALF COMEBACK

A plastic container of orange slices that was prepared as a halftime snack by Billy Tuberville's mother spurred a dramatic second-half comeback by Billy's team in an under-eight youth soccer game on Saturday afternoon.

"The other team didn't have cut-up oranges at halftime. I think all they had was water in Dixie cups," said Dave Hawkins, Billy's coach. "The oranges gave our players the energy in the second half to make the comeback."

Billy's team, the Dragons, was trailing its opponent, the Tigers, 3–1, at halftime before fueling up on Mrs. Tuberville's oranges. The Dragons stormed back to win 5–4 in the final minute when a shot by Billy slowly rolled past Tigers goalie Sarah Smyth, who was picking dandelions near the left goalpost at the time.

The Dragons managed their comeback despite losing Greg Harris, Billy's neighbor, early in the second half after he was accidentally kicked in the stomach and vomited up his halftime snack. "I really like Mrs. Tuberville's orange slices because she puts sugar on them, but I think I ate too many and now my belly hurts," said Greg.

Mrs. Tuberville is happy that her orange slices made such a difference in the team's play. "I'd bring them every week if I could," she said. "But I think I signed up for baked goods at the concession stand next week. Mrs. Preston is down for oranges for next Saturday."

Thank you for reading the soccer chapter. Now please enjoy these orange slices.

Big, fat, Greek soccer team tires in second half on way to loss . . . Young Brazilian soccer player hopes to become good enough to get his mother kidnapped some day . . . Double murder yields yellow card . . . Baseball fan passionately tries to explain why soccer is boring . . . Forty years of stoppage time added to lazy man's life . . . "Soccer sucks," claims guy who's never seen it . . .

TENNIS

ROGER FEDERER'S NEW SOFTWARE ENABLES BRIEF DISPLAYS OF HUMAN EMOTION

The makers of tennis cyborg Roger Federer say they are happy with how their new emotions-enabled operating software performed in its first test run last week at the Australian Open when Federer nearly exhibited humanlike emotions.

"During the trophy presentation ceremony he almost teared up," said Josh Lewin, CEO of TennisBorgs. "His lip quivered and everything. I can't tell you how many years and dollars went into that. Never before has software like this been developed for a robot."

Lewin hopes that within a few years, Federer's emotions-enabled software will be as powerful as his tennis operating system.

"The tennis playing system is pretty much perfect right now. He's essentially invincible on the court," he said. "But cyborgs like Federer aren't going to be truly embraced by the public until they can adequately portray human emotion and seem more lifelike. And while we're getting close, we haven't yet reached that dream with Roger."

MAN WHO FANTASIZES ABOUT SERENA WILLIAMS BEGINNING TO FEAR THAT HE'S GAY

Charles Berman, a Houston-area contractor, admits he has always been attracted to tennis star Serena Williams. But the thirty-eight-year-old bachelor didn't think anything of it until he realized his thoughts of Williams often tread dangerously close to homosexual fantasies.

"I sometimes think about her beautiful body and her curvaceous figure," said Berman. "Her long hair . . . strong jaw . . . powerful thighs . . . rippling torso . . . manly biceps—ah! There I go again!"

Berman maintains he is not homosexual. "I'm not married, but I date fairly regularly," he said. "I just haven't found the right lady. I've never found men attractive, but this Serena thing is getting weird."

Berman says he has found himself talking more to one of his employees, Al Clark—a muscular, young black man. "Put long hair and huge breasts on Al and he's practically Serena. It's creepy. And nice."

There are more men like Berman out there, though. He regularly spends evenings on an Internet message board chatting with others who are extremely attracted to Serena Williams yet feel uncomfortable about it.

"She's a beautiful woman, there's no doubt," Berman said. "It's just . . . you know . . . there's a lot of man there, too. I'm very conflicted."

While Berman and others find consolation in numbers, it doesn't make their confusion any easier when they're alone.

"I had a dream the other night that I was kissing Serena," he said. "Only her name was Sam and she didn't have breasts. I woke up screaming."

Conjoined twins make terrible doubles players.

"Ah, jeez—I got my racket stuck in my cleavage again."
—Serena Williams

"Your mother was a hamster, and your father smelt of elder-
berries."   *—Wimbledon heckler*

GREAT MOMENTS IN TENNIS HISTORY

FEBRUARY 23, 1874 English major Walter Clopton Wingfield
patents a game called "sphairistike," better known as lawn tennis.
Major Wingfield later admitted he came up with the odd name
"sphairistike" while on grass.

SEPTEMBER 20, 1973 Billie Jean King defeats fifty-five-year-old former tennis pro Bobby Riggs, 6–4, 6–3, 6–3, in the "Battle of the
Sexes." A week later, Riggs beat Betty Friedan, 6–0, 6–0, 6–0, in the
less well known "Battle of the Sexists."

JULY 2, 1988 Steffi Graf defeats Martina Navratilova in three sets to
end Navratilova's six-year reign as Wimbledon champion.
Navratilova stated she had trouble concentrating during the match
due to Graf's tight little nineteen-year-old tush.

TERMS TO KNOW

FORTNIGHT a term used by the British to make "two weeks" sound
more interesting and prestigious, as in "Wimbledon lasts a fortnight" or "Being English, I haven't brushed my teeth in a fortnight."

PEOPLE TO KNOW

ANDRE AGASSI One of only five men in history to have won the career Grand Slam, Agassi was a premier player on the men's tour
from the beginning of his pro career in the late 1980s. Early in his
career he refused to play at Wimbledon, however, citing the tournament's all-white dress code, although most likely it was really because of their staunch no-mullet policy. Agassi married actress
Brooke Shields in 1997 but filed for divorce in 1999 upon learning
she had been quite a slut while growing up at the Blue Lagoon.

Today he is married to Steffi Graf and the couple has two children with 250 mph serves they enjoy taking pictures of with a Canon EOS Rebel.

ARTHUR ASHE Ashe was both a great tennis player and a champion of social causes. In 1968 he won the U.S. Open, becoming the first Negro man to win a Grand Slam title. In the 1970s, Ashe was reclassified as the first black man to win a Grand Slam title, and then in the 1990s became the first African-American man to win a Grand Slam title. Tragically, his life was cut short by AIDS, which he had contracted from a tainted blood transfusion. His death in 1993 came at age forty-nine, just weeks after he had signed with Suge Knight to record his first gangsta rap album for Death Row Records, which was to be titled *40-Luv, Hoes.*

JIMMY CONNORS The winner of the most career men's titles with 109, Connors also won eight Grand Slam singles titles during his career. Unfortunately, like most everyone who chooses to keep the "-y" version of their name past the age of twelve, he is a bit of a dick. Since capping his career with a memorable run to the semifinals of the 1991 U.S. Open at age thirty-nine, Connors has remained active on the senior tennis tour. *Fun Fact*: Surprisingly enough, it is very easy to get tickets to senior tennis events.

CHRIS EVERT Evert invigorated women's tennis in the 1970s and early '80s through her unique talent and high-profile rivalry with Martina Navratilova. Nicknamed "the Ice Maiden" for her completely emotionless, almost sedated on-court demeanor, she was still loved by America, most likely because people could identify with her, as it's extremely difficult for any human to watch much tennis without taking on a completely emotionless, almost sedated demeanor. *Fun Fact*: Evert once dated Burt Reynolds and during their time together often used his toupee as a racket cover.

ROGER FEDERER Federer has ruled the men's game since Pete Sampras retired. Amazingly, he's somehow even more boring than Sampras. Raised on the mean streets of Basel, Switzerland, Federer began playing tennis at age eight. By age nine he had beaten Andy Roddick 468 times. His greatest season came in 2004 when he won three Grand Slam titles and earned more than $6 million. In 2003 he launched a fragrance and cosmetics line called RF Cosmetics. The signature scent suggests Swiss chocolate, brand-new tennis balls, stoicism, and sweat-drenched head scarf.

STEFFI GRAF Most believe Graf edges Margaret Court and Martina Navratilova as the greatest female tennis player of all time by a nose. (A very large, pointy, even massive, nose that dominates the face.) Graf played her first pro match at age thirteen in 1982 and lost handily to Tracy Austin, 6–4, 6–0. But in the coming years her game steadily improved as she threatened to have her fans stab anyone who stood in her way. The winner of twenty-two career Grand Slam singles titles, Graf's best year came in 1988 when she won the Grand Slam and an Olympic gold medal. *Fun Fact*: Graf practiced as a child by hitting balls off the Berlin Wall.

BILLIE JEAN KING King won twelve Grand Slam singles titles during her career and twenty-five Grand Slam doubles titles. Many of her matches were essentially over before they started, as she greatly intimidated her contemporaries, staring them down as they dressed or showered in the locker room. For all her success on the court, she may be best remembered for her 1973 "Battle of the Sexes" match, in which she beat fifty-five-year-old Bobby Riggs, 6–2, 6–1, striking a blow for women by proving that elite female athletes could, in fact, beat old men at sports. *Fun Fact*: Billie Jean King's most-prized possession is a battery-powered Maria Sharapova bobble-head doll.

ROD LAVER The diminutive Australian owned men's tennis during the 1960s, piling up eleven Grand Slam titles during the decade. His success made him hugely popular in America, where the hippie counterculture identified with no other sport as closely as tennis thanks to its antiestablishment, country club roots. In 1998 he suffered a stroke while being interviewed by ESPN, apparently unable to stand the extreme temperatures of the Budweiser Hot Seat. Now recovered, Laver has developed and sold a soap bar product, called Laver 1000. But it has not done well, as consumers eventually realize that at best it can leave only half of their 2,000 parts feeling clean.

JOHN McENROE Remembered as much for his talent as his temper—a temper which stemmed from his anger over being

cursed with a tragic fashion sense and a giant white man's Afro—
McEnroe won seven Grand Slam singles titles during his career. He
has been part of two high-profile marriages, to actress Tatum
O'Neal and singer Patty Smyth. Ten years after their 1992 divorce,
O'Neal accused McEnroe of using steroids during his career—a
charge that holds weight only if they were some rare kind of
muscle-stripping steroids that still caused wild mood swings. In recent years McEnroe has hosted two TV shows, a game show on
NBC and a talk show on CNBC that was so awful it struggled to
book even C-list celebrities like Tatum O'Neal and Patty Smyth.

MARTINA NAVRATILOVA Born in Prague in 1956, Navratilova de-
fected to the United States in 1975, achieving the dream she had of
living in America ever since hearing the Beach Boys song "California Girls" as a youth. She would win the first of her eighteen career
Grand Slam singles titles at Wimbledon in 1978, where she would
go on to win a record nine. Navratilova revolutionized the women's
game with her volleying skills and dedication to physical fitness.
But she hadn't always been in great shape. Tennis commentator
Bud Collins even referred to her as the "Great Wide Hope" early in
her career—a pretty ballsy statement coming from a short, chubby,
bald guy in a bow tie. *Fun Fact*: In 1986 Navratilova became the first
female tennis player to earn more than $10 million in her career,
money she later used to become a principal investor in the *Girls
Gone Wild* video series.

ANDY RODDICK Roddick is the best current American men's tennis
player—as depressing as that may be to admit. But as much as he is
criticized by some for being more style than substance, he does
have a Grand Slam title on his résumé—the 2003 U.S. Open, which
he won thanks in no small part to a revolutionary back-of-the-head
cooling system known to layman as the "trucker hat." The strongest
part of Roddick's game is his powerful serve, and he is the record
holder for the fastest serve ever—a 153.5 mph blast in 2004 in the
quarterfinals of the Queens Club tournament versus Paradorn
Srichaphan. Unfortunately, the excitement of the moment was
marred when the ball went clean through the tender Srichapan's
torso, killing him instantly in a violent and bloody explosion.

PETE SAMPRAS The most athletically gifted monkey ever known to man, Sampras is the winner of a record fourteen Grand Slam men's singles titles and was the top-ranked player from 1993 to 1998. During this time period there are also reports that he may have once done or said something interesting, but they aren't very credible. If there is any mark against Sampras's tennis career it is that he never won a French Open. But today he admits he feels fortunate that he did not, as the French media likely would have accused him of taking illegal performance-enhancing drugs with Lance Armstrong. *Fun Fact*: Sampras is married to actress Bridgette Wilson, but has never been able to make it through one of her movies.

MARIA SHARAPOVA Maria Sharapova exploded onto the international stage in 2004 when she won Wimbledon at the age of seventeen. Within months she became the highest-paid female athlete in the world via endorsement earnings, refreshing proof that the Madison Avenue of today is interested only in female athletes who are successful in their chosen sport, and not just those who are physically attractive. (Well, sort of.) Born in Russia in 1986, Sharapova has been compared to fellow Russian Anna Kournikova, but until Sharapova wins two Grand Slam doubles titles like Kournikova did, she will be regarded as the far inferior player. *Fun Fact*: Sharapova was born less than a year after her parents moved away from the area of the Chernobyl nuclear disaster to Russia. Some level of radiation exposure is likely why she was born with three anuses.

BILL TILDEN The dominant figure in men's tennis during the early half of the twentieth century, Tilden won every major title he competed in from 1920 to 1926. Nicknamed "Big Bill," he was tall, with broad, powerful shoulders and enormous hands, hands he could use to molest two and three boys at a time. Tilden often traveled with his own personal ball boys during his career, and was twice arrested for fondling and making unwanted advances to male teenagers. In matches he was particularly far ahead in, he was known to purposely hit balls into the net during matches so he could watch the ball boys bend over to pick them up.

SERENA WILLIAMS Thought to be a lesser talent than her older sister, Venus, at the outset of her career, Serena Williams has proven to be one of the greatest women's tennis stars ever, winning the career Grand Slam by the age of twenty. She is able to intimidate many of her opponents before they even step on the court, thanks to her 120-plus mph serve and her rare combo of 38-inch biceps and 38 double Ds. Williams has broader interests than just tennis, however. She designs clothing and even has lent her name to a line of cosmetics, including lip glosses and an Adams apple cover-up product. *Fun Fact*: Serena Williams will one day look like Aretha Franklin.

VENUS WILLIAMS Named after the planet her father is from, Venus Williams has been in the public spotlight since she was a young phenom on the tennis courts of Compton, California, a community renowned for its youth tennis programs. Her five career Grand Slam singles titles rank her behind only her sister, Serena (seven), and Eazy E (six) for the most in Compton history. From the beginning of her pro career, Williams's dynamic game and hair full of beads made her a crowd favorite, especially since she often flashed the crowd to get more beads. *Fun Fact*: Venus's matches with her sister, Serena, are prominently featured on the USTA's series of *Hilarious Tennis Bloopers* DVDs.

MARIA SHARAPOVA'S SCREAMS LESS SEXY WHEN THEY'RE COMING FROM THE CRAPPER

Tennis star Maria Sharapova's status as a sex symbol has only grown thanks to her habit of on-court grunting, moaning, and screaming with each shot—noises that sound more suited to a porno sound track than a professional tennis court.

But the young beauty doesn't refrain from screaming in other venues of her life, either, eliciting grunts and moans while doing everything from lifting a milk carton to signing an autograph. And even when—and especially when, according to reports—taking a dump.

"If people knew what Maria was really like outside of the spotlight, I can guarantee you she would not be thought of as a sexual icon," said Justin Henin-Hardenne. "She has some absolutely heinous habits in the bathroom. I've actually seen other players get nauseous and throw up after listening to her take a bowel movement in the locker room. It's like: 'Eeeeee-ahhh . . . *plop* . . . Ghhh-hhh-ahhhhh . . . *splish* . . . Mmmmm-ooooooo . . . *plap* . . . Aaaaaa-ohhhh . . . *kerplunk.*' And I won't even go into what her wiping routine sounds like. She is utterly disgusting."

"As though her screaming on the court isn't distracting enough," said Amelie Mauresmo, "but then she has to do it everywhere else, too. She'll pick up her bag—'Eeeee-ahhh'—then open the zipper—'Mmmm-baaaa'—then put it back down again—'Ruh-oooh.' Completely absurd. And that's just one example. But the worst part is in the bathroom, no doubt. It's gotten to the point that if I see her heading for a stall I leave the locker room for a while. I'd listen to my iPod, but I can hear her grunting over top of that even."

Sharapova claims she has no idea that she screams—on or off the court.

"I apologize if it's bothersome to other people, but it's something that I don't even know that I'm doing," she said. "I guess it just comes natural to me and helps me focus on the task at hand. But I do think it's a bit rude for people to be commenting on how I conduct myself when doing number two. That's very personal."

Sharapova's father, Yuri, who has guided his daughter's career and helped her become both a success on the court and off with millions in endorsement earnings, expressed concern the details of Maria's commodal exclamations could hurt her earning potential.

"Nobody wants to buy a camera or a pair of shoes from someone who has a reputation for screaming when crapping," said Yuri Sharapova. "That's something I'll have to address with her."

But it's already too late for many of Sharapova's competitors on the WTA Tour.

"The fact that she is viewed and marketed as a sex object just blows my mind," said Lindsay Davenport. "I don't know what is considered to be sexy and ladylike in Russia, but I know that in the U.S. and everywhere else it's not all that attractive to scream and grunt every time you squeeze out a log."

WIMBLEDON PLAYER SO DID NOT WANT
HER PERIOD TO COME THIS WEEK

Wimbledon contestant Elena Miricek of the Czech Republic said she's really annoyed that her period came this week, the worst possible week for it to arrive.

"No female athlete likes to play when they're bloated and uncomfortable," said Miricek. "But playing Wimbledon with your period is the absolute worst. I really wish it wasn't required for us to wear all white here."

Miricek said she had hoped her period would come last week, as scheduled, at the JP Morgan Chase Open in Los Angeles. "That's why I wore all red there," said Miricek. "It's nice to have that option. No other tournament but Wimbledon has these antiquated anti-menstruation dress codes."

When her period didn't arrive during the JP Morgan Chase Open, Miricek hoped it would hold off until the second week of the Wimbledon fortnight when she expects to be eliminated. "I'm ranked 143rd in the world, I don't expect to be here next week," said Miricek. "So at the very least I wanted it to hold off until I got eliminated. But so much for that."

Miricek said that less than forty-five minutes before her first-round match was to begin she got her period. "Not only did I have

The match was too important to rescue the ball boy that got trapped in the net.

my nerves to worry about, but then I had to worry I was going to be horribly embarrassed like I was a twelve-year-old girl in front of a worldwide TV audience. I won, but who knows what will happen next round and beyond."

Erik Magnarsson, Miricek's coach, said, while she understands her concerns, Miricek may be blowing things a bit out of proportion. "Sure, something could happen that would be very embarrassing, no doubt," said Magnarsson. "But it is these types of distractions that Elena lets get to her and prevent her from playing her best. She needs to get past it."

Miricek said she is taking all of the necessary precautions to prevent a period-related embarrassment from occurring, but she still fears the worst. "With how much running and bending you have to do, and all the exertion it takes to play, something can go wrong and that's what I fear," said Miricek. "You won't find any woman who wears all white during their period, but especially not a woman who's playing an internationally televised sporting event."

ES TOP STORIES   TOP STORIES TOP STORIES IN OTHER NEWS . . .

Reporter worried Anna Kournikova noticed his erection . . . Penis tape gives way in third set, revealing Serena Williams's secret . . . Superior intangibles not enough to allow crappy player to beat good player . . . Conjoined twins terrible doubles tennis players . . .

WOMEN'S SPORTS

WOMEN'S TEAM EMBARRASSED
TO BE DUNKED ON BY A GIRL

The Army women's basketball team was disappointed to lose 102–54 to Tennessee in the first round of the NCAA Tournament on Sunday, but not nearly as disappointed as they are about getting dunked on by a girl.

"I don't know if I'll ever be able to show myself in a gym again," said Army forward Katie Parker. "I got dunked on by a freaking girl, for crying out loud. And not just once—twice! It's just so unbelievably embarrassing."

Army's shame came from two dunks against them by Volunteers forward Candace Parker in the first quarter, the first-ever dunks in the women's tournament.

"At halftime we were all crying," said Army guard Jill Cameron. "What are we supposed to tell our children, our grandchildren— that a girl dunked on us? I don't think so. I'll lie to them before I admit something like that."

WNBA MESSAGE BOARD TURNING INTO
SOME KIND OF LESBIAN CHAT ROOM

With the WNBA off-season more than three months old, it is becoming apparent that the league's message board has become more of a lesbian chat room than a forum for discussion on league news and rumors.

The thread that received the most responses yesterday was "How to Tell Your Family," originally posted by a person with the user name "Xena" at 6:23 A.M. The post received 128 responses in twelve hours, none of which mentioned basketball even once.

Other subjects discussed on the board in the last few days include "Upcoming Adoption Legislation," "Thoughts on wearing the same bra as your partner," "I HATE MEN," "Rosie is SuperHot," and "Haircuts: tapered bowl cut or spiked?"

One visitor tried to turn the discussion back to basketball, asking, "Who do you think will be the No. 1 pick in the draft?" but received no responses, save one from Gene18 who replied: "Please, no off-topic posts on this board. Lesbian only."

FLAT-CHESTED SÖRENSTAM ONLY A PERKY SET OF C CUPS AWAY FROM SUPERSTARDOM

Despite being perhaps the most dominant female athlete of all time, LPGA golfer Annika Sörenstam will likely never achieve worldwide superstar status like that of former tennis player Anna Kournikova and others. And it's all because of her small boobies.

Regardless of how many more golf tournaments she wins, Sörenstam's lack of perky, mid- to large-sized breasts is her primary stumbling block to becoming a household name.

"Oh, man, if only Annika had a set of knockers on her, we'd be rolling in money," said her agent, Mark Steinberg. "You slap Kournikova's breasts on her or, jeez—Serena Williams's sweater puppets—and she would be the most famous female athlete in world history."

But while blessed with great athletic ability and an unmatched work ethic, Sorenstam is cursed with useless A-cup breasts.

"Look it up—there's never been a female athlete who has achieved worldwide fame that hasn't had nice, perky breasts," said Cliff Poston, a sports historian. "Well, maybe Babe Didrikson Zaharias, but she might have been a dude. But other than her, it's true. Anna Kournikova is the best example. She never won a single tournament, but she's better known than any female athlete ever. Or take Serena Williams. She may be a top player, but she's nowhere near as dominant as Sörenstam. Her fame is in large part due to her large parts. It sure doesn't have anything to do with her face. I have a more feminine mug than her."

But despite the hindrance her ironing board–like chest is to her marketability, Sörenstam has shown no willingness to get a much-needed boob job.

"I've had the conversation with her countless times," said Steinberg. "She always gives me the same line about how she wants to be remembered for her abilities as a golfer and for her personality and then some other stuff, too. I forget what exactly because I always have trouble paying attention when I talk to her because she has no cleavage to keep my attention."

Steinberg said the part that really drives him nuts is that Sörenstam has the rest of the package to become an object of sexual desire.

"She has a decent face, a nice smile, nice legs," he said. "All she needs is some bazoombas. She has a nice personality, too. I'll give her that. But nobody cares about that. Kournikova is one of the biggest bitches ever, and people still want to do her, and that's all that matters."

Marie Hodges-Hutton, a sports sociologist at Yale, says Sörenstam is fighting an all-too-common battle.

SportsPickleNation Poll

Why do you prefer watching women's sports to men's sports?

4%	Because it's funny to watch people who run like a girl
9%	It's like men's sports, but without that pretentious skill level
10%	I'm a masochist
12%	Because the media repeatedly assure me I'll start liking it if I keep watching
33%	Surely you jest
32%	I don't, but I like voting in polls

"Female athletes have come a long way, but they're still judged more by their appearance than their ability in this society, and that's both wrong and sad," said Hodges-Hutton. "Then you have male athletes, like John Daly, who are superstars even though they are not remotely attractive. That's just not fair. Although, now that I think about it, I am okay with that double standard because fat chicks are pretty disgusting."

WOMEN'S SPORTS FUN FACT

A decathlon, which men exclusively compete in, includes ten track and field events. A heptathon, which women compete in, includes seven events. The three additional events men compete in are peeing while standing up, belch talking, and fart lighting.

WOMEN'S SPORTS FUN FACT

Were you aware that Tennessee and UConn have played in every women's NCAA basketball championship game in history? It's true! (Or it could be, at least. I really can't be bothered to fact-check on women's basketball.)

WOMEN'S SPORTS FUN FACT

Hockey players adopted the tradition of play-off beards from the WNBA.

"We think our new marketing slogan is really going to raise the league's profile among men—The WNBA: If you like lesbians, then you'll love our crowds."
—Donna Orender, WNBA commissioner

The play-off beard: a WNBA tradition.

GREAT MOMENTS IN WOMEN'S SPORTS HISTORY

AUGUST 20, 1922 The first Women's Olympic Games—a one-day track meet that forced the IOC to add women's track and field events to the 1928 Olympics—is held in Paris. The opening event of the meet was the "Run-Like-a-Girl" 100-meter dash.

AUGUST 2, 1932 Stella Walsh wins the 100-meter dash at the Los Angeles Olympics, but it is found upon her death in 1980 that she was really a man. The discovery explained the confusion as to how Walsh won by a bulge.

MARCH 21, 1934 Babe Didrikson pitches one scoreless inning against the Brooklyn Dodgers in an exhibition game, escaping a jam with a triple play. Didrikson started the triple play with the hidden ball trick, concealing the baseball in a manner never before seen in a men's game.

SEPTEMBER 11, 1951 Florence Chadwick becomes the first woman to swim the English Channel from England to France. With the news of Chadwick coming ashore, France immediately surrendered the country to her.

JANUARY 8, 1980 The NCAA decides to sponsor women's championships in five sports beginning with the 1980–81 school year.

While seen by many as a major breakthrough for women's athletics, the five sports the NCAA agreed to sponsor were Jell-O wrestling, wet T-shirt competitions, mechanical bull riding, swimsuit contests, and naked Twister.

JUNE 21, 1997 The WNBA opens its first regular season, marking the beginning of the Apocalypse as prophesied in the Bible's Book of Revelation.

PEOPLE TO KNOW

(Female Olympic and tennis athletes can be found in those sections. And Anna Kournikova can be found nowhere, because she's not an athlete.)

MIA HAMM Hamm's contributions to women's sports—nay, sports as a whole—are so immense there is no way to accurately measure them. (Note: TV ratings and attendance at women's soccer games is not a good way to measure since they've always hung pretty close to zero.) The high-scoring forward and her fellow Team USA members gained attention when they won the 1999 Women's World Cup, setting off a good six years of the media trying to shove Hamm down the country's throats. Before they clinched that monumental World Cup victory, women's sports were seen as unimportant and soccer was merely a fringe sport in the United States. Today, that's all reversed—thanks to Mia—and everyone cares greatly about women's sports, especially women's soccer. (Just drink the Kool-Aid on this. It's easier.) Hamm's impact was so great that a professional women's soccer league, the WUSA, was founded in 2001 with Hamm as the primary attraction. It folded less than two years later, but only because the public was so awestruck by the greatness of women's soccer that the federal government deemed it a public health hazard to attend WUSA games or watch them on television lest people's brains literally explode when confronted with its greatness.

LISA LESLIE Leslie has dominated every level of basketball in which she has competed. In fact, she once scored 101 points in just the first half of a high school basketball game (which is less impressive when you consider she was playing against a bunch of girls). After a stellar collegiate career at Southern Cal, she joined the WNBA and has led the Los Angeles Sparks to two league championships. In 2002 she became the first woman to dunk in a WNBA game, a feat that was wildly celebrated—oddly enough—by a league that had long claimed basketball should showcase the game's fundamentals and not worry about high-flying theatrics. In Leslie's spare time, she works as a model and is considered the premier six-foot-five, black, female, dunking model in the world. *Fun Fact*: Leslie's rooting section at WNBA games is known as "Leslie's Lessies."

CHERYL MILLER Miller is without a doubt one of the greatest women's basketball players in history. An outstanding college player, she was the first Southern Cal player—male or female—to have her number retired, which is both an honor and proof of how much USC's men's program sucks. Miller was a fantastic player for Team USA after her college career ended, but her playing days were over by the time the WNBA was founded in 1997. She has participated in the league, however, coaching the Phoenix Mercury for three seasons. She resigned after the 2000 season, though, due to fatigue—apparently, the WNBA's brutal three and a half month, thirty-four-game season was quite taxing on her. *Fun Fact*: Cheryl is responsible for teaching her younger brother Reggie the fine art of flopping to the ground from even the slightest bump by a defender.

ANNIKA SÖRENSTAM Swedish but unfortunately not all that hot, Sörenstam has ruled the LPGA since turning pro in 1993. The winner of more than sixty LPGA tournaments and nine majors, Sörenstam has a friendly rivalry with PGA star Tiger Woods, both in the number of majors they can win and in who can be more boring in interviews. In 2003 at the Colonial, Sörenstam became the first female golfer to play in an event in forty-eight years. She finished ninety-sixth and missed the cut, but she beat fifteen PGA players and definitely did not look out of place, as many PGA players also have boobs. *Fun Fact*: Sörenstam is widely considered the greatest umlauted golfer of all time.

PAT SUMMITT The Tennessee women's basketball coach is arguably the greatest coach of all time. Summitt has coached more teams to the Final Four than John Wooden and has more career victories than Dean Smith and Bob Knight, two achievements that are particularly impressive considering the level of play from top to bottom is much more balanced in women's college basketball than in men's. Admired for her warm personality, Summitt is often referred to as the "Bob Knight of women's basketball." Although, unlike Knight, Summitt doesn't believe that a woman who is being raped should just sit back and enjoy it.

DIANA TAURASI Diana Taurasi is perhaps the greatest current female basketball player and may prove to be the greatest ever. She is no doubt a fan favorite, as her Phoenix Mercury jersey immediately became a WNBA top seller when she entered the league in 2004 with over a dozen purchased nationwide. Taurasi's rise to fame began during her collegiate career at UConn where she won three NCAA titles while playing from 2000 to 2004. Her fame is very meaningful in the continued rise of women's sports because it proves that in our modern society female athletes *can* manage to gain some notoriety even if they aren't all that attractive.

MICHELLE WIE Wie is a golfing phenom whose gaudy scores and prodigious drives made her a public figure in her early teens. Her star status has rubbed many of her contemporaries the wrong way, however, as she was repeatedly given exemptions to tournaments while an amateur in place of veterans. Most grievous was her exemption into several Wimbledons. In 2005 Wie was given an exemption into the PGA Tour's John Deere Classic and missed the cut, but she has continued to play in men's tournaments in her quest to make a cut and prove that the best women's golfers are almost as good as the most mediocre men's golfers. *Fun Fact*: Wie's Korean name, Wie Sung-mi, means "one who is overly hyped by the media."

BABE DIDRIKSON ZAHARIAS Given the nickname "Babe" by spiteful competitors who had nothing but her homeliness to taunt her with, Didrikson is widely regarded as the greatest female athlete of all time. Baseball, track, golf, basketball, swimming, volleyball—she could do it all. In fact, the only female sports she failed at were cooking, cleaning, and laundry. She was best at track and field—in which she won three medals at the 1932 Olympics—and golf, a sport she dominated in the 1940s and early '50s even though she didn't pick it up until she was in her twenties. Voted the Greatest Female Athlete of the first half of the twentieth century by the Associated Press, Didrikson was such an outstanding athlete that many believed she was really a man. Sadly, Didrikson died at forty-five of cancer. *Fun Fact*: Testicular cancer.

LAST-PLACE TRIATHLON FINISHER PROMISES HERSELF SHE'LL LEARN HOW TO SWIM BEFORE NEXT COMPETITION

Christy Rodgers, an American triathlete who finished dead last in the world championships at the women's triathlon on Saturday, says she has identified the problem with her performances.

"A low finish like this forces you to take stock of everything and consider your weaknesses," said Rodgers. "Whether I like it or not, I'm going to have to learn how to swim if I want to improve and get better times."

Rodgers said she noticed she fell behind the pack quickly at the beginning of the first stage—the 1.5 kilometer swim.

"I was flailing around, trying not to drown, and the field opened up a pretty sizable lead on me," said Rodgers. "By the time I was rescued and resuscitated back on shore and then pulled across the harbor by a boat, I was a good forty-five minutes behind."

Rodgers was able to close the gap to forty-three minutes after the forty-kilometer bike ride and ten-kilometer run, but couldn't come all the way back.

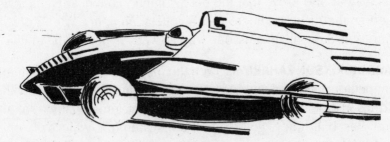

Danica Patrick is so hot! Racing can make a fortune off of her! (Assuming that was Patrick who just drove by at 220 mph and not some dude.)

"If we only had to swim maybe ten feet or so instead of 1.5 kilo-meters and then do the biking and running, I think I probably would have won. It was that close," said Rodgers.

6,465 PEOPLE YOU CAN'T IDENTIFY WITH IN ANY WAY ATTEND A WNBA GAME

A total of 6,465 people you can't identify with in any way attended a WNBA game between the Washington Mystics and Indiana Fever on Sunday in Indianapolis.

Not only did 6,465 people attend the game, but nearly all of them paid actual money for a ticket, and more than half appeared to le-gitimately be enjoying the action on the court. And some of the people were wearing WNBA licensed apparel, meaning they proudly walk around in public in that stuff.

"I love coming to WNBA games," said one fan who was sitting courtside. "I think it's the purest form of basketball out there." What's amazing, the fan didn't seem to be saying this with even the slight-est bit of sarcasm. And you'll never believe this, the fan—who was a man for crying out loud!—said he has season tickets. Seriously.

Now, of course, there was a decent amount of feminist, butchy, lesbian, athletic types there, but most of the people looked like the same kind of crowd you would see at a regular NBA game. And again, I'm not making it up, there were men there.

What would totally blow your mind is that fans enthusiastically applauded the players when they scored, apparently thinking they couldn't beat each and every one of the women on the court one-on-one just wearing their street clothes.

"The talent level in the WNBA is extremely high caliber," said Trish Adams, a fan sitting in the second deck of the arena. "I'd bet that some of the top players could hold their own in Division I men's college basketball or even in some professional leagues. These women are so exciting that it's all I can do to stay in my seat when they play." And Adams appeared even more serious about her statements than the guy who said he is a season ticket holder.

Oh—and the craziest part is that this just wasn't an Indianapolis thing. Apparently there were tens of thousands of other people you can't identify with in any way who attended WNBA games at other locations last weekend.

Women's tournament selection committee more fundamentally sound than men's . . . Softball coach asked nothing but softball questions by the media . . . TiVo refusing to record women's basketball . . . College softball team welcomes new recruits with open arms, legs . . . Michelle Wie suddenly skips off course in giggling pursuit of pretty butterfly . . .

MISCELLANEOUS SPORTS

EXTREME SPORTS ARTICLE USED FOR ROLLING PAPER

X Games skateboarder Luke Perkins used a newspaper article on the X Games as rolling paper to roll a joint and smoke it Sunday evening after his performance in the Skateboard Big Air Finals.

"I was reading an article in the *L.A. Times* about the X Games and it hit me—why not use the paper to roll a joint?" Perkins said. "It was a great idea because I had smoked a few blunts the night before and used up all my rolling papers, but I still had some primo hash to smoke. I was totally stoked when I thought of the idea."

Perkins said he wanted to chill out a little bit after getting so pumped to perform in the Big Air Finals, in which he finished fourth. "To do what you have to do to be an extreme sports athlete, you really have to pump yourself up," said Perkins. "Weed lets me mellow out so I can function normally when I'm not competing."

Despite being quite pleased with himself for thinking of the idea of using an extreme sports article for rolling paper, Perkins said newsprint isn't the best material for the job.

"It burns faster than the pot, so there was some weed that kept falling out of the tip," he said. "Plus, the ink gives off a weird smell."

But despite the problems, he said it was an ethereal experience.

"I was sitting there on my bed, staring at a screen saver on my laptop, and I realized that I was smoking an article about my sport, my livelihood, and it just totally blew my mind," he said. "I was becoming one with what I do and what I love, taking it into my lungs and blowing it back out. It was a spiritual experience."

Douglas Reynolds, who has worked security at several extreme sports events in and around Los Angeles over the last decade, says he has seen athletes make rolling papers or bongs off just about anything.

"I once saw a kid make a bong out of a skateboard wheel," he said. "And there was this one bike stunt guy who took the plastic grip off of his handlebar, stuffed it with about a pound of weed, and smoked it. He almost died from breathing in all the smoke from the melting plastic, but he claimed it was the best high he ever had."

SUDANESE REFUGEES BEG TO BE CHOSEN AS HOSTS OF NEXT COMPETITIVE EATING COMPETITION

Sudanese refugees issued a desperate plea today to the International Federation of Competitive Eating (IFOCE), begging the organization to hold a future competitive eating competition in the country's Darfur region.

IFOCE organizes dozens of the world's premier glutton events, including the Nathan's Hot Dog Eating Contest, the World Rib-Eating Championship, the GoldenPalace.com Grilled Cheese Eating Contest, and the World Shoo-Fly Pie-Eating Championship.

The tattered letter sent to the IFOCE, which was signed by more than three thousand starving Sudanese refugees, requested that just one of the organization's twenty-six competitive eating competitions be held in Darfur.

"Please, please, for the love of God and all that is good, please bring one of your events to us," read the statement. "We promise eating the likes of which you have never seen before. Most of us have been starving for years, and could easily put away hundreds upon hundreds of hot dogs, watermelons, buffalo wings, ribs, or really anything in whatever time you allot. Please, just give us a shot. We are so very hungry. We'll eat anything at all. Bugs, dirt, cow testicles. Anything. We could even eat the great eating champion Kobayashi. You people seem to have so much extra food while we have none. Please bring some to us. We will be eternally grateful."

While the IFOCE acknowledged receipt of the letter, it has no plans for holding an event in Darfur.

"Most of our events are scheduled years in advance, so if these people truly want to host an officially sanctioned competition, they need to submit a formal proposal just like everyone else," said IFOCE president Doug Bartley. "And I really doubt they could eat as much as they think they can. The best competitive eaters have undergone years of training. Plus, the stomachs of people who are starving to death, as these Sudanese refugees are, actually atrophied so they can eat very little when finally given the opportunity. They wouldn't be good enough at competitive eating for us to bother with them."

LACROSSE THE FASTEST-GROWING SPORT AMONG RICH, SNOTTY, WHITE PEOPLE

In a nine-page feature story in the most recent issue of *Sports Illustrated*, the fringe sport of lacrosse was hailed for the dramatic growth it's enjoyed in just a few years, going from being played only by rich, snotty, white people who live in the affluent Maryland and New England suburbs, to now include participation by rich, snotty, white people in other parts of the country.

"For some reason, the sport has been slow to catch on among elitists outside of the Northeast," said Bronson Stanwix, the director of U.S. Lacrosse. "But we've been working to spread the message of lacrosse at prep schools, yacht clubs, and polo matches in other parts of the country, and our efforts have begun to pay off. We always knew that rich, snotty, white people in the Northeast weren't the only ones who want to come off as smug, sanctimonious pricks—it's a universal desire of rich white people across the country."

Dubbed the "fastest-growing sport in America" in a teaser headline on the cover of *SI*, lacrosse has seen the number of youth-league players in the United States grow to more than 180,000, more than twice what it was in 2001, a period that has also seen the gap between the rich and poor in America grow dramatically—both trends the lacrosse community supports wholeheartedly.

But the *SI* article only briefly touched on the sport's elitist, upper-crust underpinnings, something that left many lacrosse fans disappointed.

"*Sports Illustrated* is a huge, mainstream publication. Sure, it's great exposure for the sport to have such a big article in the magazine, but we don't want to give the impression that lacrosse is open for the poor and middle class, or even the upper middle class," said Landon Marriott, a senior midfielder for Johns Hopkins. "We don't want our game sullied by the underclass. Let the dirty hordes, the festering proletariat, stick to boxing or whatever it is that they watch to amuse themselves and distract them from their many failures."

The sport's powers-that-be have long championed exorbitantly expensive equipment as a means to prohibit the lower classes from participating—from a $125 Brine stick to $50 Under Armour undershirts—but that tactic of preventing an influx of commoners can go only so far. "The middle class has credit cards nowadays, and they're not afraid to max them out," said Stanwix.

And as lacrosse continues to grow among rich, snotty, white people, the biggest challenge for the sport will be stemming any trickle-down popularity among the masses.

"If we're not careful, we're going go have kids without trust funds trying to play lacrosse at schools like Brown and Johns Hopkins," said Stanwix. "Or—heaven forbid—even blacks. That would be the end of us."

"Wait a minute! Are you kidding me? I did all the work and he gets the medal? This is horsesh-t."
—Cinnamon Hero, after his rider, Michael O'Connor, was presented with the gold medal for Individual Jumping at the World Equestrian Championships

GREAT MOMENTS IN MISCELLANEOUS SPORTS HISTORY

NOVEMBER 21, 1837 Thomas Morris of Australia sets a world record by skipping rope 22,806 times. The feat earned Morris the title "Gayest Man in the World."

FEBRUARY 9, 1895 In Massachusetts, W. G. Morgan invents volleyball. Morgan hoped the sport would provide him an alternative to speaking to relatives at family reunions.

MAY 3, 1997 Garry Kasparov begins a chess match with IBM supercomputer Deep Blue. Kasparov won the match with a series of brilliant moves that included spilling his water on Deep Blue, uploading a virus onto its hard drive, and unplugging it from the wall.

SportsPickleNation Poll

What is the most outrageous allegation ever levied at Lance Armstrong by the French media?

23%   While he lost a testicle due to cancer, he originally had seven

19%   He dated Sheryl Crow because he thinks she is talented

21%   He retired because the Tour de France would not allow him to put streamers on the end of his handlebars

37%   Livestrong bracelets cause cancer and release a powerful steroid into the bloodstream

PEOPLE TO KNOW

EARL ANTHONY Anthony is the reason the PBA Tour is what it is today. (Take that as a compliment or a criticism.) He helped bring the tour from small, backwater towns to major markets like Council Bluffs, Iowa; Tulsa, Oklahoma; and Grand Rapids, Michigan. Anthony won the most titles in PBA history and was the first bowler to reach $1 million in career earnings, which he, being a bowler, most likely spent on something extremely tacky. He passed away in 2001 at age sixty-three when a bowling bowl rolled off the top shelf of his hall closet and bonked him on the head. *Fun Fact*: Anthony tested positive for anabolic steroids eleven times during his pro bowling career.

LANCE ARMSTRONG Armstrong is the greatest cyclist ever. He won seven Tours de France in a row between 1999 and 2005, the last two coming on a unicycle just to make it remotely challenging for him. While Armstrong was successful during the early portion of his career, it was not until he was lucky enough to get cancer in 1996, and therefore shed some extra pounds, that he became truly great. By 1998 he was back on his bike and on his way to inspiring millions of non-French around the world. Despite all his successes, Armstrong has been plagued by drug rumors, and the French media has regularly pointed out that 10 percent of the money raised from his Live-

Looking for a challenge, Lance Armstrong rode a unicycle in his final Tour de France.

strong wristbands goes toward research to develop an undetectable strain of steroids. Now in retirement, Armstrong spends his time by taking relaxing 120-mile bike rides and educating young, attractive women about the ravages of cancer by allowing them to handle his remaining testicle.

BOBBY FISCHER In 1972 Fischer became the first American to win the World Chess Championship, ending the U.S.'s nearly 200-year run as the world's coolest country. Fischer also was the youngest grandmaster in history at age fifteen in 1958 (outside of Grandmaster Flash, of course). Later in his life he would strive to become the youngest Grand Wizard in history. While the chess genius has been shrouded by controversy and secrecy for much of the last thirty years, there is one incontrovertible fact about him: Bobby Fischer loves him some Jews. *Fun Fact*: Chess is not the only board game at which Fischer excels. He is also a former world champion in Trivial Pursuit Pop Culture Edition and Hungry Hungry Hippos.

TONY HAWK Hawk began skateboarding at the age of eleven after having his very first Mountain Dew. Fueled by its extreme flavors and with a lot of free time on his hands, thanks to not being able to fall asleep, he practiced constantly, and by the age of fourteen was a professional skateboarder. (Totally extreme career choice, dude!) He quickly became a legend in the sport, taking it from an underground activity that adults despised to an underground activity that adults still despised but could live with because they had figured how to whore it out for corporate dollars. Now nearly forty, Hawk is that creepy neighborhood older guy who still tries to hang out with the teenagers and use words like "grind" and "thrashed."

MIGUEL INDURÁIN Known for riding his bike without a seat on it, the Spanish cycling star won five Tours de France from 1991 to 1995. Despite his impressive run of dominance, he never achieved quite the same level of fame as Lance Armstrong did during his streak of seven victories a decade later—most likely because the public didn't find Induráin's fight against chronic hemorrhoids to be nearly as inspiring as Armstrong's cancer battle. *Fun Fact*: Induráin was so far superior to his contemporaries that he was able to win his Tours even with taking a two-hour siesta in the middle of each stage.

GARRY KASPAROV The dominant chess player of the past twenty years, Kasparov may be best known for his historic matches against IBM supercomputer Deep Blue. He is probably less well known for his legendary battles against the Minesweeper game on his laptop. Kasparov first became world champion in 1985 at the age of twenty-two, affording him the honor of being the youngest champion in history. But more important, it gave him something to boast about at his five-year high school reunion to all the people who had given him wedgies for being in chess club.

TAKERU KOBAYASHI A world-champion competitive eater, the thin Japanese man is able to swallow fifty hot dogs nearly whole in just a few minutes—a skill that has made him the biggest superstar ever in the gay community. In addition to winning the Nathan's Hot Dog Eating Contest multiple times, he is also a six-time winner of the World Bulimia Championship (which is held moments after the hot dog eating competition). *Fun Fact*: The founder of the Takeru Kobayashi Fan Club is Cleveland Indians minor league pitcher Kaz Tadano.

KARCH KIRALY The only athlete to have won Olympic gold medals in both indoor and beach volleyball, Kiraly is arguably the best volleyball player ever. He has had the most success in beach volleyball, winning more than 140 Association of Volleyball Professionals titles and $3 million-plus, all the while finding sand lodged deeper inside his body orifices than you could possibly imagine. Kiraly is highly skilled in virtually every aspect of the sport, but his biggest weapon is his trademark pink hat, as many competitors struggle to take a guy seriously who would willingly wear something like that. *Fun Fact*: Kiraly and his partner, Iceman, lost the 1986 world beach volleyball title to Maverick and Goose in a close match.

GREG LEMOND In 1986, LeMond was the first non-European cyclist and the first American to win the Tour de France, an achievement that went over in France about as well as would the news of Germany electing a nationalistic dictator with an eye toward expansion. In 1987 he was nearly killed when a hunting companion accidentally shot him in the chest; it would be the last time he went hunting with Bobby Knight. Luckily, LeMond recovered and won the Tour again in 1989 and 1990. In recent years he has stirred up controversy by alleging that Lance Armstrong used performance-enhancing drugs during his Tour run, stooping as low as to insist on referring to Armstrong in the media as "Druggy McOneball."

CAEL SANDERSON Sanderson completed his wrestling career at Iowa State a remarkable 159–0 and won an Olympic gold medal in 2004 but is not a household name in the United States—mainly because he doesn't hit people with chairs during his matches or wear a costume. (God, I hate this country sometimes.) In 2002, at the end of his college career, he received the honor of appearing on the cover of a Wheaties box. Fittingly, the box came with a warning instructing consumers to immediately puke up their Wheaties after eating them if they hoped to make weight. *Fun Fact*: Cauliflower ears taste best when steamed and then served with butter.

ACQUAINTANCES WORRIED GUY WITHOUT LIVESTRONG BRACELET IS PRO-CANCER

Friends and family members of San Francisco accountant Jack Robinson have begun to assume he must like cancer since he is the only person they know who isn't wearing a yellow Livestrong bracelet.

"I thought I knew Jack. I raised him better than that," said Claire Robinson, his mother. "How can he support cancer? Both of his grandfathers died of cancer. It's just despicable."

The yellow Livestrong bracelets have become a nationwide fad over the past few years, yet Robinson refuses to donate one measly dollar to the Lance Armstrong Foundation to receive his own yellow band and, in doing so, make a public stance against the disease that kills 500,000 Americans each year.

"Half a million people each year in this country alone are killed by cancer, yet he doesn't seem to care," said coworker Ron Singley. "It's as though he has no conscience. I'm disgusted by him."

But Robinson says his decision not to wear a Livestrong bracelet does not mean he is pro-cancer; in fact, he claims to be anti-cancer.

"I just don't want to wear a stupid yellow bracelet," he said. "And to be honest, I'm getting sick and tired of all these people with Livestrong bracelets looking down on those of us who don't wear them. I can't even believe I have to say this, but I'm very much against cancer. Okay? I've even donated money to cancer research in the past, I just don't want to wear one of those bracelets. They're uncomfortable and they look dumb hanging out of people's sleeves. That's all."

Robinson's wife, Molly, says she has yet to confront her husband about his Livestrong-free wrists because she is afraid of what she might hear.

"I don't want to face the truth—that he's pro-cancer," said Mrs. Robinson. "I don't think I could be married to a man who is a cancer supporter. It's like I'm living with some kind of monster."

TONY HAWK HIRES CONSULTING FIRM
TO FIND NEW WAYS FOR HIM TO SELL OUT

Skateboarding legend Tony Hawk announced today at a press conference that he has hired a high-priced New York consulting firm to help him uncover and capitalize on new ways in which to sell out.

Hawk, the father of the underground, counterculture sport, has made hundreds of millions of dollars in the last decade selling his name for use on everything from skateboards to frozen foods.

"Tony has gone above and beyond all expectations in how he has prostituted his name for the sake of a buck," said Sarah Gruver, Hawk's publicist, who opened the press conference in a ballroom at the Ritz-Carlton. "But today he is bravely taking another step to further abandon the roots of the sport he loves."

Hawk is looking to extend his revenue stream beyond the video games, clothing, shoes, toy cars, remote-controlled miniature skateboards, television shows, books, skateboards and accessories, videos, and Bagel Bites to which he has already lent his name.

"I have some ideas myself, like maybe coming out with a McDonald's burger named the Tony McHawk 'n' Cheese or something, or maybe exclusively selling my line of skateboards at Wal-Mart," said Hawk, "but I want to consult some experts first to ensure I make decisions that appropriately shame skateboarding's anticorporate ideals."

Hawk and his team of advisors tabbed the consulting firm

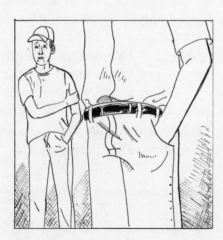

Pocket pool is the most popular game among boys ages 12 to 18.

Caulsey Partners to help him plan his next selling-out moves. The firm's founding partner, Nathan Caulsey, advised Michael Jordan in the mid-nineties to lend his name to both a signature cologne and a line of bowling balls, even though Jordan isn't a bowler.

"I'm proud of the small role I played in helping Michael Jordan pawn his name," said Caulsey, "but Mr. Hawk is an entirely different challenge. While Jordan was more greedy than a sellout, everything Tony Hawk does is intrinsically against the culture of his sport and that presents an entirely different set of challenges."

Caulsey said that Hawk could be tempted to lend his name to any product for the right price, thinking that will allow him to sell out to the highest degree, but that "we will help him choose only the right products to endorse. For instance, a line of Tony Hawk draperies sold exclusively at Nordstrom would go a much longer way toward completely destroying his credibility than would Tony Hawk-designed neckties. There are subtle differences."

Hawk said he is just excited to get started. "There's a whole lot of money I have yet to own and thousands of skateboarders left to alienate," he said.

TORIES TOP STORIES   TOP STORIES TOP STORIES **IN OTHER NEWS . . .**

World Wrestling Federation not looking forward to its day before congressional steroids panel . . . Teenagers continuing to choose skating over dying . . . Armless surfer back on her board after having her face bitten off . . . Extremely manipulative former girlfriend wins X Games . . . Match-fixing scandal rocks professional wrestling . . . Record catfish catches 230-pound man . . . Obese X Gamer considering doing the Diet Dew from now on . . .

SPORTS BUSINESS

SCHOOL LUNCH TAX TO SUPPORT NEW ARENA

The Pittsburgh City Council approved a 75-cent school lunch tax yesterday in order to support the construction of a new $360 million arena for the Pittsburgh Penguins. The hockey team will foot 2 percent of the bill.

The tax will raise the cost of school lunches from $1.40 to $2.15 for all Pittsburgh city students from kindergarten through twelfth grade. All of the surrounding counties also approved an equal increase.

"We didn't feel it was viable for the cash-strapped Penguins to finance their own arena, and they need a new facility to survive," said council president Jed Sepner. "Since school lunches are ridiculously underpriced, we felt that was the best place to find the money."

The city council also approved the suspension of any increases on educational spending through 2011 in order to raise the needed funds for the multipurpose sports arena.

"Spending on education always gets so much focus from everyone," said Sepner. "But it's getting kind of ridiculous. We've been increasing the school budgets for years and our kids aren't testing any smarter than they have before. In these tough economic times we need to finance what has the greatest need, and the Penguins have the greatest need."

Pittsburgh-area students will no longer be allowed to pack lunches in order to ensure the most possible money goes toward

Nike is able to pay its overseas laborers so well because it pays hardly a cent on advertising.

the arena. If the students want to eat, they'll have to buy the higher-priced school lunches.

"We're trying to foot the bill for this arena in less than five years," said Sepner. "If that means some of our children sacrifice a little, so be it. They're the ones who will have the new arena to enjoy for the rest of their lives."

In Pennsylvania's 180-day school year, each student will generate $135 per year for the new arena.

"These kids will be able to look back one day and know they provided a wonderful gift to the city," Sepner said. "Any hardship they or their families will experience from the lunch tax will be made up by that personal gratification, I'm sure."

SEASON TICKET HOLDER'S ANGRY LETTER TO TEAM MANAGEMENT LAUGHED AT, URINATED ON

An angry letter written by a season ticket holder about an increase in parking prices was passed around the Seattle Mariners offices yesterday so everyone could get a good laugh over it before it was set on fire in a trash basket. The team's upper-level management then took turns urinating on it to put out the flames.

"We love it when fans write in about stuff—threatening that they're going to stop coming to games or won't pay our high prices anymore, as though we really give a crap," said team president Chuck Armstrong. "Like we don't have thousands of other people who would gladly step right into their place."

"What I find so hilarious is that these people actually take the time to write an entire letter, as though their one stupid letter is going to have any impact on how we conduct business," said Sally Robinson, Seattle's director of community relations. "It can be quite a hoot sometimes."

Robinson said the team will respond to the fan with their standard form letter for complaints, which notes that the fan's letter was received and that the team will look into the complaint.

"Sending a letter usually keeps them fairly happy for a while, not that we really care either way," she said. "Of course, the letter won't mention that we made fun of it, burned it, and then pissed all over it."

YANKEES PURCHASE NAMING RIGHTS TO FENWAY PARK

The New York Yankees escalated a longtime rivalry with the Boston Red Sox on Monday when the team purchased the naming rights to Boston's Fenway Park. The stadium will now be named the New York Yankees Own Fenway Park at Suck-It Yards.

"Purchasing the naming rights to Fenway Park made good business sense for us," said George Steinbrenner, president of the Yankees. "This allows us to expand our footprint farther north along the East Coast and provides a rallying point for our many fans in New England."

The Yankees will pay $5 million per year for the naming rights to Fenway, with the contract automatically renewing each year until the Red Sox win a World Series title, upon which the stadium will revert back to its Boston ownership.

"This deal provides us a fantastic long-term situation in Boston," said Steinbrenner. "Just think what a bargain $5 million per year will be over eighty-six years when the Red Sox get around to winning another World Series."

The naming rights deal also allows the Yankees to paint Fenway's vaunted Green Monster in blue and white pinstripes. "We will enact the pinstripes clause of the deal for the play-offs, but only if the Red Sox can make it," said Steinbrenner.

Upper deck seats are the cheapest at the stadium. Unfortunately, this means upper decks usually reek of poor people. Gross.

Despite outrage from Boston fans, Red Sox management said the deal will help them beat the Yankees over the long run.

"The Yankees can name our stadium, they can buy logo space on our uniforms, I don't care what they do," said Red Sox general manager Theo Epstein. "Because that $5 million per year we're getting for the naming rights is going to allow us to acquire some players that will enable us to beat them. It was a no-brainer of a deal for us."

NBA BECOMES OFFICIAL SPONSOR OF GENITAL WARTS

The NBA announced today that it will become the official sponsor of genital warts, becoming the first professional sports league to align itself with a venereal disease. Genital warts joins Bausch & Lomb contact lenses, Gatorade, and many others as partners with the league.

"We are proud of our new relationship with genital warts and all of the trappings it brings," said Kay Leius, the NBA's marketing director. "We want people to know that having genital warts is not all that bad. Most of our players suffer from venereal disease and still live productive lives."

The decision to endorse genital warts signals an about-face in the NBA's public acceptance of the problems of its players. The league now acknowledges the fact its players are oversexed and overwhelmed by the number of groupies willing to have sex with them.

"Not only are our players unfaithful to their wives, but they seem to have very little knowledge of protecting themselves," said an NBA source. "The average player has two or three kids in different cities, and a combination of genital warts, pubic lice, herpes, syphilis, and gonorrhea.

"It's not so much that we're in favor of genital warts," said Leius. "It's just something that is easily identifiable with the NBA lifestyle and we want people to know they don't have to be ashamed of having them."

"Terrorists buy sneakers, too."   *—Michael Jordan*

SportsPickleNation Poll

What is your least favorite fan promotion?

17%   Make Out With the Umpire Night

18%   Guaranteed Loss Day

3%   Van Appreciation Night

26%   Body Cavity Search Sundays

1%   Boggle Head Night

15%   Collicky Babies Get-In-Free Night

9%   Mandatory Prostate Exam Day

11%   Free Steroids for Kids Fest

GREAT MOMENTS IN SPORTS BUSINESS HISTORY

MAY 29, 1922 The U.S. Supreme Court rules that organized baseball is a sport, and therefore not subject to antitrust laws. Microsoft used the same argument before the court in its antitrust trial in 1998, but failed to convince the justices that software programming is a sport.

JULY 12, 1979 The Detroit Tigers forfeit a game when a promotion, Disco Demolition Night, results in several small fires in the stands and a near riot. Unfortunately, the promotion's planned finale—the incineration of John Travolta—did not take place before the game was called.

MARCH 19, 1997 Major League Baseball announces a five-year, $50 million deal with Pepsi. Under the terms of the deal, Pepsi products would be sold exclusively at major-league ballparks, and players would not be able to take steroids in pill form with any other beverage.

A SPORTSPICKLE.COM INSIDE LOOK AT . . . ONLINE SPORTS MEMORABILIA SALES

The online sale of sports memorabilia is a multimillion-dollar business that continues to grow. The following is just a sample of some typical items that were purchased online in the last year.

Signed Stuart Scott edition Ebonics to English Dictionary
SELL PRICE: *1,450 cent*

Thrilla in Manila commemorative mailing envelopes (50-count box)
SELL PRICE: *$5.25*

George Foreman's grill (salvaged from his 1983 Mercedes 380SL)
SELL PRICE: *$65*

Sidd Finch 1985 Topps rookie card in mint condition
SELL PRICE: *$4,185*

Completed 2009 NCAA Tournament bracket filled out by Nostradamus in 1538
SELL PRICE: *$15,000*

Naked photo of Mike Ditka showing that Levitra works effectively
SELL PRICE: *$2.75*

One liter of Olympic pool water containing drops of Greg Louganis's blood
SELL PRICE: *$10*

Kentucky Wildcats T-shirt with Ashley Judd's pit stains
SELL PRICE: *$25*

MAY 21, 2003 Hours after signing LeBron James to a seven-year, $90 million endorsement contract, Nike signs eight-year-old Indonesian sweatshop worker Santoso Praman to a one-year, $8 contract.

PEOPLE TO KNOW

GARY BETTMAN The NHL commissioner's legacy will be defined by the lockout that canceled the entire 2004–05 season, a lockout that dragged on so long partly because the midgety Bettman was unable to see over the negotiating table. Hated by many fans and players, Bettman is widely admired among owners in all sports for breaking the players' union and implementing a salary cap—a model they all hope to use one day in almost destroying their own leagues. Bettman is also respected in many circles for his giant testicles, as he overexpanded the NHL into Arizona, Florida, Tennessee, and Texas during his tenure and then had the audacity to blame the league's economic woes on the players. *Fun Fact*: During the NHL lockout Bettman used the Stanley Cup as a birdbath in his backyard.

SCOTT BORAS The agent for many of baseball's best players, Boras had as prominent clients Carlos Beltrán, Barry Bonds, J. D. Drew, Alex Rodríguez, Gary Sheffield, and Satan, Prince of Darkness. Boras is renowned for regularly being able to get his clients signed to overpriced contracts. Examples include Bernie Williams's seven-year, $87.5 million contract with the Yankees, Magglio Ordóñez's five-year, $75 million contract with the Tigers, and Helen Keller's ten-year, $50 million contract to be an air traffic controller at La Guardia.

MARK CUBAN The billionaire tech entrepreneur is the most visible owner in the NBA, proving that weird-looking people with bad hair and creepy personalities can get on TV, too, as long as they constantly jump around, scream maniacally, and whine about everything. Cuban has taken on league referees during his time as an owner, resulting in numerous fines from commissioner David Stern. His abuse of referees has also angered mental retardation advocacy groups, who worked for years to get the mentally disabled jobs as NBA refs. Cuban is very hands-on with the Mavericks and claims to be friends with the players, sadly unaware that they all think he is an enormous dork and stand only his presence because he signs their checks. *Fun Fact*: Cuban is very interactive with Mavericks fans and it is enjoyable to contact him regularly via his e-mail address—

mark.cuban@dallasmavs.com—to remind him that he is a complete douche bag.

AL DAVIS Once one of the most powerful figures in professional football, Davis is better known to today's fans as that bespectacled old Jewish woman who wears track suits while watching Raiders games from luxury boxes. In addition to serving as commissioner of the defunct AFL in the 1960s, Davis has controlled the Raiders organization since 1967. He moved the team to Los Angeles where it played from 1980 to 1994, before moving it back to Oakland for the 1995 season—becoming the only person in recorded history to willingly move back to Oakland.

MALCOLM GLAZER Glazer owns controlling interests in both the Tampa Bay Buccaneers and Manchester United. He bought Man U in 2005 for $1.47 billion, paying with the large pot of gold found near where he lives at the end of the rainbow. The purchase of the club by an American enraged Manchester fans, who took time out from their regular routine of drunkenness, fighting, and getting laid off to burn him in effigy. Glazer is much better liked by Buccaneers fans, who laud him to this day for bringing a Super Bowl title to the city and, more important, changing the team's logo from a gay pirate.

JERRY JONES The Dallas Cowboys owner was born in Los Angeles in 1942, charting a life course that would inevitably lead him back to his L.A. roots via extreme plastic surgery. After playing football at Arkansas in the early 1960s, Jones embarked on a successful business career that culminated in buying the Cowboys in 1989. He punctuated his arrival by urinating on legendary Cowboys coach Tom Landry at the press conference announcing his purchase. The Cowboys were quickly reborn under Jones, winning three Super Bowls in the 1990s and dwarfing all sports team records for recreational drug use, even those set by major-league baseball teams of the 1970s and '80s. Jones has many detractors due to his cavalier attitude and micromanagerial style, but the charge that has stuck the most is that he is two-faced.

DON KING The boxing promoter is almost solely responsible for making boxing the highly respectable and credible industry it is today. His first major foray into the sport came in 1974 when he promoted the Rumble in the Jungle between Muhammad Ali and George Foreman. The next year he was behind the Thrilla in Manila, as well as the less well known bouts War in the Manure, Stinky in Helsinki, and Bouters with Gouters. Despite killing two people in his past—once by stabbing a man to death with his hair—links to organized crime, various lawsuits, and charges of tax evasion and insurance fraud, King has avoided lengthy jail terms and is still allowed to play an influential role in boxing. Only in America!

DREW ROSENHAUS The Tom Cruise film *Jerry Maguire* was modeled in part on Rosenhaus, the best-known agent in sports. The film even used his trademark line. (Not "Show me the money," but "Do you know that the human head weighs eight pounds?") Rosenhaus represents some of the most controversial players in the NFL, including Terrell Owens and Warren Sapp, and has regularly been accused of recruiting players away from other agents. This is a charge he denies despite flying a blimp over the Super Bowl each year with the message: "Your agent sucks. Come to Drew Rosenhaus." *Fun Fact*: Rosenhaus saved the life of a drowning boy in the summer of 2005 by administering CPR, but only after getting his parents to sign a contract guaranteeing Rosenhaus 40 percent of the child's lifetime earnings.

PETE ROZELLE Born in Compton, California, in 1926, Rozelle was a founding member of the rap group NWA and wrote such songs as "Straight Outta Compton," "F—k tha Police," and "A Bitch Iz a Bitch." Rozelle then left the group to pursue a career in sports business. Starting in the public relations office of the Los Angeles Rams in the mid-1940s, he worked his way up to NFL commissioner by 1959 at the age of just thirty-three, proving he must have been one fine piece of tail. He is credited with making the NFL into the success that it is today through consistent leadership and the negotiation of large television contracts. (The previous commissioner had saddled the NFL with exclusive broadcast deals with UPN and the WB.)

BUD SELIG The look-alike older brother of former U.S. Attorney General Janet Reno, Selig has presided over a tumultuous period in major league baseball's history, including the 1994 players' strike, steroids scandals, and the existence of the Tampa Bay Devil Rays. He began as the acting commissioner in 1992, but any hope that it was just a cruel joke was erased when he was formally appointed to the position in 1998. Selig broke into baseball in 1970 by purchasing the Seattle Pilots and moving them to Milwaukee as the Brewers. When taking the commissioner's job he transferred direction of the team to his daughter, though many believed he still played a role and that the Brewers therefore had an unfair advantage—a baseless claim considering that (1) Selig is a moron, and (2) the Brewers always suck. In 2006 Selig ordered an investigation into steroids use in baseball, saying it was something he had had on his to-do list since the early nineties but had never gotten around to it.

GEORGE STEINBRENNER The dictatorial owner of the New York Yankees, Steinbrenner runs his team like a business. Players are not even allowed to grow facial hair. (Or pubic hair, oddly enough.) Steinbrenner can be wildly temperamental and often places unrealistic expectations on his employees. He has changed managers twenty times and general managers eleven, his most infamous firing coming in 1984 when he canned the team's GM for failing to acquire Roy Hobbs. The outspoken owner has also been suspended several times by major-league baseball for infractions ranging from illegal campaign contributions to associating with gamblers to chartering a crop-dusting plan to drop thousands of gallons of urine over Fenway Park. But for all his faults, Steinbrenner will spare no expense when it comes to paying what it takes to win a championship. And not only will he spare no expense, he'll even grossly overpay if he has to for pieces of crap like Kevin Brown and Carl Pavano. *Fun Fact*: Known as "the Boss," Steinbrenner was Bruce Springsteen's ass double for the cover of Springsteen's album *Born in the U.S.A.*

DAVID STERN Stern has been credited with orchestrating the NBA's golden age of the late 1980s and early '90s, a claim the egomaniacal little troll does not dispute. But while Stern played some role in the success and rebirth of the NBA, he was more the beneficiary of good timing. His tenure as commissioner began in 1984, the same year that saw Michael Jordan, Hakeem Olajuwon, Charles Barkley, and John Stockton get drafted into the league (Portland Trail Blazers fans may recall Sam Bowie started his career in 1984, as well), supplying the league with fresh talent while Magic Johnson and Larry Bird were still in their primes. His introduction of the salary cap helped the league control spending, but anyone who refers to him as a sports marketing genius should remember that no genius of any ilk could at the same time be dumb enough to sport the porn 'stache Stern did during his early years as commissioner. His future goals for the NBA include bringing teams to Europe, as he for some reason believes other countries yearn for the opportunity to host Americans with criminal records.

PAUL TAGLIABUE The NFL commissioner from 1989 to 2006, Tagliabue continued the growth of the league's brand since taking over for Pete Rozelle. The increased success of the NFL enabled him to reach into broader areas, such as his minority hiring policy that requires all teams to interview a minority for head coaching jobs. However, he did resist calls during his tenure for minorities to be interviewed for the commissioner position. Tagliabue also built developmental leagues for the NFL, including the World League, which is widely viewed in Europe as American payback for their introducing soccer here. His time as commissioner saw parity come to the NFL, with free agency enabling teams to go from also-ran to the play-offs in a single year. (That is, all teams but the Arizona Cardinals.)

BILL VEECK Veeck was the most innovative promoter in the history of sports during his years as owner of the Cleveland Indians, St. Louis Browns, and Chicago White Sox from the 1940s to 1980s. His most memorable stunt was using three-foot-seven midget Eddie Gaedel to pinch-hit for the Browns in 1951. Upon drawing a walk, Gaedel was promptly wrapped in a wool blanket and tossed onto a Velcro wall positioned behind first base to the delight of the crowd. Ever the showman, Veeck even arranged to have his Hall of Fame induction be an event, mandating in his will that his introduction speech be given in Vulcan by a bearded female midget dressed as a clown and riding a unicycle.

DEVIL RAYS PURCHASED AT YARD SALE FOR FIVE BUCKS

The sale of the Tampa Bay Devil Rays was unanimously approved last week at the baseball owners' meetings, with team owners unanimously approving the ownership of a twelve-year-old boy who purchased them for five bucks at a yard sale.

"I think it's exciting for Major League Baseball to have some young blood with big, new ideas in the ownership ranks," said commissioner Bud Selig. "Plus, we didn't really have a choice. We're just glad somebody was willing to buy them, because it's not a very good franchise. None of us even know how the Devil Rays ended up at the yard sale, but we don't care. We're just amazed they were purchased."

The twelve-year-old owner, Matt Mitchell, said he bought the team on a whim when he saw it for sale in a neighbor's yard.

"My dad had just given me twenty bucks for my allowance and I saw that the Wilsons across the street were having a yard sale, so I went and checked it out," he said. "I spent fifteen on a used Xbox game they were selling, and I had five dollars left and saw they had the Devil Rays sitting there, so I thought, 'Hey, why not?' I don't really know what I'm going to do with them, though. I guess I just thought it would be cool to own a baseball team. Too bad they suck. Maybe I can trade them to a friend for a skateboard or something."

FUBU-NASCAR PARTNERSHIP SEEN AS POOR MATCH

NASCAR announced this morning that it will buy out its contract with circuit sponsor Nextel, and instead begin a new partnership with FUBU, the popular urban clothing apparel company. Beginning in 2008, the NASCAR Winston Cup circuit will be known as FUBU-NASCAR.

But despite the apparent joy over the deal felt by NASCAR and FUBU officials, industry observers immediately proclaimed the partnership a poor match. "What we have here is an organization that appeals primarily to lower-class Southern white people, teamed with an apparel company created solely to provide clothing for young blacks. It's a sports marketing disaster of unparalleled proportions," said Mickey Armstrong, editor of *The Sports Business Today*.

FUBU, which took its name from the phrase "For Us By Us," has created an urban apparel empire less than fifteen years after it was launched with clothes designed by African-Americans for African Americans, as the company's mission outlines.

FUBU agreed to pay $50 million a year for twenty years to NASCAR in order to place its name on the circuit and must outfit all of the drivers in FUBU wear. Despite the third-party statements to the contrary, both FUBU and NASCAR officials say it is a perfect deal for both parties.

"This opens up NASCAR to untapped markets," said Richie Winstott, NASCAR's marketing director. "If we can convince young black men that NASCAR is cool, stock car racing will grow beyond anyone's wildest imagination."

FUBU's marketing director, Jayson Mitchell, said the FUBU-NASCAR deal will one day be seen as a stroke of genius.

"Not only does this make marketing sense and financial sense, but this signifies a major bridge between two races and classes in this country," said Mitchell. "Most NASCAR fans probably hate people in FUBU gear, and most people in FUBU gear probably hate NASCAR fans, but we hope to change that by showing we can have something in common. And we hope we can make that commonality be stock car racing."

NIKE DEBUTS THE FIRST ALL-AIR SHOE

Just days after releasing its first shoe with an all-air sole, the Air Max 360, Nike announced today the release of the world's first-ever all-air shoe, the new Nike Air Max Barefoot. The shoe, a bare foot with a swoosh sticker attached to both sides, will retail for $180.

"The new Air Max Barefoot will provide comfort and performance never before seen in a shoe," said Phil Knight, Nike's chairman and cofounder. "Nike's patented Air support is found on all sides of the foot—an unprecedented and historic step in shoe design. We are confident the Air Max Barefoot will be a huge seller, regardless of its hefty price tag."

While the all-air sole Air Max 360 weighs less than thirteen ounces, the Air Max Barefoot weighs less than an ounce, the only weight coming from the swoosh stickers—a required accessory for anyone around the world who goes barefoot from now on.

"We put countless hours of research and design into developing this shoe," said Knight. "That's why we are requiring everyone to purchase the $180 swoosh stickers to place on their feet if they choose to go barefoot. Thanks to our pull with copyright and trademark offices around the globe, this is not only a requirement, but it is now punishable by law for a person to not wear a swoosh on their bare feet. It's the least we deserve for all the expenses we put into designing this—quote, unquote—shoe."

The company admits enforcement of their sticker-wearing mandate may be difficult, but early data suggests consumers are more than willing to part with $180 due to their confidence in, and loyalty to, the Nike brand.

"I've loved Nike shoes since I was a little kid," David Garrith, a recreational jogger from San Francisco. "I'm sure these are going to be their best shoes yet, and even though they're a little pricey I'm sure they're more than worth the cost. My feet sweat a lot when I run, and this will probably put an end to that with all the air circulation the shoe provides. Just an amazing design on their part."

Nike put the Air Max Barefoot through a rigorous round of testing and put it before focus groups before finalizing the design, and claims to have received extremely positive feedback on all accounts.

"My favorite part of the shoe is that there is no insole. Insoles always make my foot feel constricted," said Claire Shipp, who participated in an early round of product testing. "I guess the only negative thing I can say about it is that the one time I went running I stepped on a shard of glass and it went right through my foot and severed some nerves. I had to get surgery. But even that felt very natural and organic to me. It's a great shoe."

While the initial retail price for the Air Max Barefoot is set at $180, Nike may push it over the $200 mark if it seems the market can bear it.

"Trust me on this—the Air Max Barefoot is the best shoe we've ever made," said Knight.

MARK CUBAN SECRETLY FANTASIZING THAT A DEAD
DAVID STERN WOULDN'T BE ABLE TO FINE HIM

While pleased with his team's continued improvement, Dallas Mavericks owner Mark Cuban finds himself increasingly consumed by thoughts of how his life would be better if NBA commissioner David Stern happened to die in a sudden and unexplained accident.

"I dream about it, think about it all the time," says Cuban. "It consumes me. That son of a bitch has cost me millions and millions of dollars in fines since I became on owner in this league—all because I see things a little bit differently than he does. But that wouldn't be the case if he wasn't around anymore, would it? Say his glasses get knocked off somehow when he walks by me before one of the games, and I pick them up for him. And as I'm handing them to him, he starts to bend down to pick them up, too, and one of the stems of his glasses plunges deep into his neck, right into his jugular vein—accidentally, of course—and he drops over dead, painfully gurgling and spouting blood. That would just be an accident, right? No one could be blamed for that, don't you think? Hypothetically speaking, of course."

Those close to the Mavericks owner say he has been increasingly talking about Stern's death in recent weeks.

"It's a scary sight to see when he talks about Stern," said Dave Hunter, a business associate. "His eyes get this really creepy, crazed look in them. And not the regular crazed look that they normally have. That one creeps me out, for sure. But it goes to a whole different level of creepiness when he talks about Stern, as hard as that may be to believe. I really think he wants to do him harm."

In the weeks since his latest six-figure fine, Cuban has called several meetings with team officials to brainstorm ways Stern could be murdered without the killer ever being discovered.

"Again, this is all hypothetical stuff," said Cuban. "I mean, no one has ever wanted to kill someone just because they've taken millions and millions of dollars from them without provocation, right? That would be absurd for me to want to kill him for that. Absurd. I just use these 'How Can We Kill David Stern?' brainstorming sessions as a way to have some fun around the office and bond with one another. But I make it a requirement that my secretary take notes. Very detailed notes. And then I've been bouncing some of the best ideas off of my attorneys to see which they think are the most viable. You know, just for giggles."

As much as the billionaire businessman tries to downplay his desire to see the NBA commissioner die a horrible death, he admits Stern's passing would benefit him in many ways, including financially.

"The way I see it, if Stern stays alive I'm looking at another $5 to $10 million in fines in the coming years," said Cuban. "But if I kill him, I might spend 200 grand on bail, and three or four million in attorneys' fees to get myself off. That means I'm saving myself more than five million. So it just makes good business sense to kill him. And I'm a good businessman."

STORIES TOP STORIES   TOP STORIES TOP STORIES **IN OTHER NEWS . . .**

Intravenous fluid named the official sports drink of the Israeli-Palestinian conflict . . . Man's investment in baseball cards as a child not enough to retire on as hoped . . . Bin Laden bobble-head giveaways selling out Middle East sporting events . . . Charlotte Bobcats to wear throwback jerseys commemorating their inaugural season . . . Long-estranged from Michael Jordan, Nike pitchmen and Brooklyn resident Mars Blackmon found dead in a gutter . . . Mark Cuban changing the world one blog entry at a time . . .

SPORTS IN AMERICA

Not all of the most important sports stories make it into the national media. The following are news items from local papers across the country.

SIX-FOOT-FOUR, 255-POUND THIRD-GRADER WINS SCIENCE FAIR WITH STEROIDS EXPERIMENT

Ryan Miller, a third-grader at tiny Meadow Park Elementary in Lawrence, Nebraska, won first prize at the school's science fair yesterday by making steroids and using them to transform himself into a six-foot-four, 255-pound muscled behemoth.

"I am very proud of Ryan for winning the science fair," said his mother, Cathy. "Although I am a bit concerned that all the steroids he took may affect his long-term health."

The boy's project, titled "The Human Body and Steroids," was approved by his teacher, Mrs. Claire Rinaldi, back in September, when the children had to select their science fair experiments.

"No doubt this is the most remarkable and impressive science fair project I have seen in my thirty-five years of teaching," said Rinaldi. "But perhaps I should have asked more questions about what exactly Ryan planned with his project. I thought it was just going to be some charts and an article or two pasted to a poster board like many of the other children do. I didn't realize he was going to make his own anabolic steroids and human growth hormone, and then ingest large doses of them and gauge the results by the changes they made in his own body. I probably would not have signed off on that if I had known his intentions ahead of time."

The eight-year old Miller, four foot two and 74 pounds before beginning his experiment, grew more than two feet and gained nearly 200 pounds of pure muscle in just five months.

"It wasn't all the steroids that made me so big and strong, though," said Ryan. "People want to say that, but they have to realize I worked really hard to get like this. I lifted weights and worked out several hours a day. The steroids only played a small part."

He found the chemical makeups for various steroids on the Internet and ordered the chemicals needed to make them from a company in Hungary.

"My dad let me use his credit card to pay for all the stuff," said Ryan. "Once they arrived, I followed the directions I printed out from the Internet, and within a few hours I had enough steroids to last me through high school."

With his lunchbox filled with various steroid cocktails and a protein shake each day, in place of his normal turkey sandwich and apple sauce, and then another round of steroid injections before bed each night, Ryan said he began noticing changes in his body right away.

"Things that were heavy to me all of a sudden became light. Like lifting up a gallon of milk with one arm was a lot easier than before," he said. "Then, before I knew it, I was covered in big muscles. Just the other day I was late for the bus, and I ran it down and made it stop by grabbing on to the back bumper and digging in my heels. It ground to a stop and I jumped on."

The boy's mother noticed changes in her son almost immediately as well.

"Boys his age grow fast, but we went through about six wardrobes and eight pairs of shoes since he started his science fair experiment," said Claire Miller. "He's been a little bit more moody than normal, too, but he's been a great help around the house, moving the piano into the basement for me and ripping out an old, dead tree we had in the backyard."

Leonard Witman, Meadow Park Elementary's principal and the lead judge of the science fair, said he was most impressed by Ryan's attention to detail in his experiment.

"Most of the projects were the same old, same old—a crappy papier-mâché volcano spewing steam, a bunch of stuff with mice—but then I turn the corner to Ryan's display and there he is bending a steel pipe into a knot and I was intrigued. Then I saw the before picture and it was an easy decision for me. And I thought the tanning lotion and body oil he applied to his body was the coup de grâce—that's the kind of extra effort I notice as a judge."

DEBATE TEAM UNABLE TO TALK ITS WAY OUT OF BEATING BY FOOTBALL TEAM

The debate team at Mountain Spring High School in Rochester, New York, was unable to talk its way out of a severe beating by the MSHS football team during sixth-period lunch yesterday. All six male members of the county championship–winning debate team were treated for injuries by the school nurse. The two female members were unharmed.

The confrontation began early in the lunch period when members of the MSHS football team heard the debate teamers congratulating one another on the championship they won over the weekend.

According to debate team president Martin Schlitzer, junior linebacker Mark Hutchen came over to the debaters' lunch table and said: "Hey, nerds, think you can debate your way out of a beating?"

Schlitzer responded to the challenge by referencing Martin Luther King Jr.'s example of nonviolence as the impetus for progress, which in turn caused Hutchen's fists to rain down upon him.

Hutchen was then joined by other members of the football team in pummeling Schlitzer and his friends. During the melee, debate team members could be heard—between whimpers and shrieks of pain—alluding to the teachings of Mahatma Gandhi, Jesus Christ, and even Hemchandra, an eighth-century Jainist philosopher who espoused the oneness of all peoples and religions.

Despite the reasoned pleas given during the beating, the debate teams' words only enraged the football team further. "With each smart-guy thing those dorks said we just hit them harder," said Hutchen.

GUY MUCH TOUGHER ON SPORTS MESSAGE BOARDS THAN IN REAL LIFE

Gary Mueller, who is known by the moniker "KillSmackPapa" on-line, has built up a reputation as a cocky, belligerent loose cannon on the on the sports message boards he frequents. But in real life Mueller exhibits a completely different persona.

The five-foot-six, 140-pound, thirty-three-year-old manager at a Chicago-area Dairy Queen lives with his widowed mother and is a longtime choir member at his church, where he often plays accordion solos for special music. He has an extensive comic book collection and goes to and from work in a pale blue 1987 Ford Festiva that he purchased in high school with money earned from a paper route. And despite not having a girlfriend since the fourth grade, Mueller, by all accounts, is seen as a pleasant soul, if a bit uncomfortable in social situations.

But not when he has his computer on. Each day before and after work, Mueller becomes KillSmackPapa and fills sports message boards with venomous posts.

"You #$!%ers over here on the Packers board suck" read a post this morning on the Green Bay Packers message board on ESPN .com. "The Bears are going to be back this year and will beat the %&$^ out of you losers."

Mueller's post on the Packers board is similar to the type of confrontational language he leaves all over the Web as KillSmack-Papa.

"KillSmackPapa seems like a very angry dude," said Mike Letner, or MiLet18, a Detroit Red Wings fan and frequent recipient of Mueller's vitriol on hockey message boards. "He is always talking smack and trying to pick a fight."

Robert Wystrom, a Chicago sports fan who reads many of the message boards that Mueller frequents, says even those who support the same teams as Mueller find him annoying.

"He is extremely cocky and confrontational and often drives other users away from the message board because he can't discuss things civilly," said Wystrom. "A lot of people just wish he would post elsewhere."

KillSmackPapa often claims in his posts that he would "beat the #!&% out of" those he exchanges messages with as he escalates the war of words, "but can't, because we're only online and not face-to-face. But if I met you I would destroy you."

Both Wystrom and Letner were interested to learn that, in real life, Mueller is just a spindly fast-food worker who lives with his mom and has no athletic ability.

"That's some great information to have," said Letner. "Next time he says he would beat me up I'm going to give him my address and invite him over."

"Yeah, I kind of figured he was a dork," said Wystrom. "A lot of the guys like him that you come across online are. They're overcompensating and lashing out from being made fun of their whole life. Online they can pretend to be someone else."

Mueller refused comment for this story, but sent an e-mail to the reporter saying, "You better hope that KillSmackPapa doesn't find out you're writing this story or he's going to be pissed and come after you. But if you do write it, please don't mention that I don't have a girlfriend or that I spend ten hours a day online or that I like to post completely naked. Thanks. AND GO CUBS! EVERYONE ELSE SUCKS! KillSmackPapa out."

HANDICAPPED ATHLETE COURAGEOUS, YET REALLY EASY TO BEAT

Michael Lewster, a former high school basketball star who lost a leg in an auto accident three years ago, has made a courageous recovery through months of grueling rehab. Fitted with a prosthetic limb, Lewster returned to the court last week and is playing pickup games with his old teammates.

"What can you say about Michael," said Jake Lowell, a former teammate. "He's an inspiration to all of us. A true hero. Only now he's really bad at basketball. He's slow and can't jump hardly at all and he's really easy to beat, but he's still an amazing, courageous person, of course. Stinking at basketball doesn't diminish the courageous part."

Lewster said he hopes to be back at full speed in time for the spring rec league basketball season: "It would be great to be out there with the guys and playing together again like it was old times. And I think I can do it if I keep working hard."

"I don't think he can do it, regardless of how hard he works," said Rob Mitchell, another former teammate. "He's simply a terrible, terrible player right now, and I just don't think he's ever going to be good enough again. And frankly, we don't want him on our team. It's hard to tell him that, but we don't. He's a liability. None of this takes away from what a wonderful and inspiring guy he is. He's a better person than all of us. But we're just much better at basketball."

HUNTER MOCKS SLAIN DEER WITH CELEBRATORY DANCE

Hunter Jonathan Frederick celebrated his shooting of a seven-point buck on Monday by executing a fifteen-second celebratory dance directly in front of the deer, mocking it as it lay dying.

"I've been waiting for the opportunity to unveil that dance," said Frederick, of Ambler, Wisconsin. "I really showed that deer what kind of hunter he was dealing with."

Frederick said his routine opened with numerous hip thrusts and climaxed by holding his fingers up to his head like deer antlers before grabbing at his heart and falling to the ground.

"I could tell by looking into the deer's eyes that when I did that last part he was pretty angry," said Frederick. "If he wasn't two or three breaths away from dying, I'm sure he would have jumped up and gored me. But that's why it was so fun to do because he wasn't able to. All he could do is lay there helplessly and die. But I'll always have that satisfaction that his last memory in this world was of me mocking him. Boo-yah!"

Frederick said he was happy that the deer didn't die before he got up to it after firing the fatal shot: "I wanted him to see my dance before he died," he said.

The twenty-eight-year-old construction worker has been practicing a kill dance since last deer season. "I'm a big football fan, and I love how those guys dance it up after they score a touchdown or make a big tackle, so I wanted to do the same with my hunting," he said. "I remember last year when I got a doe and then realized I didn't have any dance to do in front of it. I got a really condescending look from the deer, and I promised myself I would never be disrespected like that by an animal again."

Walter Reman, the director of the Wisconsin Game Commission, said that while dances such as Frederick's are not condoned, they are not illegal.

"There's really nothing we can do to stop stuff like that," said Reman. "God knows I'd like to. I wish people like him had more respect for the animals, but we can't control everything. All I know is that twenty or thirty years ago, hunters didn't go around doing dances every time they killed something. But these days it's different with this new breed of hunter."

Frederick says his only regret is that he didn't get his performance on film.

"My friend Ron, who went out with me, was supposed to bring along his digital camcorder, but he forgot it in the car. All he had was a 35-millimeter camera," said Frederick. "I was hoping he would be able to videotape it and then I could put it on the Internet or something. Maybe become the Terrell Owens of hunting. But I'm not too disappointed. I'll get it on film next year. I'm already thinking of new dance ideas."

JACK STILL THINKS HE'S GONNA BE A FOOTBALL STAR

Jack, the Indiana high school football player who was brought to fame by John Mellencamp's 1982 hit song "Jack & Diane," still claims he's gonna be a football star, despite being thirty-seven years old and out of the game for two decades.

"Mellencamp said it best—'Oh yeah, life goes on; long after the thrill of livin' is gone,'" said Jack. "I've definitely done a lot of living since '82."

Jack was a sixteen-year-old junior quarterback on his high school team in 1982 when Mellencamp penned the song about him and his girlfriend Diane. He was set to take over as the starting quarterback in his senior season, 1983, and achieve football greatness.

"Jack had a cannon for an arm," said Jim Dalrymple, Jack's high school coach. "His potential was limitless. We expected to win districts with him in 1983 and take a run at states. But he just threw it all away."

Less than six weeks after "Jack & Diane" hit number one on the charts, Jack found out Diane was pregnant.

"Diane was the debutante of the backseat of my car," said Jack. "Sometimes we'd run off behind a shady tree. I'd dribble off her Bobby Brooks and she'd let me do what I pleased. Life went on, but spending too much time in the backseat of my car and behind shady trees got her pregnant."

Jack was forced to get a job the summer before his senior year in order to support his pregnant girlfriend, leaving little time for him to prepare for the football season.

"I had certain responsibilities after Diane got pregnant and I needed to uphold them. Football became second then," he said.

The diminished importance of football in Jack's life was obvious on the field; his team went only 7–4 in 1983. And after Jack Jr. was born in mid-October, the team spiraled to a 0–3 finish, failing to the win the district title or qualify for states.

"I wish I could have held on to sixteen longer," said Jack. "Changes came around real soon and made us women and men."

Jack received minimal interest from college football programs following his disappointing senior season. He enrolled for one semester at Division III Meshaw State in Indiana in 1984 and rode the bench on the football team before quitting school before the end of the spring semester.

"Jack had some real talent, better than most you see in Division III," said Charles Duhauser, Jack's college coach. "But you could tell his mind was elsewhere."

"When I realized I wasn't going to play right away in college, I made the decision to quit school and head back home to take care of Diane and Jackie Jr.," said Jack. "It's not a decision I regret." Jack and Diane got married and Jack began working double shifts at a local auto parts factory to support his family. The seventeen years of backbreaking manual labor has left Jack looking much older than his thirty-seven years.

"It hasn't been easy. Diane wasn't able to work for a long time after having Jack Jr. due to some complications with the delivery," said Jack. "So the responsibility for making a living fell to me. I guess we were just two American kids doing the best we could."

Today, with Jackie Jr. off to college and with more time to devote to his own endeavors, Jack wants to revisit his football career.

"I know I can still play," said Jack. "I may not look all that good for my age, and I know teams are going to be apprehensive to take a shot on a forty-one-year-old who hasn't played in twenty-five years, but I've always had the talent and I still do. My goal is to make the NFL, but I've still got college eligibility left, too, so I can go that route first."

Jack has cut back his schedule at the factory in order to allow time for training. And he says he has Diane's full support.

"I just want a shot," he said. "Mellencamp knew what he saw in me when I was sixteen. I'm still gonna be a football star."

SPELLING BEE FINALIST ELIMINATED ON THE WORD "GIRLFRIEND"

Christopher Heck, a finalist at last week's Scripps National Spelling Bee, was eliminated when he was unable to spell the word "girlfriend." Bee champion David Tidmarsh then clinched the title by successfully spelling "autochthonous," a word meaning "indigenous."

Heck, thirteen, gamely tried to spell "girlfriend" for several minutes, asking its origin (English), definition ("a favored female companion or sweetheart") and its use in a sentence. Bee Master Michael Winchester provided Heck with the sentence "You will never have a girlfriend," prompting the boy to break into tears and run off the stage.

Heck's mother, Bonnie, who homeschools her three children in the dining room of their Peoria, Illinois, home, said this is not the first time her son has been tripped up by a seemingly simple word.

"Last year in the Illinois state competition he was knocked out when he failed to spell 'popularity' correctly," she said. "It was a word he had no concept of or experience with."

Spelling Bee officials say it is an unwritten rule that Bee Masters do not ask spellers words that may have negative emotional connotations for the children. "It is our goal to not upset the children or remind them of their status as social outcasts," said Beth Riley, director of the Spelling Bee. "That's why you'll never see words like 'dork,' 'gayboy,' 'nerd,' 'wedgie,' or 'loser' in a spelling bee. These kids hear those words enough on a day-to-day basis and don't need to deal with hearing them in the one place their special talents are celebrated."

Riley also stated that while such words may be simple for most people to spell, they can provide an enormous challenge to even the best child spellers. "You have to realize what these kids go through each day in school," she said. "If you ask them to spell an easy word like 'queerbate' or 'retard,' a lot of them will freeze up because of all the emotional baggage they have tied to a word like that. They're completely unable to spell it, and many of them will wet their pants upon hearing such words. I've seen it happen."

But Heck said he was unable to spell "girlfriend" simply because the word is foreign to him and because girls think he is weird, not because he is taunted about it. "My mother homeschools me because she says I'm special and that the normal kids at public school would be a detriment to my educational well-being, so I don't get ridiculed too much—except when my family takes its monthly trip to the shopping mall," he said. "Then I get my share of abuse if I stray away from mother or father."

Heck claims the Spelling Bee was only the second time he ever heard the word "girlfriend." "I once heard it on television when I was staying at my cousin's house while my mother was giving birth to my little sister, so I know what it means," he said. "But that was the only time. We don't have a television at my house because my parents say TV is for proletariat ignoramuses."

Riley said the Bee Master Winchester has been reprimanded about his choice of context sentence for Heck's word. "Not only did he use a word that is a bit risky with most of these kids," said Riley, "but the sentence he used to describe it was highly inappropriate. I can assure you it won't happen again."

"I apologized to Heck about making him cry," said Winchester. "I didn't mean to do it, I just couldn't find the paper with the context sentence, so I simply said what came to my mind first. I looked up at that kid and all I could think was: 'You will never have a girlfriend.' I'm sorry he took it so personally."

STUDY: GAY CHILDREN DISLIKE PLAYING SMEAR THE QUEER

A joint study released today by the National Recess Board, the Gym Teacher Association of America, and GLAAD found that homosexual children dislike playing smear the queer by an almost three-to-one margin.

The findings come after a ten-year study looked at more than 50,000 grade school children across the country and studied their feelings toward the popular schoolyard game in which one child is arbitrarily deemed the "queer," and then is repeatedly tackled, thrown to the ground, or pelted with kick balls, depending on local rules. The study was funded by a $40 million federal grant.

"The research proves what many have long suspected: gay children feel excluded, even targeted, by their classmates from smear the queer," said Mary Levine, president of the National Recess Board. "What some see as a harmless child's game is really a societal mechanism to discriminate against homosexuals at an early age. The queer smearing needs to stop in this country immediately."

Seventy-four percent of gay children surveyed said that they feel either "sad," "different," or "disliked" when their peers play smear the queer. A majority also reported they often found themselves to be the target of the game, with gay or effeminate boys being deemed the "queer" more than 90 percent of the time.

"The other kids always smear me. I hate that game," said an eight-year-old gay boy from Nebraska in the report (no names were disclosed). "Everyone makes me the queer 'cause they say I run weird

BOOTH THROWS IT DOWN TO SIDELINE REPORTER FOR UPDATE ON HER DELICIOUS BREASTS

ABC play-by-play announcer Mike Tirico tossed it down to sideline reporter Erin Andrews in the first quarter of last night's Orange Bowl broadcast, not to hear how an injured player was doing, though, but to get an update on Andrews's wonderful, voluptuous bosom.

"I was supposed to turn it over to Erin under the guise of her letting us know when a Florida State defensive back who had twisted his ankle would be back in the game," said Tirico, "but I decided to cut through all the crap and get to the point, so I said: 'And now down to Erin Andrews for an update on her exquisite jugs.' And as the professional she is, Erin took it in stride and ran with it."

"They're spectacular as ever, Mike, thanks for asking," Andrews said. "A perky C cup to die for, each breast topped with a perfect, small, rosey nipple you would only believe if you saw them with your own eyes. In fact, you may be interested to know that since it's a bit cold in here, my nipples are hard right now. I can barely contain them. And if viewers were lucky enough to bury their face in my delicious cleavage, I'm sure they would note my breasts naturally exude the scent of cocoa butter. It's true. Now back up to you so I can take off my top and rub lotion all over my chest. Oh, and the injured player is expected to be back for the second half."

Tirico said he hopes his novel approach doesn't make anyone think he lacks respect for Andrews as a broadcaster.

"She's proved time and time again that she has what it takes as a sideline reporter, but there's also a reason she's wearing a low-cut shirt every broadcast that shows off her flawless cleavage," said Tirico. "I mean, come on—it's not a coincidence that almost all sideline reporters are females that

male viewers would be excited to see naked."

Tirico's unique interplay with Andrews continued into the fourth quarter.

"In the third quarter I sent it to Erin with: 'Now let's go down to Erin Andrews to find out if it's possible to bounce a quarter of off her butt,'" said Tirico. "And she countered with: 'Indeed it is, Mike. And not only that, but I've been known to let people eat soup out of it, it's so clean. I've never pooed in my life, Mike. Never pooed. Back to you for now. But stay tuned for a gratuitous beaver shot.'"

But before Tirico could deliver on Andrews's titillating promise, the pair was told to stick to only game updates by their producer.

"I think we made broadcast history tonight, and I'm proud of that," said Tirico. "Hopefully our producer will reconsider and we can do more of the same in the future."

NATIONAL GEOGRAPHIC SWIMSUIT ISSUE KIND OF DISGUSTING

As the latest edition of Sports Illustrated*'s popular swimsuit issue hits newsstands this week,* National Geographic *is looking for a sales boost of its own with its first-ever swimsuit edition. But early reviews of the magazine's swimsuit photos are mixed at best.*

"Saggy breasts, bloated bellies and wrinkled, weathered faces," read a description of National Geographic*'s swimsuit edition in today's* New York Times. *"If that's what's to be found at beaches around the world, we don't want to travel out of the U.S., thank you very much. And we don't want to see another* National Geographic *swimsuit issue, either."*

Reactions from people on the street have been even harsher.

"I understand other cultures having different viewpoints on what is attractive. Really, I understand that," said Thomas Williamson, a New York bonds trader. "But—yikes. Those chicks weren't even remotely hot. Not only did looking at them make me never want to have sex again, but I also feel guilty now for living in a wealthy country. I mean, come on—these tribes can't even afford one bra for the woman to pass around so they at least get some support every once in a while?"

Larry Canon, a New York lawyer, said he picked up copies of both the Sports Illustrated *and* National Geographic *issues at a newsstand on his way back to the office from lunch.*

"I always get SI's issue, and then I saw the headline on the front of National Geographic's *issue, 'Exotic Women from Around the World: Our First Swimsuit Issue,' and decided to get that one, too," he said. "I was thinking there'd be some hot Brazilian women in bikinis, or maybe some Asian women or Eastern Europeans or something, but then I crack it open back in my office and they're, like, really exotic. I wanted exotic, but not that exotic, you know? This was exotic like, women with miniature spears through their nipples and women breastfeeding newborn pigs kind of exotic. Not really my cup of coffee."*

The publisher and editors of National Geographic *said they are not expecting the magazine's foray into sexy swimsuit shots to be without challenges.*

"You have to realize that Sports Illustrated's *swimsuit issue was not an overnight sensation," said Leo Hall,* National Geographic's *editor-in-chief. "It took them forty years to get it to be the cultural staple that it is today. We plan to wait just as long if we have to."*

Publisher Michael Barros says the goal of the swimsuit issue is profit and education.

"Sex sells. There's no denying that," said Barros. "What we want to do with this annual issue is teach people something about different cultures while getting them sexually stimulated at the same time. I acknowledge, based on early reactions, that perhaps we need to use more discretion next year in the photos we choose in hopes of better meeting the 'sexually stimulated' part of that equation."

Hall and other top-level editors at National Geographic *also see the swimsuit issue as an extension of the magazine's brand.*

"When I was a kid, the only place you could see a woman's breasts without getting in trouble was in National Geographic," *he said. "All we're doing now is providing an entire issue of breasts for those kids who have grown into adults. We realize that as adults they probably have other means for seeing female nudity, but we think they'll enjoy reminiscing about their perverted youth while paging through our swimsuit issue."*

and because I design stylish clothing for my GI Joes during lunch. They tackle me and kick me and punch me. I wish we never played that stupid smear the queer."

"Every day when we go out for recess or have a free day during gym class all of the bigger boys point at me and say: 'Let's play smear the queer everybody. [Name withheld]'s the queer. Get him!'" said a ten-year-old Maryland boy. "Then they chase me around for a half hour, tackling me and jumping on me. It is my least favorite part of school."

Of the 26 percent of homosexual children who said they "enjoyed" smear the queer, 80 percent were girls, a segment the study found is rarely made the "queer" in the game and, in fact, often hands out a disproportionate amount of the beatings.

"Of those who do the smearing of the queer, most were extremely homophobic straight boys, but we also found many gay girls, who in grade school often seem to be quite brawny, did heavy amounts of queer smearing," said Larry Childs of GLAAD.

The other 20 percent of those who said they "enjoyed" smear the queer were gay boys who claimed they believed the game rightly punished them for their homosexuality.

"I know from what my dad says sometimes about the people on the TV that I shouldn't be gay," said a seven-year-old Texas boy. "So when we play smear the queer I always pray that the other kids will beat the queer out of me so I can be a normal boy. But it hasn't happened yet."

"My Sunday school teacher told us that being gay is wrong," said an eleven-year-old Ohio boy, "so I see smear the queer as God punishing me for not stopping my gayness. And also, I like it because sometimes I can kiss the other boys when they tackle me."

The idea that the playing of smear the queer should be stopped has not been met with unanimous support, however. Antihomosexual and faith-based family groups across the country said that the results of the study prove that smear the queer serves a valuable purpose.

"Smear the queer is the first line of defense against the scourge of homosexuality," said Dick Platt, director of the Family Foundation Association. "Who knows how many gay children have been turned back on the straight path by being smeared at an early age."

"Playing smear the queer is an important part of growing up in America," said Rodney Richards, president of AmeriFam. "Of course, gay children don't like smear the queer. It's because they know that their lifestyle is wrong. If we outlaw the game we'll have written a free pass for queerdom to take over this great country."

Yet despite such protests, it appears smear the queer's last days are on the horizon; researchers have already received a federal grant to conduct a fifteen-year study to find ways in which children can be discouraged from playing the game.

"We hope that by 2020, our nation's young queers will feel free to walk their schoolgrounds without the fear of being smeared," said GLAAD's Childs.

Father distraught to learn his son is playing right field on Little League team . . . Tall black guy tired of people asking him if he plays basketball . . . Company softball team hungover again . . . Chess club wiped out by tetherball . . . Teenage athlete really going to regret it in the future if he doesn't take steroids . . .

STADIUMS AND ARENAS

The stadiums and arenas in which we watch sporting events are just as important as the teams and athletes we cheer for. They are where our voices come together as one. Where shared experiences can form an unbreakable bond between people young and old, rich and poor. Where we can become children again and dare to dream. And where the identity of our team and city is whored out to whatever corporation is willing to pay enough money to slap their name on the side of the building.

GREAT MOMENTS IN THE HISTORY OF STADIUMS AND ARENAS

JUNE 15, 1938 In the first night game at Brooklyn's Ebbets Field, Johnny Vander Meer of the Cincinnati Reds throws his second-straight no-hitter. Vander Meer's feat was helped by the fact that the lights at Ebbets Field were not installed until a week later.

APRIL 9, 1965 Mickey Mantle hits the first indoor home run in history as the Yankees beat Houston in the debut game at the Astrodome. Mantle's blast was met with a loud ovation from the crowd, which was quickly chastised by the public address announcer for not using its "inside voice."

APRIL 4, 1971 Veterans Stadium in Philadelphia is dedicated with a ribbon-booing ceremony.

SEPTEMBER 13, 1991 A fifty-five-ton concrete beam falls in Montreal's Olympic Stadium. The incident tragically wiped out the entire crowd watching that evening's Expos game, killing four people, including Montreal's mascot and a beer vendor.

THE STADIUMS

AIR CANADA CENTRE Home of the Toronto Maple Leafs and Toronto Raptors

Home to some of the most supportive hockey fans in the world, the Air Canada Centre routinely draws standing-room-only crowds for Maple Leafs games. Basketball is another story, however, with just 85 percent of the seats being filled, or twice the percentage of effort that Vince Carter gave while he played for the Raptors. Ground was broken for the venue in 1997 and opened two years later at a cost of $265 million Canadian ($3.19 US).

ALLEN FIELDHOUSE Home of Kansas basketball

The Fieldhouse was opened March 1, 1955, with a win over Kansas State, marking the last time the Jayhawks would defeat the powerful Wildcats, their rivals and cross-state nemesis in basketball. A rich sense of history fills the building, with banners hanging in the rafters to honor Kansas greats such as Wilt Chamberlain and Danny Manning. Former coach Roy Williams is also hung in effigy from the center court scoreboard.

ARROWHEAD STADIUM Home of the Kansas City Chiefs

Despite opening in 1972, Arrowhead Stadium is far from outdated, thanks to the foresight and vision of its designers. In fact, in many ways Arrowhead is still ahead of its time, with its "hover garages" built for flying cars still standing vacant. Same with the soma concession stands and the stadium's robot-seating-only sections. The Chiefs thrive off their sold-out home crowds, which are regarded as the NFL's loudest, at more than 100 decibels, a noise level experts liken to the sound of 79,000 people simultaneously vomiting up the five pounds of barbecue and six-pack of Bud they ingested in the parking lot before the game.

AT&T CENTER Home of the San Antonio Spurs

The arena was completed in 2002 at a cost of $186 million and financed through a local sales tax. (Every San Antonio resident who had entered the country illegally was forced to pay $100, giving the city the $186 million plus an additional $15 million to put up more bilingual street signs.) The AT&T Center was built to replace the Alamodome, opened less than ten years earlier, in 1993, because the Spurs said the venue did not offer revenue streams competitive with other teams' homes. And the claim of not being able to be competitive was more than backed up on the court, as the Spurs managed only a 400–224 record, five division titles, and just one measly championship in their eight years at the Alamodome.

AT&T PARK Home of the San Francisco Giants

Although still a young ballpark, AT&T has become one of the most recognizable stadium in all of sports. The huge Coke bottle and baseball mitt—which are to-scale with Barry Bonds's actual hat—found behind the left-field bleachers are easily identified by most baseball fans. As are the waters beyond the right-field fence, where Bonds has hit home run after home run into "McCovey Cove"—so named because destitute ex-Giants slugger Willie Mc-Covey lives in those waters on a dilapidated raft. But despite Bonds's many feats at the stadium, it is by no means considered a homer-friendly park. Homo-friendly, perhaps.

BEAVER STADIUM Home of Penn State football

With a capacity of 107,282, it is the second largest stadium in the United States, behind only Michigan's football stadium, and is thought to have taken in more people than any other beaver outside of Paris Hilton's. The stadium has endured numerous renovations over the years, growing from 46,284 seats in 1960 to 60,203 in 1976, to 76,203 in 1978, to 83,770 in 1980, and finally to today's current capacity—a rate of growth that should see Beaver Stadium with some 250,000 seats when Joe Paterno finally keels over on the sidelines in the early twenty-second century.

BEN HILL GRIFFIN STADIUM Home of Florida football

Named after British comedian Benny Hill, who offered to sponsor the stadium in exchange for the lifetime rights to grope the breasts of any Florida cheerleader, the Gators football home is nick-named "the Swamp" because, like everything in the state of Florida, it was built on top of one. Tailgating is a major part of the atmosphere before games, as many residents of Gainesville tow their trailer homes right up to the stadium.

BRONCO STADIUM Home of Boise State football

In addition to hosting Broncos football, the stadium is the home of the annual MPC Computers Bowl and is recognized for its distinctive blue field, which is the leading cause of televisions being sent for repairs. Installed in 1986, the surface is widely referred to as "Smurf-Turf" after the term the male Smurfs used for Smurfette's pube-covered pleasure trail in the 1980s cartoon series.

BUSCH STADIUM Home of the St. Louis Cardinals

Opened for the 2006 season, the new Busch Stadium has no seats so the ever-supportive Cardinals fans can give constant standing ovations, as they are known to do for everything from a home run to a player running hard when hitting into a game-ending double play. The new venue is also positioned perfectly so fans can get views of downtown St. Louis and the Gateway Arch, because as any St. Louisian knows, one can never get enough views of the freaking arch.

CAMERON INDOOR STADIUM Home of Duke University basketball

With only 9,314 seats, Cameron Indoor is practically tiny. In fact, nearly every seat is within earshot of Mike Krzyzewski's expletive-filled tirades, making it illegal for those under the age of seventeen to enter the building if not accompanied by a parent or guardian. The student crowd, known as the Cameron Crazies, is famous for its enthusiastic and undying support of the Blue Devils, support that is bested only by that of referees and broadcasters.

CARRIER DOME Home of Syracuse University basketball and football

The largest on-campus basketball arena in the country, with 33,000 seats, it is also the only venue that can boast that it has more fans who are unable to see the court from their nosebleed upper-deck seats than most schools have in their entire arena. The dome is also the site of many concerts. Some notable appearances from the past include Elton John, Frank Sinatra, Billy Joel, Rod Stewart, and many other stars of the entertainment industry that Jim Boeheim got to know while playing the role of the father on ALF in the late 1980s.

CITIZENS BANK PARK Home of the Philadelphia Phillies

While most cities have constructed their new ballparks in scenic and convenient downtown locations in recent years, Philadelphia bravely bucked that trend in 2004 when it plopped Citizens Bank Park down in the middle of acres of parking lots, four miles from Philly's downtown. The stadium has taken flak for being a bandbox and marking its fence distances as deeper than they really are, although those factors likely won't hurt the Phillies much due to the team's historically stellar pitching.

COMERICA PARK Home of the Detroit Tigers

Criticized upon its 2000 opening for its enormous field dimensions, Comerica may be partly to blame for baseball's steroids problem, as players were forced to bulk up to have even the slightest chance of hitting a home run there. The stadium includes a Ferris wheel, carousel, and dozens of stone tiger sculptures, leading Siegfried and Roy to endorse Comerica as "the greatest and gayest stadium in all the land."

CONTINENTAL AIRLINES ARENA Home of the New Jersey Devils and New Jersey Nets

Continental Airlines Arena is part of the Meadowlands complex in East Rutherford, New Jersey. It is named "Meadowlands" because the more accurate "Industrial Swamplands" sounds less appealing. Since opening in 1981 the arena has witnessed three Stanley Cup championships by the Devils and, up until recently, about as many wins by the Nets. Bruce Springsteen has sold out more than thirty concerts there, although that's less impressive considering the New Jersey–bred Springsteen could get a standing-room-only crowd in the state if he took his bowel movements in public. The arena will be without permanent tenants in the coming years when the Nets move to Brooklyn and the Devils to Newark, leading the New Jersey Sports and Exposition Authority to consider asking Springsteen to take his bowel movements at Continental Airlines Arena.

COORS FIELD Home of the Colorado Rockies

It was obvious from the first at-bat in the stadium on April 17, 1995, that Coors Field would be a hitter's ballpark. Mets leadoff hitter Brett Butler opened the game with a bunt that landed in the third deck in right field for a home run. And while it is a homer-friendly park, Coors Field has seen some of the game's elite hitters don a Rockies uniform: Jeffrey Hammonds, Dante Bichette, Vinny Castilla, and more, all sluggers who must be listed among the game's all-time greats regardless of where they played their home games. But while the Rockies lineup has boasted some of baseball's premier hitters, the team has failed to produce many winning seasons in its history—although the team's high altitude means it has probably been building endurance and may be ready to break through with a wildcard berth by the year 2050 or so.

DEAN SMITH CENTER Home of UNC basketball

Filled with splashes of paint in the wussiest shade of blue known to man, the "Dean Dome" opened in 1986 with number one Carolina beating number three Duke, 95–92. Former Tar Heels head coach Dean Smith originally balked at the idea of naming the arena after him, but was persuaded by the school's administration that the drive to fund the building's construction would be more successful with his name attached to it. Plus, Smith was against the backup choice: The UNC Sucks Pavilion, which was proposed by a wealthy Duke alum who promised to pay the cost of the entire facility if that name was used.

DOAK CAMPBELL STADIUM Home of Florida State football

Since its debut in 1950 to the present day the stadium has filled its mission of providing recreation grounds for young men with a violent criminal past. A statue of head coach Bobby Bowden was unveiled outside the stadium in 2004 with his right arm pointing forward, depicting what some think is him giving a player direction, when in fact it is meant to show Bowden telling one of his charges which way to run to avoid the cops. *Fun Fact*: The Seminoles locker room is trimmed in garnet, gold, and concertina wire.

DODGER STADIUM Home of the Los Angeles Dodgers

Huge photographic banners on the outside of the stadium featuring current Dodger players greeting fans as they arrive in the third inning and waving good-bye as they exit in the seventh. Inside, however, the huge stadium struggles with intimacy, especially since smog makes it difficult to even see the Dodger Dog in front of your face, never mind the baseball diamond five decks below. Dodger Stadium seats 56,000, or enough to hold 1.46 percent of the illegal immigrant population of Los Angeles.

FENWAY PARK Home of the Boston Red Sox

The oldest active ballpark in the major leagues, Fenway is most famous for its imposing left-field wall—the Green Monster, named for the benevolent monster of Irish folklore who was said to bless well-behaved children by giving them alcoholism. Seats were added above the Green Monster after the 2002 season so fans could hock loogies on Yankees left fielders. In 2005, after years of discussion about replacing the stadium, Red Sox ownership announced that Fenway would remain the team's home, thanks in part to aggressive campaigning by the Urine Stench, Cramped Seating and Obstructed Sightline Lovers Society of Boston.

GIANTS STADIUM Home of the New York Jets and New York Giants

The shared stadium setup creates quite a dilemma for New York bookies in determining who has home field advantage when the teams meet every few years. Rumors have swirled for years that Jimmy Hoffa is buried under one of the end zones, but no bodies have been found in or around the stadium, other than the thousands of hookers that Lawrence Taylor killed when he was finished with them. While large crowds routinely fill the stadium, the largest gathering ever there came in 1995 when Pope John Paul II celebrated Mass before 82,948. But the event was unfortunately marred when former Jets quarterback Joe Namath drank all the communion wine and tried to kiss His Holiness.

GREAT AMERICAN BALL PARK Home of the Cincinnati Reds

Perhaps the cockiest of all stadiums, the originally proposed name for Great American Ball Park was All Other Stadium's Suck Compared to This One, So Bite Us Park. The stadium opened in

2003 and was built so the Reds could have a stadium separate from the Bengals. (Primarily because the Reds feared the Bengals suckosity was starting to rub off on them.) Great American Ball Park is a cozy venue with just 42,059 seats. In fact, Ken Griffey's Jr.'s hamstrings can be heard tearing even in the upper deck. *Fun Fact*: Former Reds owner Marge Schott dreamed of one day moving the team into a stadium named Adolf Hitler Memorial Park.

HEINZ FIELD Home of the Pittsburgh Steelers and University of Pittsburgh football

Opened just a few years ago, in 2001, Heinz Field has still been around long enough for Steelers head coach Bill Cowher to lose multiple AFC Championship Games there. The 64,450-seat stadium regularly sells out for Steelers games, but has had trouble getting filled for Pitt games. (And most of the people who show up for Pitt games are only there to keep their seats warm for the following day's Steeler game.) *Fun Fact*: The Steelers are planning to install a cost-effective, retractable roof over Heinz Field by using an enormous Terrible Towel.

HUBERT H. HUMPHREY METRODOME Home of the Minnesota Twins and Minnesota Vikings

The building's unique Teflon fabric roof stays up only because of air pressure; former Vikings receiver Randy Moss and a dozen or so friends routinely inflated the entire roof before games by simultaneously exhaling a bong hit. The roof also contributes to a deafening roar in the building with noise levels reaching more than 100 decibels, approximately the same amount of noise generated from one Kent Hrbek fart. Because of the intense noise, Twins fans often use their "Homer Hankies" to dab at the blood dribbling out of their ears. The dome seats 48,000 for baseball and 63,000 for football, with the vast majority of football fans getting their tickets by scalping them from former Vikings head coach Mike Tice.

HUSKY STADIUM Home of University of Washington football

Situated high above Lake Washington's Union Bay, Husky Stadium is perhaps the most scenic football stadium in the entire country. Or at least it could potentially be scenic if it wasn't always freaking raining or overcast in Seattle. When the stadium was originally built in 1920 it contained 30,000 seats. Its most recent expansion in 1987 put the figure at its current 72,500, although the '87 construction project was marred when 13,000 seats collapsed. The expansion was then taken away from the freshman Engineering 101 class and given to an actual architectural firm.

JACOBS FIELD Home of the Cleveland Indians

The opening of the pristine Jacobs Field in 1994 coincided with a crop of Indians prospects coming of age, making the Indians the hottest ticket Cleveland had seen in years—even hotter than riverside seats to watch the Cuyahoga catch fire in the '60s. The draw of "the Jake" has waned a bit since the Indians division title run ended in 1999, but the team still gets solid crowds due to its ingenious advertising tagline: "Come see the Indians! (At least we don't suck like the Browns)." In 2004 the stadium was updated with the installation of the largest sports venue video display in the world, allowing fans to see in giant size how stupid C. C. Sabathia's hat looks.

JOE LOUIS ARENA Home of the Detroit Red Wings

Opened in 1978, the arena is named after the legendary heavyweight and Detroit native Joe Louis, playing off the obvious synergy between a black boxer and the exclusive home of a hockey team. Replacing the arena with a more modern facility has been discussed for years, as the JLA is woefully short on luxury boxes and other revenue-generating amenities. For this reason, the Red Wings have historically had one of the lowest payrolls in hockey and are never able to add high-priced veterans to their roster before the play-offs. *Fun Fact*: Red Wings fans like smuggling dead octopuses in their pants.

KAUFFMAN STADIUM Home of the Kansas City Royals

Thousands of people zip past the park each day on I-70, many of whom are shocked to see that Kansas City still has a major-league baseball team. The centerfield scoreboard is shaped like the Royals logo and topped by a giant crown, cruelly mocking the franchise's lone championship. But Kauffman's most recognizable feature isn't the scoreboard, but its outfield system of erupting fountains and gently trickling waterfalls, an atmosphere that makes Kaufmann the nation's most wizzed-at stadium.

LAMBEAU FIELD Home of the Green Bay Packers

It is a federal crime to not mention the words "frozen tundra" when speaking of Lambeau Field, so now that that's out of the way ... Lambeau Field is the crown jewel of NFL stadiums, even though it reeks of cheese. In 2003 a massive renovation project was completed which left most of the interior of the stadium untouched while adding a myriad of modern amenities. Included were a Packers Hall of Fame, numerous eating options, and event facilities for 25 to 1,200 people—therefore enough space to fit the entire population of Green Bay three times over. Also unveiled were statues of legendary coach Vince Lombardi and team founders Curly Lambeau, Moe Lambeau, and Larry Fine.

LINCOLN FINANCIAL FIELD Home of the Philadelphia Eagles

"The Linc" was built along with the Phillies Citizen's Bank Park at the beginning of the decade to replace Veterans Stadium, which the VFW had complained for decades was disgracing the memory of U.S. servicemen and women. While a vast improvement over its predecessor in terms of design and amenities, Lincoln Financial Field also retains much of what made the Vet a unique venue, such as crowd noise and an overwhelming sense of impending failure.

LOUISIANA SUPERDOME Home of the New Orleans Saints

Opened in 1975, the Superdome got off to a bad start when at the grand opening it was discovered all of the stadium's signage had a typo in it that read: "The Louisiana Superdome: Home of the Taints." The NFL has scheduled more Super Bowls at the Superdome than any other venue, confident that it won't have to deal with the possibility of the Saints ever having an unfair home field advantage in the game since they would never make it to a Super Bowl. In 2005 the building was almost destroyed by Hurricane Katrina as tens of thousands were huddled inside hoping to stay safe from the storm. Rescue workers were able to lure the people into the Superdome only by promising them the Saints would not be playing.

M&T BANK STADIUM Home of the Baltimore Ravens

Opened in 1998, the stadium has 68,915 seats that give each fan the impression that they are peering down from a prison tower at a collection of dangerous criminals because—outside of their not being in an actual prison yard—that's exactly what they're doing when the Ravens are on the field. Before each game begins, star linebacker Ray Lewis performs an end-zone dance routine and the crowd dutifully whips itself into a frenzy, each person fearful they could be harmed or even killed if they don't respond in the manner Lewis wishes. The stadium's two state-of-the-art, 24-by-100-foot high-definition video screens make it seem all the more to fans like they're watching an episode of *Playmakers*.

MADISON SQUARE GARDEN Home of the New York Knicks and New York Rangers

Dubbed "the World's Most Famous Arena," Madison Square Garden has truly been home to some of sport's most memorable moments: Ali-Frazier in 1971, the Rangers winning the Stanley Cup in 1994, and

Isiah Thomas being announced as the first mentally retarded team president in history when he was hired by the Knicks in 2004. In addition to concerts, the Garden hosts the Ringling Brothers and Barnum and Bailey Circus, which fills the building with the literal stench of crap instead of just the figurative one left there by the play of the Knicks. *Fun Fact*: For some reason, many Chinese restaurants post signs stating that they are opposed to Madison Square Garden.

McAFEE COLISEUM Home of the Oakland A's and Oakland Raiders

One of the last remaining multipurpose monstrosities from the 1960s, the stadium unfortunately was not destroyed by the 1989 earthquake that struck during the A's-Giants World Series. The stadium became even more of an eyesore in 1995 when the Raiders returned to Oakland from Los Angeles and had a massive wall of seats built in place of the centerfield bleachers. Nicknamed "Mt. Davis" for Raiders owner Al Davis, the addition can fit 22,000 A's fans, or 11,000 fully-costumed Raiders fans.

MELLON ARENA Home of the Pittsburgh Penguins

Perhaps the most antiquated venue still in use today by a major sports franchise, Mellon Arena was actually ahead of its time when it

was opened in 1961. Built with a state-of-the-art retractable roof, the roof has not been opened to its surrounding skyline in years—mostly because the Penguins can barely afford the electricity to keep their lights on, let alone what it would cost to slide around a multiton roof for fun. While the Penguins have won two Stanley Cups championships in their time at Mellon Arena, the venue's most memorable moment came in 1995 when a disgraced former fireman defeated a group of terrorists holding the vice president hostage during the seventh game of the Stanley Cup Finals—an event that was captured in the documentary *Sudden Death* with Jean-Claude Van Damme.

MEMORIAL STADIUM Home of Nebraska football

The Cornhuskers home field holds the record for most consecutive sellouts in NCAA football, dating back to 1962, which is great and all, but what else is there really to do in Nebraska? So wrapped up in the support of their team are Cornhusker fans that for most the embarrassment of showing up in the same exact red shirt as every other person in the stadium doesn't even register.

MICHIE STADIUM Home of Army football

The pageantry and excitement of the pregame festivities at Michie are unmatched in college football. Cadets march in a full-dress parade before the game, the band plays the Army fight song, and skydivers jump into the stadium to deliver the game ball, all of which is almost enough to compensate for the fact that the Black Knights will start getting pummeled as soon as play begins. And after each Army score, members of the Corps of Cadets do as many push-ups as the Knights point total, a feat that has become much easier to pull off in recent decades.

MICHIGAN STADIUM Home of University of Michigan football

Nicknamed "the Big House," Michigan Stadium is the largest football stadium in the United States, with an official capacity of 107,501. The 107,501st seat is supposedly "saved" each game for former head coach Fritz Crisler, but the jerk hasn't showed up to claim it in more than twenty years. The latest expansion project at Michigan Stadium is set to be completed in 2008 and will add even more seats, which will enable even more fans to watch Michigan underachieve each season live and in person.

MINUTE MAID PARK Home of the Houston Astros

Originally named Enron Field when the stadium opened before the 2000 season, it was built with money taken from the pension accounts of low-level Enron staffers. The company had to pull out of the naming deal in 2001 when its whiny employees began complaining that they had no money for retirement. The field is the quirkiest in all of baseball by design, with a short porch in left field, a train beyond the outfield, and a hill in centerfield with a flagpole in the middle of it. Future design elements include the installation of an alligator-filled moat in the infield and a giant, 400-foot Ferris wheel in right-center. Above all else, Minute Maid Park is about baseball in its purest form.

NEYLAND STADIUM Home of University of Tennessee football

The biggest stadium in the South, Neyland can fit more than 104,000 Volunteer faithful—all of whom would think getting mooned by Peyton Manning to be the greatest moment of their lives. Sixteen expansion projects in the stadium's eighty-plus years have gotten it to its current capacity, the most recent coming in 2000 when seventy-eight sideline skyboxes were added. Also installed was surveillance equipment in the visitor's locker room so head coach Phil Fulmer could keep an eye on his opponents and report any violations to the NCAA.

NOTRE DAME STADIUM Home of Notre Dame football

Many believe that God has actually interceded here in the past to help the Irish win. Although if that's true, the team's play for most of the past decade may be the greatest proof yet for Nietzsche's claim that God is dead. Perhaps the most recognizable element of a Notre Dame home football game is found outside the stadium, where the mural of "Touchdown Jesus" peers out from the school library. The mural honors Jesus Velazquez, who in 1934 became the first Latino player ever to win the Heisman, and is said to bring the Golden Domers good luck and a large family.

OHIO STADIUM Home of Ohio State football

Perhaps the single greatest tradition in college football is the dotting of the "i" in "Ohio" by the school marching band during halftime of home games at Ohio Stadium. In fact, at Ohio State this tradition is second only to giving blue-chip recruits cars, jewelry, and expensive electronic equipment. "The Horseshoe" underwent a major renovation before the 2001 season that cost $187 million, although Ohio State student athletes generously pitched in by agreeing to have 10 percent withheld from their paychecks to use toward building costs.

ORANGE BOWL Home of Miami football

Known by the majority of Miami residents as Cuenco de Naranja, the Orange Bowl was the host of the bowl game of the same name until 1995. It has been played at Dolphins Stadium since then because the aging Orange Bowl is starting to look like a piece of *mierda*. *Fun Fact*: Playing varsity football counts for 120 credits at "the U."

ORIOLE PARK AT CAMDEN YARDS Home of the Baltimore Orioles

The first of the retro parks when it was opened in 1992, Camden Yards is now horribly outdated and lacks the revenue streams needed for a team to be competitive. (Or at least someone will no doubt make this argument soon.) The focal point of the stadium is the B&O Warehouse beyond the right-field wall, a massive structure stadium designers wisely utilized to block fans' views of the crime and urban decay that was all around them in 1990s Baltimore. A favorite ballpark eatery for O's fans is Boog's Barbecue in the right-field concourse, although it's much less popular among out-of-towners who fear the possibility of eating a booger-filled sandwich.

PALACE OF AUBURN HILLS Home of the Detroit Pistons

Built in suburban Detroit because no one in their right mind would want to go into downtown Detroit after dark, the Palace has seen three NBA championships since opening in 1988. On the negative side, however, it also saw one of the darkest moments in recent sports history when in 2004 a near-riot broke out between the fans and the Indiana Pacers. It was an incident that sadly tainted the image Detroiters had built over the years as the best-behaved and most respectful fans in the world.

PAULEY PAVILION Home of UCLA basketball

Pauley became the home of the greatest college basketball team in history upon its opening in 1965. (No, seriously. Ask your grandfather. UCLA used to be really good every year.) The building oozes the history of that championship era, with eleven NCAA title banners hanging from the rafters, including the retired jerseys of Kareem Abdul-Jabbar (Lew Alcindor) and Bill Walton, who insisted his retired jersey be made out of tie-dyed hemp.

PETCO PARK Home of the San Diego Padres

As fans step inside beautiful Petco Park they are immediately struck by an overwhelming stench of dog food and kitty litter. Petco is unique among many of its retro brethren with its stucco walls, white exposed steel, and dark blue seats, which are meant to represent the color of the surrounding landscape, white boat sails, the blue of the Pacific ocean, and a bunch of other stupid artsy junk like that. The team honored former Padres star Tony Gwynn by making the official stadium address 19 Tony Gwynn Way. They honored him further by giving him a full-size replica of Petco made out of delicious milk chocolate.

THE PIT Home of New Mexico basketball

One of college basketball's best known venues, the Pit is built in a thirty-seven-foot hole in the ground, presumably dug by workers who, delirious from the oppressive heat, were trying to dig their way out of the godforsaken state. The Pit is attributed to the Lobos fantastic home court advantage—a winning percentage over .800—since moving into the building in 1966. And, of course, their impressive record at home is all about the Pit and has nothing to do with getting to play Mountain West crap teams such as Air Force, Brigham Young, Colorado State, San Diego State, and Wyoming every year.

PNC PARK Home of the Pittsburgh Pirates

No other Triple-A team can claim to have a stadium as beautiful as the Pittsburgh Pirates'. Fans are greeted at the stadium's various gates by statues of past Pirate greats Honus Wagner, Roberto Clemente, and Willie Stargell. And more are planned, too, with a statue commemorating the fifteenth anniversary of Barry Bonds not being able to throw out Sid freaking Bream at home set to be unveiled in 2007, as well as one scheduled for 2008 that will depict Dave Parker smoking crack. Once inside the park, fans are treated to a view that is unmatched in baseball, with the Clemente Bridge,

Allegheny River, and Pittsburgh skyline seemingly painted in the sky beyond centerfield—a view that provides a welcome diversion from watching the Pirates get pummeled on the field. *Fun Fact*: The PIN "3481" works at all PNC Bank ATM machines. Give it a try!

QUICKEN LOANS ARENA Home of the Cleveland Cavaliers

Once named Gund Arena after former Cavaliers owner Gordon Gund, the building was renamed in 2005 because Gund Arena unfortunately sounds like a venereal disease. The downtown Cleveland venue seats 20,562 for basketball, although 10 percent of that number is tied up in comped tickets for LeBron James's entourage. *Fun Fact*: Gundarena is treatable with penicillin.

RALPH WILSON STADIUM Home of the Buffalo Bills

Named Rich Stadium at its opening in 1973, the stadium was renamed in 1998 in honor of Bills founder and owner Ralph C. Wilson Jr.—although a fan poll favored the name: F–k You, Scott Norwood Field at We Hope You Die Stadium by a wide margin. Rich Stadium provided the Bills with a strong home field advantage, as the team did not lose a play-off game there until December 1996. Unfortunately for the Bills, however, Super Bowls were played elsewhere. *Fun Fact*: Ralph Wilson Stadium is a great place to go if you want to freeze your nuts off.

RAYMOND JAMES STADIUM Home of the Tampa Bay Buccaneers

The most recognizable element of this stadium, opened in 1998, is a massive replica pirate ship beyond the north end zone that fires footballs and confetti each time Tampa Bay scores. Interestingly, the team's former stadium had the same pirate ship, but the Bucs offense never provided the opportunity for it to fire for years upon coming into the league in 1976. The pirate ship is not the stadium's only fanciful element, however. Beyond the south end zone is a giant rainbow and a pot of gold where team owner Malcom Glazer lives year round.

ROGERS CENTRE Home of the Toronto Blue Jays

Widely hailed when it was opened as SkyDome in 1989, the retractable-roofed venue is essentially now a massive relic of the multisport facility era. And worse, at least for Torontonians, is that one of the sports played there is not hockey. The facility offers a myriad of amenities, and even includes a hotel with rooms that overlook the field. Former Blue Jays second baseman Roberto Alomar actually lived in the stadium, primarily so he could spit on umpires when they passed him in the halls.

ROSE BOWL Home of UCLA football

Known for hosting the bowl game of the same name, the Rose Bowl has also been the site of five Super Bowls, men's and women's soccer World Cup matches, and Olympic action. On the down side, it also is the home of UCLA's football team. The stadium can also lay claim to being the site of the most-attended women's sports event in history, the 1999 women's World Cup final, at which 90,185 showed up after hearing that Brandi Chastain was going to show some tit.

RUPP ARENA Home of Kentucky basketball

Named in honor of former Kentucky coach Adolph Rupp, the school has dishonored Rupp's legacy not only by allowing black people through the doors of the arena, but by letting one down on the floor to coach(!). But the Wildcats' loud and supportive fans make it hard to make out the sound of Rupp rolling over in his grave. The arena's 23,000 seats are divided into two sections. There are 10,000 cushioned theater seats in the lower bowl and 13,000 bleacher seats in the upper level. But the best seats are anywhere one might get a chance to cop a feel of Ashley Judd as she is passed through the crowd.

SHEA STADIUM Home of the New York Mets

What Shea Stadium may lack in prestige compared to historic New York ballparks such as the Polo Grounds, Ebbets Field, and Yankee Stadium, it more than makes up for in concrete. But Shea has seen greatness. For instance, the Yankees played there during the 1974 and 1975 seasons while Yankee Stadium was being renovated. And the 1986 Mets team won the World Series, with Shea becoming the first stadium ever with a cocaine vending machine in the home team locker room. *Fun Fact*: Queens smells slightly less than the Bronx.

SOLDIER FIELD Home of the Chicago Bears

Opened in 1924 and modeled after ancient Greek and Roman stadiums with its colonnades, Soldier Field serves as a memorial to fallen American soldiers. Following the stadium's ultramodern reconstruction before the 2003 NFL season, Soldier Field now serves as a memorial to those who will lose their lives in the future fighting alien spacecraft in the great war against the planet Mezzatron 7. The widely panned rebuild is seen by many as karmic payback for the Bears 1985 release of "The Super Bowl Shuffle."

STAPLES CENTER Home of the Los Angeles Clippers, Los Angeles Kings, and Los Angeles Lakers

Opened in 1999, the Staples Center is the only arena to house three major professional teams: the Lakers, Clippers, and Kings. (Note: The Clippers did not become a "major professional" team until recently.) Attending a Lakers game at the Staples Center affords not only the opportunity to see a game, but the chance to gaze at the many Hollywood stars sitting courtside. Similarly, attending a Clippers or Kings game there affords not only the opportunity to see a game, but the chance to maybe see a supporting actor from a cancelled UPN show sitting somewhere in the upper deck.

TD BANKNORTH GARDEN Home of the Boston Bruins and Boston Celtics

Opened in 1995 as a replacement for the historic Boston Garden, the arena has quickly come to play an essential role in the New England sports scene. Unlike Fenway Park or Gillette Stadium in recent years, TD Banknorth's hosting of the Celtics and Bruins allows fans to conduct the activity that is essential to being a Boston sports fan: whining and complaining incessantly about your team's lousiness. Called FleetCenter upon its opening, the arena was actually without a name for several months in 2005 after Fleet's deal expired before a new sponsor was found. The building's operators auctioned off one-day naming rights to the arena during this time with the proceeds going to charity, but the idea backfired when wealthy fans of Boston rivals bought up most of the days and named the venue everything from The Larry Bird Sucks Center to the Boston Is Wicked Retahded Arena.

WRIGLEY FIELD Home of the Chicago Cubs

So famous that people crowd the roofs of neighboring houses during games just to look at it, Wrigley Field is referred to as the "friendly confines" by visiting teams who are fortunate enough to play there. Best known for its ivy-covered outfield wall, atop which sit the stadium's famed "bleacher bums," whose unconditional support for their team is surpassed only by their drunkenness. Late broadcaster Harry Caray famously led the Wrigley crowd in singing "Take Me Out to the Ball Game" during the seventh-inning stretch because he was way too hammered to even realize he was already at the ball game. *Fun Fact*: Popular local boy Ferris Bueller interfered with a foul ball during Game 6 of the Cubs 2003 NLCS series against the Florida Marlins.

YANKEE STADIUM Home of the New York Yankees

Since Babe Ruth and his construction crew stayed up all night putting the finishing touches on the structure in April of 1923, Yankee Stadium has been home to sport's most successful franchise. The team memorializes its rich history beyond the left-center field fence in Monument Park, an area with plaques honoring Ruth, Miller Huggins, Lou Gehrig, Joe DiMaggio, Mickey Mantle, and the 2004 Yankees squad, the only team in history to blow a 3–0 lead in

the play-offs. The team is planning to open a new Yankee Stadium in 2009 one lot over from the current structure, but that plan has hit a snag thanks to a lawsuit from PETA that claims the construction of a new park will displace thousands of city rats from their natural habitat in the Bronx.

(Note: Ninety percent of the stadiums and arenas will likely be named by different corporations by the time you read this, whereas the remaining 10 percent will likely change their names while you are reading this.)

SPORTS CALENDAR

Major events to keep an eye out for in the coming year.

JANUARY

BCS BOWL GAMES Nothing builds excitement for college football's showcase games like a month's worth of inactivity by all of the involved teams. Kudos, NCAA marketing department!

NFL PLAY-OFFS Detroit Lions—free, since, well . . . pretty much forever.

BASEBALL HALL OF FAME VOTING RESULTS ANNOUNCED At least Pete Rose will always have the Gambling Hall of Fame.

AUSTRALIAN OPEN Holding a tennis major in the middle of the winter? Yeah, there's a good idea, stupid Aussie morons.

WINTER X GAMES It's pretty much the same as the Summer X Games, except the bong water is frozen.

MLB SALARY ARBITRATION HEARINGS HELD Nothing builds team unity quite like making a case in public about why your players don't deserve to get a raise.

FEBRUARY

SUPER BOWL The only thing the Roman Empire gave the world was a means to track Super Bowls. Well, that and vomituriums.

COLLEGE FOOTBALL NATIONAL LETTER OF INTENT DAY It's always an exciting day in the state of Florida to see how Miami, Florida State, and Florida handle their recruit commitments, since most of them can't sign their own names.

NBA ALL-STAR GAME Don't bother trying to get tickets—90 percent of the crowd is comped player posse, groupies, and pot dealers.

NHL ALL-STAR GAME They've tried Wales vs. Campbell, East vs. West, and North America vs. the World. Next up is Whites vs. Jarome Iginla.

PRO BOWL Where tackling by the lei is a 15-yard penalty.

DAYTONA 500 Nicknamed the "Great American Race," and nothing shows the melting pot that is America more than NASCAR's diverse fan base.

MARCH

COLLEGE BASKETBALL CONFERENCE TOURNAMENTS Mid- and low-major conferences battle for the right to get blown out in the first round of the NCAA Tournament.

NCAA TOURNAMENT SELECTIONS SUNDAY But more important, it's NIT Selection Sunday, too.

NCAA TOURNAMENT BEGINS And employee absenteeism skyrockets. Especially among all the parents of Duke players that Mike Krzyzewski got jobs for.

SPRING TRAINING GAMES BEGIN The media begins preparing for the baseball season as well by running countless Red Sox-Yankees stories.

NHL TRADE DEADLINE Look for recaps of all the blockbusters on page 38 of your local newspaper's sports section.

IDITAROD BEGINS Alaska gets its annual covering of frozen dog poo.

MCDONALD'S HIGH SCHOOL BASKETBALL ALL-AMERICAN GAME Of course, one of the keys to being an elite athlete is eating lots of McDonald's food.

APRIL

BASEBALL OPENING DAY And come the end of the month, the Devil Rays will be mathematically eliminated in the AL East.

FINAL FOUR Unlike college football, the NCAA apparently doesn't care if college basketball players miss weeks of classes due to a play-off system.

NHL PLAYOFFS BEGIN When defenses tighten up, proving those 3–2 scoring fests were just a regular season luxury.

THE MASTERS I hear there are rumors that it's a tradition unlike any other.

NFL DRAFT And following its completion, Mel Kiper is returned to a cold storage facility far below ESPN headquarters in Bristol, Connecticut.

NBA PLAYOFFS BEGIN Beginning just weeks after the Final Four is held, which is almost enough time to forget how bad the NBA game sucks compared to college basketball.

BOSTON MARATHON Held on Patriots' Day in Boston, it also always seems to coincide with Kenyan National Pride Day.

MAY

KENTUCKY DERBY The pageantry, the excitement, the intrigue. And that's just the hats.

PREAKNESS STAKES Where Triple Crown dreams go to die. Or, at the very best, where they go to be falsely flamed only to die at Belmont.

WNBA SEASON BEGINS Ruining the sports scores ticker at the bottom of your television screen since 1997.

INDIANAPOLIS 500 It's always held over the Memorial Day weekend to memorialize way back when people actually cared about the Indy 500.

JUNE

BELMONT STAKES Belmont steaks taste like horse meat.

FRENCH OPEN Perhaps the only place in the world where one can be unashamed of their brown, skid mark–covered undies.

STANLEY CUP FINALS Don't wear sweat pants, Canada. We'll see your boner.

NBA FINALS After somehow completing three rounds of play-offs in just two short months, the NBA Finals begin.

U.S. OPEN GOLF The USGA doesn't want anyone to finish under par at the U.S. Open, which should give David Duval a lifetime exemption.

COLLEGE WORLD SERIES It could be argued that the Little League World Series is the greatest amateur baseball tourney in America, but at least the players in the CWS admit to being in their twenties.

WIMBLEDON BEGINS Nothing's hotter than girls dressed in white with grass stains on their knees.

NHL DRAFT It's the day some Canadian boy will have his childhood dream realized by getting drafted by the Nashville Predators.

NBA DRAFT Where the Utah Jazz look to pick the best white guy available.

JULY

WIMBLEDON FINALS It's full of tradition, but none more than the tradition of a Brit not winning it.

BRITISH OPEN Look for Prince Harry relaxing in a pot bunker.

MLB ALL-STAR GAME The winning league gets home field advantage for the World Series, something that's always great motivation for All-Star reps from the Devil Rays, Royals, and Rockies.

ESPY AWARDS SHOW Helping athletes build their low self-esteem since 1993.

TOUR DE FRANCE Riders can hit speeds above 60 mph simply in hopes of escaping the smell of French people.

NFL TRAINING CAMPS OPEN At least for everyone who's not a Drew Rosenhaus client.

BASEBALL TRADE DEADLINE It's the last day for the Yankees and Red Sox to call up players from their minor-league affiliates in Pittsburgh and Milwaukee.

COLLEGE FOOTBALL PRESEASON POLLS RELEASED Wow, what a shock—the media thinks Notre Dame is going to be good this season.

AUGUST

SUMMER X GAMES Honoring the athletic pursuits of the late black leader Malcolm X for more than a decade.

NFL HALL OF FAME INDUCTION Former players can't be voted in until they've been out of the NFL for five years or crippled by arthritis for three.

PGA CHAMPIONSHIP It may not be golf's most prestigious major, but winners get to have their names etched alongside some of the sport's all-time greats, like Shaun Micheel, Rich Beem, and Mark Brooks.

U.S. OPEN TENNIS BEGINS Where Serena Williams historically debuts risqué outfits, ones that barely conceal her penis.

LITTLE LEAGUE WORLD SERIES Sobbing kids are hilarious.

COLLEGE FOOTBALL SEASON BEGINS And with it, players start getting paid time-and-a-half.

SEPTEMBER

NFL REGULAR SEASON BEGINS After an off-season of conditioning and film study, more than a month of grueling practices in the summer heat, and four exhibition games, it's time for NFL players to begin providing stats for your fantasy league.

NASCAR'S "CHASE FOR THE NEXTEL CUP" BEGINS Started in 2004, the circuit's play-off participants are determined by a mathematical formula . . . oops, sorry—I lost some NASCAR fans there with the "mathematical formula" stuff.

RYDER CUP An entire continent versus one little country? Yeah, that's fair.

U.S. OPEN TENNIS FINALS Featuring courts that are slightly softer than the greens at the golf U.S. Open.

WNBA FINALS They may not appeal to everyone, but the WNBA Finals get huge ratings among those who have fetishes for sweaty chicks with knee braces who can't jump.

OCTOBER

NHL REGULAR SEASON BEGINS After its seemingly endless nine-day off-season, the NHL drops the puck.

MLB PLAYOFFS BEGIN All we can hope is that one day soon a flesh-eating bacterium will attack Tim McCarver's throat.

WORLD SERIES Two teams battle for their very own hardbound *Sports Illustrated* Commemorative Edition.

NOVEMBER

NEW YORK CITY MARATHON P. Diddy ran the 2003 marathon, although it should be known that he sampled other runners for twenty-four of the miles and actually ran only two all by himself.

NBA REGULAR SEASON BEGINS Since only sixteen teams make the play-offs, these early season games really mean a lot.

MLS CUP Yes, I'm aware you probably don't care. But it's rude not to include it.

COLLEGE BASKETBALL SEASON BEGINS And Bob Huggins's players get a five-month break from having to attend class.

DECEMBER

HEISMAN TROPHY AWARDED And the winner's draft stock immediately plummets.

BASEBALL'S WINTER MEETINGS General managers gather to put up decorations, sing carols, and exchange gifts, all in hopes of winning the affections of Scott Boras. And every year they conclude with a flurry of trades of Christmas cookie recipes.

COLLEGE BOWL GAMES BEGIN Sure, even if your favorite team wins its non-BCS bowl game it has no chance of winning the national championship, but it's an honor just to be asked to appear in the Gaylord Hotels Music City Bowl.

THE FUTURE

**A LOOK AT WHAT WILL BE THE BIGGEST STORIES
IN THE COMING YEAR . . .**

Jose Canseco's new children's book, *Oh! The Places You'll Grow*, hits the top of the bestsellers list.

The U.S. government comes to a halt after the president hires Drew Rosenhaus and holds out for a new contract.

ESPN and MTV launch a network together that shows no sports or music.

The NBA will release a new logo that more accurately captures its modern players than the current silhouette of Jerry West.

Major League Baseball requires Barry Bonds to replace his uniform number with a huge asterisk.

The New England Patriots fire Bill Belichick after their draft receives only a C grade from Mel Kiper Jr.

John Madden nearly chokes to death on-air when he tries to swollen an entire turducken whole.

The Colts sign Tee Martin in hopes of getting better play out of the quarterback position in the postseason.

AND BEYOND . . .

2014 Men's pairs figure skating debuts at the Olympics.

2017 Angered that Augusta National still does not admit women, activist Martha Burk unleashes the fury of another fourteen-person protest outside the Masters.

2060 Joe Paterno's cryogenically frozen head announces it will coach five more years.

2075: Jesus Christ returns to Earth. The Yankees ink him to a 10-year, $50 billion contract.

NAME INDEX